Frommer's®

S0-CFR-435

PORTABLE
San Francisco

7th Edition

by Matthew Richard Poole

Here's what critics say about Frommer's:

"Amazingly easy to use. Very portable, very complete."

—*Booklist*

"Detailed, accurate, and easy-to-read information for all price ranges."

—*Glamour Magazine*

WILEY

Wiley Publishing, Inc.

WILEY PUBLISHING, INC.

111 River St.
Hoboken, NJ 07030-5774

ISBN 978-0-470-38220-2

Editor: Marc Nadeau
Production Editor: Erin Amick
Cartographer: Liz Puhl
Photo Editor: Richard Fox
Production by Wiley Indianapolis Composition Services

For information on our other products and services or to obtain technical support, please contact our Customer Care Department within the U.S. at 800/762-2974, outside the U.S. at 317/572-3993 or fax 317/572-4002.

Wiley also publishes its books in a variety of electronic formats. Some content that appears in print may not be available in electronic formats.

Manufactured in the United States of America

5   4   3   2   1

Contents

List of Maps

ABOUT THE AUTHOR

Matthew Richard Poole, a native Californian, has authored more than two dozen travel guides to California, Hawaii, and abroad, and is a regular contributor to radio and television travel programs, including numerous guest appearances on the award-winning *Bay Area Backroads* television show. Before becoming a full-time travel writer and photographer, he worked as an English tutor in Prague, a ski instructor in the Swiss Alps, and a scuba instructor in Maui and Thailand. He currently lives in San Francisco but spends most of his time on the road searching for new adventures. His other Frommer's titles include *California, San Francisco, Irreverent Guide to San Francisco,* and *Portable Disneyland*®.

AN INVITATION TO THE READER

In researching this book, we discovered many wonderful places—hotels, restaurants, shops, and more. We're sure you'll find others. Please tell us about them, so we can share the information with your fellow travelers in upcoming editions. If you were disappointed with a recommendation, we'd love to know that, too. Please write to:

Frommer's Portable San Francisco, 7th Edition
Wiley Publishing, Inc. • 111 River St. • Hoboken, NJ 07030-5774

AN ADDITIONAL NOTE

Please be advised that travel information is subject to change at any time—and this is especially true of prices. We therefore suggest that you write or call ahead for confirmation when making your travel plans. The authors, editors, and publisher cannot be held responsible for the experiences of readers while traveling. Your safety is important to us, however, so we encourage you to stay alert and be aware of your surroundings. Keep a close eye on cameras, purses, and wallets, all favorite targets of thieves and pickpockets.

FROMMER'S STAR RATINGS, ICONS & ABBREVIATIONS

Every hotel, restaurant, and attraction listing in this guide has been ranked for quality, value, service, amenities, and special features using a **star-rating system.** In country, state, and regional guides, we also rate towns and regions to help you narrow down your choices and budget your time accordingly. Hotels and restaurants are rated on a scale of zero (recommended) to three stars (exceptional). Attractions, shopping, nightlife, towns, and regions are rated according to the following scale: zero stars (recommended), one star (highly recommended), two stars (very highly recommended), and three stars (must-see).

In addition to the star-rating system, we also use **seven feature icons** that point you to the great deals, in-the-know advice, and unique experiences that separate travelers from tourists. Throughout the book, look for:

Finds	Special finds—those places only insiders know about
Fun Fact	Fun facts—details that make travelers more informed and their trips more fun
Kids	Best bets for kids and advice for the whole family
Moments	Special moments—those experiences that memories are made of
Overrated	Places or experiences not worth your time or money
Tips	Insider tips—great ways to save time and money
Value	Great values—where to get the best deals

The following **abbreviations** are used for credit cards:

AE	American Express	DISC	Discover	V	Visa
DC	Diners Club	MC	MasterCard		

FROMMERS.COM

Now that you have this guidebook to help you plan a great trip, visit our website at **www.frommers.com** for additional travel information on more than 3,600 destinations. We update features regularly to give you instant access to the most current trip-planning information available. At Frommers.com, you'll find scoops on the best airfares, lodging rates, and car rental bargains. You can even book your travel online through our reliable travel booking partners. Other popular features include:

- Online updates of our most popular guidebooks
- Vacation sweepstakes and contest giveaways
- Newsletters highlighting the hottest travel trends
- Online travel message boards with featured travel discussions

Planning Your Trip to San Francisco

1 Visitor Information

Thee **San Francisco Visitor Information Center,** on the lower level of Hallidie Plaza, 900 Market St., at Powell Street (© **415/ 391-2000;** www.onlyinsanfrancisco.com), is the best source of specialized information about the city. Even if you don't have a specific question, you might want to request the free *Visitors Planning Guide* and the *San Francisco Visitors* kit. The kit includes a 6-month calendar of events; a city history; shopping and dining information; and several good, clear maps; plus lodging information. The bureau highlights only its members' establishments, so if it doesn't have what you're looking for, that doesn't mean it's nonexistent.

You can also get the latest on San Francisco at the following online addresses:

- The *Bay Guardian,* the city's free weekly paper: **www.sfbg.com**
- *SF Gate,* the city's *Chronicle* newspaper: **www.sfgate.com**
- CitySearch: sanfrancisco.citysearch.com

2 Money

ATMS

In San Francisco and nationwide, the easiest and best way to get cash away from home is from an ATM, sometimes referred to as a "cash machine," or "cashpoint." The **Cirrus** (© **800/424-7787;** www. mastercard.com) and **PLUS** (© **800/843-7587;** www.visa.com) networks span the country; you can find them even in remote regions. Be sure you know your daily withdrawal limit before you depart.

Note: Many banks impose a fee every time you use a card at another bank's ATM, and that fee is often higher for international transactions (up to $5 or more) than for domestic ones (where they're rarely more than $2). In addition, the bank from which you withdraw cash may charge its own fee. To compare banks' ATM fees within the U.S., use **www.bankrate.com**. Visitors from outside the U.S. should also find out whether their bank assesses a 1% to 3% fee on charges incurred abroad.

Tip: One way around these fees is to ask for cash back at grocery, drug, and convenience stores that accept ATM cards and don't charge usage fees (be sure to ask). Of course, you'll have to purchase something first.

CREDIT CARDS & DEBIT CARDS

Credit cards are the most widely used form of payment in the United States: **Visa** (Barclaycard in Britain), **MasterCard** (Eurocard in Europe, Access in Britain, Chargex in Canada), **American Express, Diners Club,** and **Discover.** They also provide a convenient record of all your expenses, and offer relatively good exchange rates. You can withdraw cash advances from your credit cards at banks or ATMs, but high fees make credit-card cash advances a pricey way to get cash.

It's highly recommended that you travel with at least one major credit card. You must have a credit card to rent a car, and hotels and airlines usually require a credit card imprint as a deposit against expenses.

TRAVELER'S CHECKS

Traveler's checks are something of an anachronism from the days before the ATM made cash accessible at any time. Traveler's checks used to be the only sound alternative to traveling with dangerously large amounts of cash. They were as reliable as currency, but, unlike cash, could be replaced if lost or stolen.

These days, traveler's checks are less necessary because most cities have 24-hour ATMs that allow you to withdraw small amounts of cash as needed. However, keep in mind that you will likely be charged an ATM withdrawal fee if the bank is not your own, so if you're withdrawing money every day, you might be better off with traveler's checks—provided that you don't mind showing identification every time you want to cash one. Visitors should make sure that traveler's checks are denominated in U.S. dollars; foreign-currency checks are often difficult to exchange.

3 When to Go

If you're dreaming of convertibles, Frisbee on the beach, and tank-topped evenings, change your reservations and head to Los Angeles. Contrary to California's sunshine-and-bikini image, San Francisco's weather is "mild" (to put it nicely) and can often be downright bone-chilling because of the wet, foggy air and cool winds—it's nothing like that of Southern California. Summer, the most popular time to visit, is often characterized by damp, foggy days; cold, windy nights; and crowded tourist destinations. A good bet is to visit in spring or, better yet, autumn. Every September, right about the time San Franciscans mourn being cheated (or fogged) out of another summer, something wonderful happens: The thermometer rises, the skies clear, and the locals call in sick to work and head for the beach. It's what residents call "Indian summer." The city is also delightful during winter, when the opera and ballet seasons are in full swing; there are fewer tourists, many hotel prices are lower, and downtown bustles with holiday cheer.

CLIMATE

San Francisco's temperate, marine climate usually means relatively mild weather year-round. In summer, chilling fog rolls in most mornings and evenings, and if temperatures top 70°F (21°C), the city is ready to throw a celebration. Even when autumn's heat occasionally stretches into the 80s (upper 20s Celsius) and 90s (lower 30s Celsius), you should still dress in layers, or by early evening you'll learn firsthand why sweatshirt sales are a great business at Fisherman's Wharf. In winter, the mercury seldom falls below freezing and snow is almost unheard of, but that doesn't mean you won't be whimpering if you forget your coat. Still, compared to most of the states' weather conditions, San Francisco's are consistently pleasant.

San Francisco's Average Temperatures & Rainfall

	Jan	Feb	Mar	Apr	May	June	July	Aug	Sept	Oct	Nov	Dec
High °F	56	59	61	64	67	70	71	72	73	70	62	56
Low °F	43	46	47	48	51	53	55	56	55	52	48	43
High °C	13	15	16	18	19	21	22	22	23	21	17	13
Low °C	6	8	8	9	11	12	13	13	13	11	9	6
Rain (in.)	4.5	4.0	3.3	1.2	0.4	0.1	0.1	0.1	0.2	1.0	2.5	2.9
Rain (mm)	113.0	101.9	82.8	30.0	9.7	2.8	0.8	1.8	5.1	26.4	63.2	73.4

SAN FRANCISCO CALENDAR OF EVENTS

For more information, visit www.sfvisitor.org for an annual calendar of local events.

February

Chinese New Year, Chinatown. In 2009, public celebrations will again spill onto every street in Chinatown. Festivities begin with the "Miss Chinatown USA" pageant parade, and climax a week later with a celebratory parade of marching bands, rolling floats, barrages of fireworks, and a block-long dragon writhing in and out of the crowds. The revelry runs for several weeks and wraps up with a memorable parade through Chinatown that starts at Market and Second streets and ends at Kearny Street. Arrive early for a good viewing spot on Kearny Street. You can purchase bleacher seats online starting in December. Make your hotel reservations early. For dates and information, call © **415/982-3000** or visit www.chineseparade.com.

March

St. Patrick's Day Parade, Union Square and Civic Center. Everyone's an honorary Irish person at this festive affair, which starts at 11:30am at Market and Second streets and continues to City Hall. But the party doesn't stop there. Head down to the Civic Center for the post-party, or venture to The Embarcadero's Harrington's bar (245 Front St.) and celebrate with hundreds of the Irish-for-a-day yuppies as they gallivant around the closed-off streets and numerous pubs. For information, call © **415/675-9885;** www.sfstpatricksdayparade.com. Sunday before March 17.

April

Cherry Blossom Festival, Japantown. Meander through the arts-and-crafts and food booths lining the blocked-off streets around Japan Center and watch traditional drumming, flower arranging, origami making, or a parade celebrating the cherry blossom and Japanese culture. Call © **415/563-2313** for information. Mid- to late April.

San Francisco International Film Festival, around San Francisco with screenings at the AMC Kabuki 8 Cinemas (Fillmore and Post sts.), and at many other locations. Begun in 1957, this is America's oldest film festival. It features close to 200 films and videos from more than 50 countries. Tickets are relatively inexpensive, and screenings are accessible to the public. Entries include new films by beginning and established directors. For a schedule or information, call © **415/561-5000** or visit www. sffs.org. Mid-April to early May.

May

Cinco de Mayo Festival, Mission District. This is when the Latino community celebrates the victory of the Mexicans over the French at Puebla in 1862; mariachi bands, dancers, food, and a parade fill the streets of the Mission. The parade starts at 10am at 24th and Bryant streets and ends at the Civic Center, though rumor has it that in 2009 the Festival will be held on Harrison and Mission Streets. Contact the Mission Neighborhood Center for more information at ℭ **415/206-0577.** First Sunday in May.

Bay to Breakers Foot Race, The Embarcadero through Golden Gate Park to Ocean Beach. Even if you don't participate, you can't avoid this run from downtown to Ocean Beach, which stops morning traffic throughout the city. More than 75,000 entrants gather—many dressed in wacky, innovative, and sometimes X-rated costumes—for the approximately 7½-mile run. If you don't want to run, join the throng of spectators who line the route. Sidewalk parties, bands, and cheerleaders of all ages provide a good dose of true San Francisco fun. For recorded information, call ℭ **415/359-2800,** or check their website www.baytobreakers.com. Third Sunday of May.

Carnaval Festival, Harrison Street between 16th and 23rd streets. The Mission District's largest annual event, held from 9:30am to 6pm, is a day of festivities that includes food, music, dance, arts and crafts, and a parade that's as sultry and energetic as the Latin American and Caribbean people behind it. For one of San Franciscans' favorite events, more than half a million spectators line the parade route, and samba musicians and dancers continue to entertain on 14th Street, near Harrison, at the end of the march where you'll find food and craft booths, music, and more revelry. Call the hot line at ℭ **415/920-0125** for information. Celebrations are held Saturday and Sunday of Memorial Day weekend, but the parade is on Sunday morning only. See www.carnavalsf.com for more information.

June

Union Street Art Festival, Pacific Heights, along Union Street from Steiner to Gough streets. This outdoor fair celebrates San Francisco with themes, gourmet food booths, music, entertainment, and a juried art show featuring works by more than 250 artists. It's a great time and a chance to see the city's young well-to-dos partying it up. Call the **Union Street Association** (ℭ **415/441-7055**) for more information or see www.unionstreetfestival.com. First weekend of June.

Haight-Ashbury Street Fair, Haight-Ashbury. A far cry from the froufrou Union Street Fair, this grittier fair features alternative crafts, ethnic foods, rock bands, and a healthy number of hippies and street kids whooping it up and slamming beers in front of the blaring rock-'n'-roll stage. The fair usually extends along Haight between Stanyan and Ashbury streets. For details and the exact date, call ℭ **415/863-3489** or visit www.haightstreetfair.org.

North Beach Festival, Grant Avenue, North Beach. In 2009, this party will celebrate its 55th anniversary; organizers claim it's the oldest urban street fair in the country. Close to 100,000 city folk meander along Grant Avenue, between Vallejo and Union streets, to eat, drink, and browse the arts-and-crafts booths, poetry readings, swing-dancing venue, and arte di gesso (sidewalk chalk art). But the most enjoyable parts of the event are listening to music and people-watching. Call ℂ **415/989-2220** or visit www. sfnorthbeach.org/NBFestival for details. Usually Father's Day weekend, but call to confirm.

Stern Grove Music Festival, Sunset District. Pack a picnic and head out early to join the thousands who come here to lie in the grass and enjoy classical, jazz, and ethnic music and dance in the grove, at 19th Avenue and Sloat Boulevard. The Festival's 70th year was marked in 2007. The free concerts take place every Sunday at 2pm between mid-June and August. Show up with a lawn chair or blanket. There are food booths if you forget snacks, but you'll be dying to leave if you don't bring warm clothes—the Sunset District can be one of the coldest parts of the city. Call ℂ **415/252-6252** for listings; www.sterngrove.org. Sundays, mid-June through August.

San Francisco Lesbian, Gay, Bisexual, Transgender Pride Parade & Celebration, downtown's Market Street. This prideful event draws up to one million participants who celebrate all of the above—and then some. The parade proceeds west on Market Street until it gets to the Civic Center, where hundreds of food, art, and information booths are set up around several soundstages. Call ℂ **415/864-3733** or visit www.sfpride.org for information. Usually the third or last weekend of June.

July

Fillmore Jazz Festival, Pacific Heights. July starts with a bang, when the upscale portion of Fillmore closes to traffic and the blocks between Jackson and Eddy are filled with arts and crafts, gourmet food, and live jazz from 10am to 6pm. Call ℂ **510/ 970-3217** for more information; www.fillmorejazzfestival.com. First weekend in July.

Fourth of July Celebration & Fireworks, Fisherman's Wharf. This event can be something of a joke—more often than not, fog comes into the city, like everyone else, to join in the festivities. Sometimes it's almost impossible to view the million-dollar pyrotechnics from Pier 39 on the northern waterfront. Still, it's a party, and if the skies are clear, it's a darn good show. Visit www.visitfishermanswharf.com and click on "Events" for more info.

San Francisco Marathon, San Francisco and beyond. This is one of the largest marathons in the world. It starts and ends at the Ferry Building at the base of Market Street, winds 26-plus miles through virtually every neighborhood in the City, and crosses the Golden Gate Bridge. For entry information, visit www.runsfm. com. Usually the last weekend in July.

September

Sausalito Art Festival, Sausalito. A juried exhibit of more than 20,000 original works of art, this festival includes music—provided by jazz, rock, and blues performers from the Bay Area and beyond—and international cuisine, enhanced by wines from some 50 Napa and Sonoma producers. Parking is impossible; take the **Blue & Gold Fleet ferry** (© 415/705-5555) from Fisherman's Wharf to the festival site. For more information, call © 415/332-3555 or log on to www.sausalitoartfestival.org. Labor Day weekend.

Opera in the Park, usually in Sharon Meadow, Golden Gate Park. Each year the San Francisco Opera launches its season with a free concert featuring a selection of arias. Call © 415/861-4008 to confirm the location and date. Usually the Sunday after Labor Day.

San Francisco Blues Festival, on the grounds of Fort Mason, the Marina. The largest outdoor blues music event on the West Coast turned 35 years old in 2007 and continues to feature local and national musicians performing back-to-back during the 3-day extravaganza. You can charge tickets by phone at © 415/421-8497 or online at www.ticketmaster.com. For information, call © 415/979-5588 or visit www.sfblues.com. Usually in late September.

Folsom Street Fair, along Folsom Street between 7th and 12th streets, SoMa, from 11am to 6pm. This is a local favorite for its kinky, outrageous, leather-and-skin gay-centric blowout celebration. It's hard-core, so only open-minded and adventurous types need head into the leather-clad and partially dressed crowds. For info call © 415/861-3247 or visit www.folsomstreetfair.org. Last Sunday of September.

October

Fleet Week, Marina and Fisherman's Wharf. Residents gather along the Marina Green, The Embarcadero, Fisherman's Wharf, and other vantage points to watch incredible (and loud!) aerial performances by the Blue Angels, flown in tribute to our nation's marines. Call 🕿 **650/599-5057** or visit www.fleetweek.us/fleetweek for details and dates.

Artspan Open Studios, various San Francisco locations. Find an original piece of art to commemorate your trip, or just see what local artists are up to by grabbing a map to over 800 artists' studios that are open to the public during weekends in October. Call 🕿 **415/861-9838** or visit www.artspan.org for more information.

Castro Street Fair, the Castro. Celebrate life in the city's most famous gay neighborhood. Call 🕿 **415/841-1824** or visit www.castrostreetfair.org for information. First Sunday in October, from 11am to 6pm.

Italian Heritage Parade, North Beach and Fisherman's Wharf. The city's Italian community leads the festivities around Fisherman's Wharf, celebrating Columbus's landing in America. The year 2008 marked the festival's 140th, and as usual included a parade along Columbus Avenue. But for the most part, it's a great excuse to hang out in North Beach and people-watch. For information, call 🕿 **415/587-8282** or visit www.sfcolumbusday.org. Observed the Sunday before Columbus Day.

Exotic Erotic Halloween Ball, The Cow Palace, on the southern outskirts of San Francisco. Thousands come here dressed in costume, lingerie, and sometimes even less than that. It's a wild fantasy affair with bands, dancing, and costume contests. *Beware:* It can be somewhat cheesy. Advance tickets range from $60 to $125 per person. For information, call 🕿 **415/567-BALL** or visit www.exoticeroticball.com. One or two Friday or Saturday nights before Halloween.

Halloween, the Castro. This is a huge night in San Francisco, especially in the flamboyant gay community of the Castro. Drop by for music, costume contests, and all-around revelry when streets are shut down and filled with a mixed crowd reveling in costumes of extraordinary imagination. For info visit www.halloweeninthecastro.com. October 31.

San Francisco Jazz Festival, various San Francisco locations. This festival presents eclectic programming in an array of fabulous jazz venues throughout the city. With close to 3 weeks of nightly entertainment and dozens of performers, the jazz festival is a hot ticket. Past events have featured Herbie Hancock, Dave Brubeck, the Modern Jazz Quartet, Wayne Shorter, and Bill Frisell. For information, call ✆ **800/850-SFJF** or 415/788-7353; or visit www.sfjazz.org. Also check the website for other events throughout the year. Late October and early November.

December

The Nutcracker, War Memorial Opera House, Civic Center. The **San Francisco Ballet** (✆ **415/865-2000**) performs this Tchaikovsky classic annually. Order tickets to this holiday tradition well in advance. Visit www.sfballet.org for information.

4 Specialized Travel Resources

TRAVELERS WITH DISABILITIES

Most disabilities shouldn't stop anyone from traveling. There are more options and resources out there than ever before.

The San Francisco Convention and Visitors Bureau (p. 1) should have the most up-to-date information on accessible options for travelers with disabilities.

Travelers in wheelchairs can request special ramped taxis by calling **Yellow Cab** (✆ 415/626-2345), which charges regular rates for the service. Travelers with disabilities can also get a free copy of the *Muni Access Guide,* published by the San Francisco Municipal Transportation Agency, Accessible Services Program, One South Van Ness, third floor (✆ 415/923-6142), which is staffed weekdays from 8am to 5pm. Many of the major car-rental companies offer hand-controlled cars for drivers with disabilities. **Alamo** (✆ 800/651-1223), **Avis** (✆ 800/331-1212, ext. 7305), and **Budget** (✆ 800/314-3932) have special hot lines that help provide such a vehicle at any of their U.S. locations with 48 hours' advance notice; **Hertz** (✆ 800/654-3131) requires between 24 and 72 hours' advance notice at most locations.

GAY & LESBIAN TRAVELERS

If you head down to the Castro—an area surrounding Castro Street near Market Street—you'll understand why the city is a mecca for gay and lesbian travelers. Since the 1970s, this unique part of town has remained a colorfully festive neighborhood, teeming with "out" city folk who meander the streets shopping, eating, partying, or cruising. If anyone feels like an outsider in this part of town, it's heterosexuals, who, although warmly welcomed in the community, may feel uncomfortable or downright threatened if they harbor any homophobia or aversion to being checked out. For many San Franciscans, it's just a fun area (especially on Halloween) with some wonderful shops.

Gays and lesbians make up a good deal of San Francisco's population, so it's no surprise that clubs and bars all over town cater to them. Although lesbian interests are concentrated primarily in the East Bay (especially Oakland), a significant community resides in the Mission District, around 16th and Valencia streets.

Several local publications concentrate on in-depth coverage of news, information, and listings of goings-on around town for gays and lesbians. The *Bay Area Reporter* (www.ebar.com) has the most comprehensive listings, including a weekly calendar of events. Distributed free on Thursday, it can be found stacked at the corner of 18th and Castro streets and at Ninth and Harrison streets, as well as in bars, bookshops, and stores around town. It may also be available in gay and lesbian bookstores elsewhere in the country.

SENIOR TRAVEL

Nearly every attraction in San Francisco offers a senior discount; age requirements vary, and specific prices are listed in chapter 4. Public transportation and movie theaters also have reduced rates. Don't be shy about asking for discounts, but always carry some kind of identification that shows your date of birth.

Members of **AARP**, 601 E St. NW, Washington, DC 20049 (*©* **888/687-2277;** www.aarp.org), get discounts on hotels, airfares, and car rentals. AARP offers members a wide range of benefits, including *AARP The Magazine* and a monthly newsletter. Anyone over 50 can join.

Recommended publications offering travel resources and discounts for seniors include the quarterly magazine **Travel 50 & Beyond** (www.travel50andbeyond.com) and the bestselling paperback **Unbelievably Good Deals and Great Adventures That You Absolutely Can't Get Unless You're Over 50** (McGraw-Hill), by Joann Rattner Heilman.

Frommers.com offers more information and resources on travel for seniors.

FAMILY TRAVEL

San Francisco is full of sightseeing opportunities and special activities geared toward children. See **Frommer's San Francisco with Kids** (Wiley Publishing, Inc.) for good, kid-specific information for your trip.

5 Getting There

BY PLANE

The northern Bay Area has two major airports: San Francisco International and Oakland International.

SAN FRANCISCO INTERNATIONAL AIRPORT Almost four dozen major scheduled carriers serve **San Francisco International Airport** or **SFO** (© 650/821-8211; www.flysfo.com), 14 miles directly south of downtown on U.S. 101. Travel time to downtown during commuter rush hour is about 40 minutes; at other times, it's about 20 to 25 minutes.

You can also call **511** or visit www.511.org for up-to-the-minute information about public transportation and traffic.

GETTING INTO TOWN FROM SAN FRANCISCO INTERNATIONAL AIRPORT

The fastest and cheapest way to get from SFO to the city is to take **BART** (Bay Area Rapid Transit; © 415/989-2278; www.bart.gov), which offers numerous stops within downtown San Francisco. This route, which takes about 35 minutes, avoids traffic on the way and costs a heck of a lot less than taxis or shuttles (about $6 each way, depending on exactly where you're going). Just jump on the airport's free shuttle bus to the International terminal, enter the BART station there, and you're on your way to San Francisco. Trains leave approximately every 15 minutes.

A **cab** from the airport to downtown costs $35 to $40, plus tip, and takes about 30 minutes, traffic permitting.

SuperShuttle (© 800/BLUE-VAN or 415/558-8500; www.supershuttle.com) is a private shuttle company that offers door-to-door airport service, in which you share a van with a few other passengers. They will take you anywhere in the city, charging $15 per person to a residence or business. On the return trip, add $8 to $15 for each additional person depending on whether you're traveling from a hotel or a residence. The shuttle stops at least every 20 minutes, sometimes sooner, and picks up passengers from the marked areas outside the terminals' upper levels. Reservations are required for the return trip to the airport only and should be made 1 day before departure. These shuttles often demand they pick you up 2 hours before your domestic flight and 3 hours before international flights and during holidays. Keep in mind that you could be the first one on and the last one off, so this trip could take a while; you might want to ask before getting in. For $65, you can either charter the entire van for up to seven people or an Execucar private sedan for up to four people. For more info on the Execucar, call (C) **800/410-4444.**

The San Mateo County Transit system, **SamTrans** ((C) **800/660-4287** in Northern California, or 650/508-6200; www.samtrans.com), runs two buses between the San Francisco Airport and the Transbay Terminal at First and Mission streets. Bus no. 292 costs $1.50 and makes the trip in about 55 minutes. The KX bus costs $4 and takes just 35 minutes but permits only one carry-on bag. Both buses run daily. The no. 292 starts at 5:25am Monday through Friday and 5:30am on weekends; both run until 1am and run every half-hour until 7:30pm, when they run hourly. The KX starts at 5:53am and ends at 10:37pm Monday through Friday. On weekends, service runs from 7:19am to 9:30pm, runs every half-hour until 6:30pm, and then changes to an hourly schedule.

OAKLAND INTERNATIONAL AIRPORT About 5 miles south of downtown Oakland, at the Hegenberger Road exit of Calif. 17 (U.S. 880; if coming from south, take 98th Ave.), **Oakland International Airport** ((C) **800/247-6255** or 510/563-3300; www.oaklandairport.com) primarily serves passengers with East Bay destinations. Some San Franciscans prefer this less-crowded, more accessible airport, although it takes about half an hour to get there from downtown San Francisco (traffic permitting). The airport is also accessible by BART via a shuttle bus.

GETTING INTO TOWN FROM OAKLAND INTERNATIONAL AIRPORT

Taxis from the Oakland Airport to downtown San Francisco are expensive—approximately $50, plus tip.

Bayporter Express ((C) **877/467-1800** in the Bay Area, or 415/467-1800 elsewhere; www.bayporter.com) is a shuttle service that charges $26 for the first person and $12 for each additional person for the ride from the Oakland Airport to downtown San Francisco. Children under 12 pay $7. The fare for outer areas of San Francisco is higher. The service accepts advance reservations. To the right of the Oakland Airport exit, there are usually shuttles that take you to San Francisco for around $20 per person. The shuttles in this fleet are independently owned, and prices vary.

The cheapest way to reach downtown San Francisco is to take the shuttle bus from the Oakland Airport to **BART** (Bay Area Rapid Transit; (C) **510/464-6000;** www.bart.gov). The AirBART shuttle bus runs about every 15 minutes Monday through Saturday from 5am to 12:05am and Sunday from 8am to 12:05am. It makes pickups in front of terminals 1 and 2 near the ground transportation signs. Tickets must be purchased at the Oakland Airport's vending machines prior to boarding. The cost is $2 for the 10-minute ride to BART's Coliseum station in Oakland. BART fares vary, depending on your destination; the trip to downtown San Francisco costs $3.15 and takes 15 minutes once you're on board. The entire excursion should take around 45 minutes.

BY CAR

San Francisco is easily accessible by major highways: **Interstate 5,** from the north, and **U.S. 101,** which cuts south–north through the peninsula from San Jose and across the Golden Gate Bridge to points north. If you drive from Los Angeles, you can take the longer coastal route (437 miles and 11 hr.) or the inland route (389 miles and 8 hr.). From Mendocino, it's 156 miles and 4 hours; from Sacramento, 88 miles and 1½ hours; from Yosemite, 210 miles and 4 hours.

If you are driving and aren't already a member, it's worth joining the **American Automobile Association (AAA;** ✆ **800/922-8228;** www.csaa.com). It charges $49 to $79 per year (with an additional one-time joining fee), depending on where you join, and provides roadside and other services to motorists. **Amoco Motor Club** (✆ **800/334-3300;** www.bpmotorclub.com) is another recommended choice.

6 Orientation

VISITOR INFORMATION

The **San Francisco Visitor Information Center,** on the lower level of Hallidie Plaza, 900 Market St., at Powell Street (✆ **415/391-2000;** www.onlyinsanfrancisco.com), has brochures, discount coupons, and advice on restaurants, sights, and events in the city; their website offers an incredible amount of information as well. The on-site staff can provide answers in German, Japanese, French, Italian, and Spanish. To find the office, descend the escalator at the cable car turnaround. The office is open Monday through Friday from 9am to 5pm, and Saturday and Sunday from 9am to 3pm, May through October. However, it is closed on Sundays during winter and Easter, Thanksgiving Day, and Christmas Day. Phones are answered in person Monday through Friday only. Otherwise, dial ✆ **415/391-2001** any time, day or night, for a recorded message

San Francisco Neighborhoods

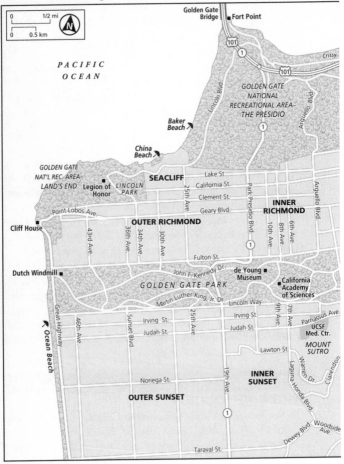

about current cultural events, theater, music, sports, and other special happenings.

Pick up a copy of the **Bay Guardian** (www.sfbg.com) or the **S.F. Weekly** (www.sfweekly.com), the city's free alternative papers, to get listings of all city happenings. You'll find them in kiosks throughout the city and in most cafes.

For specialized information on Chinatown's shops and services, and on the city's Chinese community in general, contact the **Chinese**

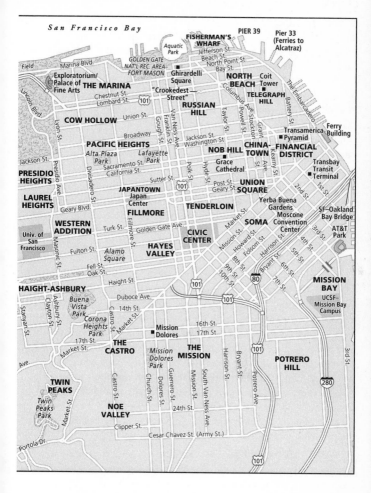

Chamber of Commerce, 730 Sacramento St. (© **415/982-3000**), open daily from 9am to 5pm.

CITY LAYOUT

San Francisco occupies the tip of a 32-mile peninsula between San Francisco Bay and the Pacific Ocean. Its land area measures about 46 square miles, although the city is often referred to as being 7 square miles. At more than 900 feet high, the towering Twin Peaks marks the geographic center of the city and is a killer place to take in a vista of San Francisco.

With lots of one-way streets and plenty of nooks and crannies, San Francisco might seem confusing at first, but it will quickly become easy to negotiate. The city's downtown streets are arranged in a simple grid pattern, with the exceptions of Market Street and Columbus Avenue, which cut across the grid at right angles to each other. Hills appear to distort this pattern, however, and can disorient you. As you learn your way around, the hills will become your landmarks and reference points. But even if you get lost, it's no big deal: San Francisco's a small town—so much so, in fact, that I've run from one end to the other (during the Bay to Breakers Foot Race) in an hour flat.

MAIN ARTERIES & STREETS **Market Street** is San Francisco's main thoroughfare. Most of the city's buses travel this route on their way to the Financial District from the outer neighborhoods to the west and south. The tall office buildings clustered downtown are at the northeast end of Market; 1 block beyond lies The Embarcadero and the bay.

The Embarcadero 𝄞—an excellent strolling, skating, and biking route (thanks to recent renovations)—curves along San Francisco Bay from south of the Bay Bridge to the northeast perimeter of the city. It terminates at Fisherman's Wharf, the famous tourist-oriented pier. Aquatic Park, Fort Mason, and the Golden Gate National Recreation Area are on the northernmost point of the peninsula.

From the eastern perimeter of Fort Mason, **Van Ness Avenue** runs due south, back to Market Street. The area just described forms a rough triangle, with Market Street as its southeastern boundary, the waterfront as its northern boundary, and Van Ness Avenue as its western boundary. Within this triangle lie most of the city's main tourist sights.

FINDING AN ADDRESS Because most of the city's streets are laid out in a grid pattern, finding an address is easy when you know the nearest cross street. Numbers start with 1 at the beginning of the street and proceed at the rate of 100 per block. When asking for directions, find out the nearest cross street and the neighborhood where your destination is located, but be careful not to confuse numerical avenues with numerical streets. Numerical avenues (Third Ave. and so on) are in the Richmond and Sunset Districts in the western part of the city. Numerical streets (Third St. and so on) are south of Market Street in the east and south parts of town.

NEIGHBORHOODS IN BRIEF

Union Square Union Square is the commercial hub of San Francisco. Most major hotels and department stores are crammed into the area surrounding the actual square, which was named for a series of violent pro-union mass demonstrations staged here on the eve of the Civil War. A plethora of upscale boutiques, restaurants, and galleries occupy the spaces tucked between the larger buildings. A few blocks west is the **Tenderloin** neighborhood, a patch of poverty and blight where you should keep your wits about you. The **Theater District** is 3 blocks west of Union Square.

The Financial District East of Union Square, this area, bordered by The Embarcadero and by Market, Third, Kearny, and Washington streets, is the city's business district and the stamping grounds for many major corporations. The pointy Transamerica Pyramid, at Montgomery and Clay streets, is one of the district's most conspicuous architectural features. To its east sprawls The Embarcadero Center, an 8½-acre complex housing offices, shops, and restaurants. Farther east still is the old Ferry Building, the city's pre-bridge transportation hub. Ferries to Sausalito and Larkspur still leave from this point. However, in 2003, the building became an attraction in itself when it was completely renovated, jampacked with outstanding restaurant and gourmet food- and wine-related shops, and surrounded by a farmers' market a few days a week, making it a favorite place of San Francisco's residents seeking to stock their kitchens.

Nob Hill & Russian Hill Bounded by Bush, Larkin, Pacific, and Stockton streets, Nob Hill is a genteel, well-heeled district still occupied by the city's major power brokers and the neighborhood businesses they frequent. Russian Hill extends from Pacific to Bay and from Polk to Mason. It contains steep streets, lush gardens, and high-rises occupied by both the moneyed and the bohemian.

Chinatown A large red-and-green gate on Grant Avenue at Bush Street marks the official entrance to Chinatown. Beyond lies a 24-block labyrinth, bordered by Broadway, Bush, Kearny, and Stockton streets, filled with restaurants, markets, temples, shops, and, of course, a substantial percentage of San Francisco's Chinese residents. Chinatown is a great place for exploration all along Stockton and Grant streets, Portsmouth Square, and the alleys that lead off them, like Ross and Waverly. This district has a maddening combination of incessant traffic and horrible drivers, so don't even think about driving around here.

North Beach This Italian neighborhood, which stretches from Montgomery and Jackson to Bay Street, is one of the best places in the city to grab a coffee, pull up a cafe chair, and do some serious people-watching. Nightlife is equally happening in North Beach; restaurants, bars, and clubs along Columbus and Grant avenues attract folks from all over the Bay Area, who fight for parking places and romp through the festive neighborhood. Down Columbus toward the Financial District are the remains of the city's Beat Generation landmarks, including Ferlinghetti's City Lights Bookstore and Vesuvio's Bar. Broadway—a short strip of sex joints—cuts through the heart of the district. **Telegraph Hill** looms over the east side of North Beach, topped by Coit Tower, one of San Francisco's best vantage points.

Fisherman's Wharf North Beach runs into Fisherman's Wharf, which was once the busy heart of the city's great harbor and waterfront industries. Today it's a kitschy and mildly entertaining tourist area with little, if any, authentic waterfront life, except for a small fleet of fishing boats and some lethargic sea lions. What it does have going for it are activities for the whole family, with attractions, restaurants, trinket shops, and beautiful views and walkways everywhere you look.

The Marina District Created on landfill for the Pan Pacific Exposition of 1915, the Marina District boasts some of the best views of the Golden Gate, as well as plenty of grassy fields alongside San Francisco Bay. Elegant Mediterranean-style homes and apartments, inhabited by the city's well-to-do singles and wealthy families, line the streets. Here, too, are the Palace of Fine Arts, the Exploratorium, and Fort Mason Center. The main street is Chestnut, between Franklin and Lyon, which abounds with shops, cafes, and boutiques. Because of its landfill foundation, the Marina was one of the hardest-hit districts in the 1989 quake.

Cow Hollow Located west of Van Ness Avenue, between Russian Hill and the Presidio, this flat, grazable area supported 30 dairy farms in 1861. Today, Cow Hollow is largely residential and largely yuppie. Its two primary commercial thoroughfares are Lombard Street, known for its many relatively inexpensive motels, and Union Street, a flourishing shopping sector filled with restaurants, pubs, cafes, and shops.

Pacific Heights The ultra-elite, such as the Gettys and Danielle Steel—and those lucky enough to buy before the real-estate boom—reside in the mansions and homes in this neighborhood. When the rich meander out of their fortresses, they wander down to Union Street and join the pretty people who frequent the street's long stretch of chic boutiques and lively neighborhood restaurants, cafes, and bars.

Japantown   Bounded by Octavia, Fillmore, California, and Geary, Japantown shelters only a small percentage of the city's Japanese population, but exploring these few square blocks and the shops and restaurants within them is still a cultural experience.

Civic Center   Although millions of dollars have gone toward brick sidewalks, ornate lampposts, and elaborate street plantings, the southwestern section of Market Street can still feel a little sketchy due to the large number of homeless who wander the area. The Civic Center at the "bottom" of Market Street, however, is a stunning beacon of culture and refinement. This large complex of buildings includes the domed and dapper City Hall, the Opera House, Davies Symphony Hall, and the Asian Art Museum. The landscaped plaza connecting the buildings is the staging area for San Francisco's frequent demonstrations for or against just about everything.

SoMa   No part of San Francisco has been more affected by recent development than the area south of Market Street (dubbed "SoMa"), the area within the triangle of The Embarcadero, Highway 101, and Market Street. Until a decade ago it was a district of old warehouses and industrial spaces, with a few scattered underground nightclubs, restaurants, and shoddy residential areas. But when it became the hub of dot-commercialization and half-million-dollar-plus lofts, its fate changed forever. Today, though dot-coms don't occupy much of the commercial space, the area is jumping thanks to fancy loft residents, the baseball stadium, and surrounding businesses, restaurants, and nightclubs in addition to urban entertainment such as the Museum of Modern Art, Yerba Buena Gardens, Metreon, and a slew of big-bucks hotels that make tons of money from businesspeople. Though still gritty in some areas, it's growing more glittery by the year.

Mission District   This is another area that was greatly affected by the city's new wealth. The Mexican and Latin American populations here, with their cuisine, traditions, and art, make the Mission District a vibrant area to visit. Some parts of the neighborhood are still poor and sprinkled with the homeless, gangs, and drug addicts, but young urbanites have also settled in the area, attracted by its "reasonably" (a relative term) priced rentals and endless oh-so-hot restaurants and bars that stretch from 16th and Valencia streets to 25th and Mission streets. Less adventurous tourists may just want to duck into Mission Dolores, cruise by a few of the 200-plus amazing murals, and head back downtown. But anyone who's interested in hanging with the hipsters and experiencing the hottest restaurant and bar nightlife should definitely beeline it here. Don't be afraid to visit this area, but do use caution at night.

The Castro   One of the liveliest streets in town, the Castro is practically synonymous with San Francisco's gay community (even though it is technically a street in the Noe Valley District). Located at the very end of Market Street, between 17th and 18th streets, the Castro has dozens of shops, restaurants, and bars catering to the gay community. Open-minded straight people are welcome, too.

Haight-Ashbury   Part trendy, part nostalgic, part funky, the Haight, as it's most commonly known, was the soul of the psychedelic, free-loving 1960s and the center of the counterculture movement. Today, the gritty neighborhood straddling upper Haight Street on the eastern border of Golden Gate Park is more gentrified, but the commercial area still harbors all walks of life. Leftover aging hippies mingle with grungy, begging street kids outside Ben & Jerry's Ice Cream Store (where they might still be talking about Jerry Garcia), nondescript marijuana dealers whisper "Buds" as shoppers pass, and many people walking down the street have Day-Glo hair. But you don't need to be a freak or wear tie-dye to enjoy the Haight—the ethnic food, trendy shops, and bars cover all tastes. From Haight Street, walk south on Cole Street for a more peaceful and quaint neighborhood experience.

Richmond & Sunset Districts   San Francisco's suburbs of sorts, these are the city's largest and most populous neighborhoods, consisting mainly of small (but expensive) homes, shops, and neighborhood restaurants. Although they border Golden Gate Park and Ocean Beach, few tourists venture into "The Avenues," as these areas are referred to locally, unless they're on their way to the Cliff House, zoo, or Palace of the Legion of Honor.

7 Getting Around

BY PUBLIC TRANSPORTATION

The **San Francisco Municipal Transportation Agency,** 1 S. Van Ness Ave., better known as "Muni" (© **415/673-6864;** www.sfmuni.com), operates the city's cable cars, buses, and streetcars. Together, these three services crisscross the entire city. Fares for buses and streetcars are $1.50 for adults; 50¢ for seniors over 65, children 5 to 17, and riders with disabilities. Cable cars, which run from 6:30am to 12:50am, cost a whopping $5 for all people over 5 ($1 for seniors and riders with disabilities 9pm–7am). Needless to say,

---

⟨Value⟩ Muni Discounts

Muni discount passes, called **Passports**, entitle holders to unlimited rides on buses, streetcars, and cable cars. A Passport costs $11 for 1 day, $18 for 3 days, and $24 for 7 consecutive days. Another option is buying a **CityPass**, which entitles you to unlimited Muni rides for 7 days, plus admission to numerous attractions (p. 20). Passports are also sold every day from 8am to midnight at the information booths in the baggage claim areas at San Francisco International Airport. You can also buy a Passport or CityPass at the San Francisco Visitor Information Center, Powell/Market cable car booth, Holiday Inn Civic Center, and TIX Bay Area booth at Union Square, among other outlets.

---

they're packed primarily with tourists. Exact change is required on all vehicles except cable cars. Fares are subject to change. If you're standing waiting for Muni and have wireless Web access (or from any computer), check www.nextmuni.com to get up-to-the-minute information about when the next bus or streetcar is coming. Muni's NextBus uses satellite technology and advanced computer modeling to track vehicles on their routes. Each vehicle is fitted with a satellite tracking system so the information is constantly updated.

For detailed route information, phone Muni or consult the Muni map at the front of the San Francisco Yellow Pages. If you plan to use public transportation extensively, you might want to invest in a comprehensive transit and city map ($2), sold at the San Francisco Visitor Information Center (p. 1), Powell/Market cable car booth, and many downtown retail outlets. Also, see the "Muni Discounts" box for more information.

CABLE CAR San Francisco's cable cars might not be the most practical means of transport, but the rolling historic landmarks are a fun ride. The three lines are concentrated in the downtown area. The most scenic, and exciting, is the **Powell-Hyde line,** which follows a zigzag route from the corner of Powell and Market streets, over both Nob Hill and Russian Hill, to a turntable at gaslit Victorian Square in front of Aquatic Park. The **Powell-Mason line** starts at the same intersection and climbs Nob Hill before descending to Bay Street, just 3 blocks from Fisherman's Wharf. The least scenic is the **California Street line,** which begins at the foot of Market Street and

San Francisco Mass Transit

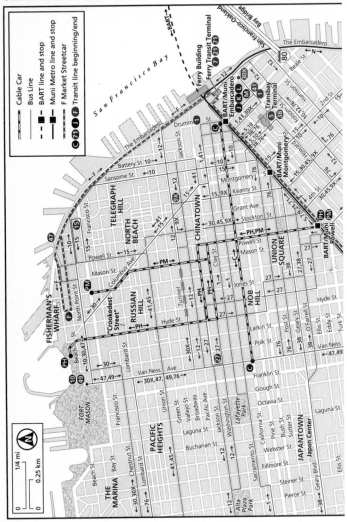

runs a straight course through Chinatown and over Nob Hill to Van Ness Avenue. All riders must exit at the last stop and wait in line for the return trip. The cable car system operates from approximately 6:30am to 12:50am, and each ride costs $5.

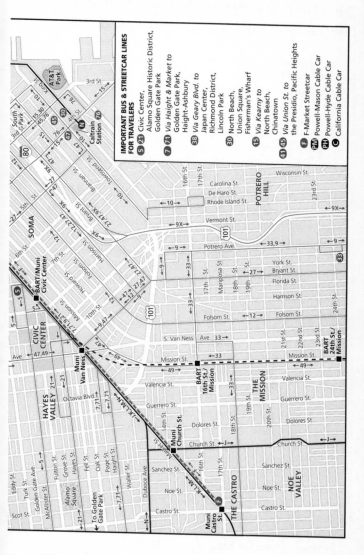

IMPORTANT BUS & STREETCAR LINES FOR TRAVELERS

⑤ ㉑ Civic Center, Alamo Square Historic District, Golden Gate Park

⑦ ㉞ *Via Haight & Market to* Golden Gate Park, Haight-Ashbury

㊳ *Via Geary Blvd. to* Japan Center, Richmond District, Lincoln Park

㉚ North Beach, Union Square, Fisherman's Wharf

⑮ *Via Kearny to* North Beach, Chinatown

㊶ ㊺ *Via Union St. to* the Presidio, Pacific Heights

Ⓕ F-Market Streetcar

ⓅⓂ Powell-Mason Cable Car

ⓅⒽ Powell-Hyde Cable Car

Ⓒ California Cable Car

BUS Buses reach almost every corner of San Francisco and beyond—they even travel over the bridges to Marin County and Oakland. Overhead electric cables power some buses; others use conventional gas engines. All are numbered and display their destinations on the front. Signs, curb markings, and yellow bands on adjacent utility poles designate stops, and most bus shelters exhibit Muni's transportation map and schedule. Many buses travel along Market Street or pass near Union Square and run from about 6am to midnight. After midnight, there is infrequent all-night "Owl" service. For safety, avoid taking buses late at night.

Popular tourist routes include bus nos. 5, 7, and 71, all of which run to Golden Gate Park; 41 and 45, which travel along Union Street; and 30, which runs between Union Square and Ghirardelli Square. A bus ride costs $1.50 for adults and 50¢ for seniors over 65, children 5 to 17, and riders with disabilities.

STREETCAR   Five of Muni's six streetcar lines, designated J, K, L, M, and N, run underground downtown and on the streets in the outer neighborhoods. The sleek rail cars make the same stops as BART (see below) along Market Street, including Embarcadero Station (in the Financial District), Montgomery and Powell streets (both near Union Square), and the Civic Center (near City Hall). Past the Civic Center, the routes branch off: The J line takes you to Mission Dolores; the K, L, and M lines run to Castro Street; and the N line parallels Golden Gate Park and extends all the way to The Embarcadero and AT&T Park. Streetcars run about every 15 minutes, more frequently during rush hours. They operate Monday through Friday from 5am to 12:15am, Saturday from 6am to approximately 12:15am, and Sunday from approximately 8am to 12:20am. The L and N lines operate 24 hours a day, 7 days a week, but late at night, regular buses trace the L and N routes, which are normally underground, from atop the city streets. Because the operation is part of Muni, the fares are the same as for buses, and passes are accepted.

The most recent new line to this system is not a newcomer at all, but is, in fact, an encore performance of San Francisco's beloved rejuvenated 1930s streetcar. The beautiful, retro multicolored F-Market streetcar runs from 17th and Castro streets to Beach and Jones streets; every other streetcar continues to Jones and Beach streets in Fisherman's Wharf. This is a quick and charming way to get up- and downtown without any hassle.

BART   BART, an acronym for **Bay Area Rapid Transit** (© 415/ 989-2278; www.bart.gov), is a futuristic-looking, high-speed rail network that connects San Francisco with the East Bay—Oakland, Richmond, Concord, and Fremont. Four stations are on Market Street (see "Streetcar," above). Fares range from $1.45 to $7.35, depending on how far you go. Machines in the stations dispense tickets that are magnetically encoded with a dollar amount. Computerized exits automatically deduct the correct fare. Children 4 and under ride free. Trains run every 15 to 20 minutes, Monday through Friday from 4am to midnight, Saturday from 6am to midnight, and Sunday from 8am to midnight. In keeping with its futuristic look, BART now offers online trip planners that you can download to your PDA, iPod, or phone.

The 33-mile BART extension, which extends all the way to San Francisco International Airport, opened in 2003. See p. 11, for information on getting into town from the airport.

BY TAXI

This isn't New York, so don't expect a taxi to appear whenever you need one—if at all. If you're downtown during rush hour or leaving a major hotel, it won't be hard to hail a cab; just look for the lighted sign on the roof that indicates the vehicle is free. Otherwise, it's a good idea to call one of the following companies to arrange a ride; even then, there's been more than one time when the cab never came for me. What to do? Call back if your cab is late and insist on attention, but don't expect prompt results on weekends, no matter how nicely you ask. The companies are: **Veteran's Cab** (© 415/552-1300), **Luxor Cabs** (© 415/282-4141), and **Yellow Cab** (© 415/626-2345). Rates are approximately $2.85 for the first mile and 45¢ each fifth of a mile thereafter.

BY CAR

You don't need a car to explore downtown San Francisco. In fact, with the city becoming more crowded by the minute, a car can be your worst nightmare—you're likely to end up stuck in traffic with lots of aggressive and frustrated drivers, pay upwards of $30 a day to park (plus a whopping new 14% parking lot tax), and spend a good portion of your vacation looking for a parking space. Don't bother. However, if you want to venture outside the city, driving is the best way to go.

Before heading outside the city, especially in winter, call © 800/427-7623 for California **road conditions.** You can also call 511 for current traffic information.

CAR RENTALS   All the major rental companies operate in the city and have desks at the airports. When we last checked, you could get a compact car for a week for anywhere from $165 to $315, including all taxes and other charges, but prices change dramatically on a daily basis and depend on which company you rent from.

Some of the national car-rental companies operating in San Francisco include **Alamo** (© 800/327-9633; www.alamo.com), **Avis** (© 800/331-1212; www.avis.com), **Budget** (© 800/527-0700; www.budget.com), **Dollar** (© 800/800-4000; www.dollar.com), **Enterprise** (© 800/325-8007; www.enterprise.com), **Hertz** (© 800/654-3131; www.hertz.com), **National** (© 800/227-7368; www.nationalcar.com), and **Thrifty** (© 800/367-2277; www.thrifty.com).

Car-rental rates vary even more than airline fares. Prices depend on the size of the car, where and when you pick it up and drop it off, the length of the rental period, where and how far you drive it, whether you buy insurance, and a host of other factors. A few key questions can save you hundreds of dollars, but you have to ask—reservations agents don't often volunteer money-saving information:

- Are weekend rates lower than weekday rates? Ask if the rate is the same for pickup Friday morning, for instance, as it is for Thursday night. Reservations agents won't volunteer this information, so don't be shy about asking.
- Does the agency assess a drop-off charge if you don't return the car to the same location where you picked it up?
- Are special promotional rates available? If you see an advertised price in your local newspaper, be sure to ask for that specific rate; otherwise, you could be charged the standard rate. Terms change constantly.
- Are discounts available for members of AARP, AAA, frequent-flier programs, or trade unions? If you belong to any of these organizations, you may be entitled to discounts of up to 30%.
- How much tax will be added to the rental bill? Will there be local tax and state tax?
- How much does the rental company charge to refill your gas tank if you return with the tank less than full? Most rental companies claim their prices are "competitive," but fuel is almost always cheaper in town, so you should try to allow enough time to refuel the car before returning it.

Some companies offer "refueling packages," in which you pay for an entire tank of gas upfront. The cost is usually fairly competitive with local prices, but you don't get credit for any gas remaining in the tank. If a stop at a gas station on the way to the airport will make you miss your plane, then by all means take advantage of the fuel purchase option. Otherwise, skip it.

(*Tips* **Safe Driving**

Keep in mind the following handy driving tips:

- California law requires that both drivers and passengers wear seat belts.
- You can turn right at a red light (unless otherwise indicated), after yielding to traffic and pedestrians, and after coming to a complete stop.
- Cable cars always have the right of way, as do pedestrians at intersections and crosswalks.
- Pay attention to signs and arrows on the streets and roadways, or you might suddenly find yourself in a lane that requires exiting or turning when you want to go straight. Whats more, San Francisco 's many one-way streets can drive you in circles, but most road maps of the city indicate which way traffic flows.

Most agencies enforce a minimum-age requirement—usually 25. Some also have a maximum-age limit. If you're concerned that these limits might affect you, ask about rental requirements at the time of booking to avoid problems later.

Make sure you're insured. Hasty assumptions about your personal auto insurance or a rental agency's additional coverage could end up costing you tens of thousands of dollars, even if you are involved in an accident that is clearly the fault of another driver.

If you already have your own car insurance, you are most likely covered in the United States for loss of or damage to a rental car and liability in case of injury to any other party involved in an accident. Be sure to check your policy before you spend extra money (around $10 or more per day) on the **collision damage waiver (CDW)** offered by all agencies.

Most major credit cards (especially gold and platinum cards) provide some degree of coverage as well—if they were used to pay for the rental. Terms vary widely, however, so be sure to call your credit card company directly before you rent and rely on the card for coverage. If you are uninsured, your credit card may provide primary coverage as long as you decline the rental agency's insurance. If you already have insurance, your credit card may provide secondary coverage, which basically covers your deductible. However, note that *credit cards will not cover liability*, which is the cost of injury to an outside party and/or damage to an outside party's vehicle. If you do not hold an insurance policy, you should seriously consider buying additional liability insurance from your rental company, even if you decline the CDW.

PARKING   If you want to have a relaxing vacation, don't even attempt to find street parking on Nob Hill, in North Beach, in Chinatown, by Fisherman's Wharf, or on Telegraph Hill. Park in a garage or take a cab or a bus. If you do find street parking, pay attention to street signs that explain when you can park and for how long. Be especially careful not to park in zones that are tow areas during rush hours. And be forewarned, San Francisco has instituted a 14% parking tax, so don't be surprised by that garage fee!

Curb colors also indicate parking regulations. *Red* means no stopping or parking; *blue* is reserved for drivers with disabilities who have a disabled plate or placard; *white* means there's a 5-minute limit; *green* indicates a 10-minute limit; and *yellow* and *yellow-and-black* curbs are for stopping to load or unload passengers or luggage only. Also, don't park at a bus stop or in front of a fire hydrant, and watch out for street-cleaning signs. If you violate the law, you might get a hefty ticket or your car might be towed; to get your car back, you'll have to get a release from the nearest district police department and then go to the towing company to pick up the vehicle.

When parking on a hill, apply the hand brake, put the car in gear, and *curb your wheels*—toward the curb when facing downhill, away from the curb when facing uphill. Curbing your wheels not only prevents a possible "runaway" but also keeps you from getting a ticket—an expensive fine that is aggressively enforced.

BY FERRY

TO/FROM SAUSALITO, TIBURON, OR LARKSPUR   The **Golden Gate Ferry Service** fleet (© 415/455-2000; www.golden gateferry.org) shuttles passengers daily between the San Francisco Ferry Building, at the foot of Market Street, and downtown Sausalito and Larkspur. Service is frequent, departing at reasonable intervals every day of the year except January 1, Thanksgiving Day, and December 25. Phone or check the website for an exact schedule. The ride takes half an hour, and one-way fares are $6.45 for adults; $3.35 for seniors, passengers with disabilities, and youth 6 to 18. Children 5 and under travel free when accompanied by a full-fare paying adult (limit two children per adult). Family rates are available on weekends.

Ferries of the **Blue & Gold Fleet** (*©* **415/773-1188** for recorded info, or 415/705-5555 for tickets; www.blueandgoldfleet.com) also provide round-trip service to downtown Sausalito and Tiburon, leaving from Fisherman's Wharf at Pier 41. The one-way cost is $8.50 for adults, $4.50 for kids 5 to 11. Boats run on a seasonal schedule; phone for departure information. Tickets can be purchased at Pier 41.

2

Where to Stay

Whether you want a room with a view or just a room, San Francisco is more than accommodating to its 15.7 million annual guests. Most of the city's 200-plus hotels cluster near Union Square, but some smaller independent gems are scattered around town.

When reading over your options, keep in mind that prices listed are "rack" (published) rates. At big, upscale hotels, almost no one actually pays them—and with the dramatic travel downturn of late, there are still deals to be had. Therefore, you should always ask for special discounts or, even better, vacation packages. It's often possible to get the room you want for $100 less than what is quoted here, except when the hotels are packed (usually during summer and due to conventions) and bargaining is close to impossible. Use the rates listed here for the big hotels as guidelines for comparison only; prices for inexpensive choices and smaller B&Bs are closer to reality, though.

Hunting for hotels in San Francisco can be a tricky business, particularly if you're not a seasoned traveler. What you don't know—and the reservations agent may not tell you—could very well ruin your vacation, so keep the following pointers in mind when it comes time to book a room:

- Prices listed below do not include state and city taxes, which total 14%. Other hidden extras include parking fees, which can be up to $45 per day (also subject to 14% tax!), and hefty surcharges—up to $1 per local call—for telephone use.
- San Francisco is Convention City, so if you want a room at a particular hotel during high season (summer, for example), book well in advance.
- Be sure to have a credit card in hand when making a reservation, and know that you may be asked to pay for at least 1 night in advance (this doesn't happen often, though).
- Hotels usually hold reservations until 6pm. If you don't tell the staff you're arriving late, you might lose your room.

Pricing Categories

The accommodations listed below are classified first by area, and then by price, using the following categories: **Very Expensive,** more than $250 per night; **Expensive,** $200 to $250 per night; **Moderate,** $150 to $200 per night; and **Inexpensive,** less than $150 per night. These categories reflect the rack rates for an average double room during the high season, which runs approximately from April to September.

- Almost every hotel in San Francisco requires a credit card imprint for "incidentals" (and to prevent walkouts). If you don't have a credit card, be sure to make special arrangements with the management before you hang up the phone, and make a note of the name of the person you spoke with.
- When you check in, if your room isn't up to snuff, politely inform the front desk of your dissatisfaction and ask for another. If the hotel can accommodate you, they almost always will—and sometimes will even upgrade you!

Read the following entries carefully: Many hotels also offer rooms at rates above and below the price category that applies to most of the units. If you like the sound of a place that's a bit over your budget, it never hurts to call and ask a few questions. Also note that we do not list single rates. Some hotels, particularly more affordable choices, do charge lower rates for singles, so inquire about them if you are traveling alone.

San Francisco is a wildly popular destination year-round so though there are bargains available, rooms here will still seem expensive compared to many other U.S. destinations. Still, you should always ask about weekend discounts, corporate rates, and family plans; most larger hotels, and many smaller ones, offer them, but many reservations agents don't mention them unless you ask about them specifically.

You'll find nonsmoking rooms available in all larger hotels and many smaller hotels; reviews indicate establishments that are entirely nonsmoking. Nowadays, the best advice for smokers is to confirm a smoking-permitted room in advance.

While you'll find that most accommodations have an abundance of amenities (including phones, unless otherwise noted), don't be

---

Value   **Dial Direct**

When booking a room in a chain hotel, call the hotel's local line and the toll-free number and see where you get the best deal. A hotel makes nothing on a room that stays empty. The clerk who runs the place is more likely to know about vacancies than someone from the toll-free number and will often grant deep discounts in order to fill up rooms.

---

alarmed by the lack of air-conditioned guest rooms. San Francisco weather is so mild, you'll never miss them.

Most larger hotels can accommodate guests who use wheelchairs and those who have other special needs. Ask when you make a reservation to ensure that your hotel can accommodate your needs, especially if you are interested in a bed-and-breakfast.

HELPING HANDS   Having reservations about your reservations? Leave it up to the pros:

San Francisco Reservations, 360 22nd St., Suite 300, Oakland, CA 94612 (© **800/677-1500** or 510/628-4450; www.hotelres.com), arranges reservations for more than 150 of San Francisco's hotels and often offers discounted rates. Their nifty website allows Internet users to make reservations online.

Other good online sites with discounted rates include **www.hotels.com** and **www.placestostay.com**.

1 Union Square

VERY EXPENSIVE

Campton Place Hotel *&&*   This luxury boutique hotel offers some of the best accommodations in town—not to mention the most expensive. Rooms are compact but comfy, with limestone, pear wood, and Italian-modern decor. The two executive suites and one luxury suite push the haute envelope to even more luxurious heights. Discriminating returning guests will still find superlative service, California king-size beds, exquisite bathrooms, bathrobes, top-notch toiletries, slippers, and every other necessity and extra that's made Campton Place a favored temporary address. Alas, Campton Place Restaurant lost its award-winning chef Daniel Humm in 2005, but the restaurant still offers a respectable French/California menu. The jury's still out on whether it's a destination in its own right.

Where to Stay near Union Square & Nob Hill

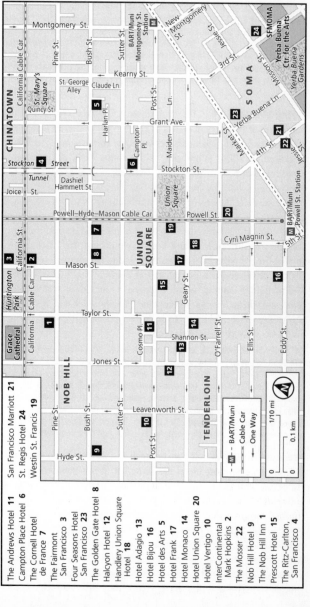

The Andrews Hotel **11**
Campton Place Hotel **6**
The Cornell Hotel
de France **7**
The Fairmont
San Francisco **3**
Four Seasons Hotel
San Francisco **23**
The Golden Gate Hotel **8**
Halcyon Hotel **12**
Handlery Union Square
Hotel **18**
Hotel Adagio **13**
Hotel Bijou **16**
Hotel des Arts **5**
Hotel Frank **17**
Hotel Monaco **14**
Hotel Union Square **20**
Hotel Vertigo **10**
InterContinental
Mark Hopkins **2**
The Mosser **22**
Nob Hill Hotel **9**
The Nob Hill Inn **1**
Prescott Hotel **15**
The Ritz-Carlton,
San Francisco **4**

San Francisco Marriott **21**
St. Regis Hotel **24**
Westin St. Francis **19**

33

340 Stockton St. (btw Post and Sutter sts.), San Francisco, CA 94108. ℰ **866/ 332-1670** or 415/781-5555. Fax 415/955-5536. www.camptonplace.com. 110 units. $350–$485 double; $585–$2,000 suite. American breakfast $18. AE, DC, MC, V. Valet parking $38. Bus: 2, 3, 4, 30, 38, or 45. Cable car: Powell–Hyde or Powell–Mason lines (1 block west). BART: Market St. **Amenities:** Restaurant; outdoor fitness terrace; concierge; secretarial services; room service; laundry service; same-day dry cleaning. *In room:* A/C, TV w/pay movies, dataport, T1 line, minibar, hair dryer, iron, safe.

Hotel Monaco 𝘙𝘙 This remodeled 1910 Beaux Arts building has plenty of atmosphere thanks to a whimsically ethereal lobby with a two-story French inglenook fireplace. The guest rooms, which were upgraded in 2006, follow suit, with canopy beds, Asian-inspired armoires, bamboo writing desks, lively stripes, and vibrant color. Everything is bold but tasteful, and as playful as it is serious, with nifty extras like flatscreen TVs, complimentary Wi-Fi, and two-line cordless phones. The decor, combined with the truly grand neighboring Grand Café restaurant that's ideal for cocktails and mingling (but also serves breakfast and lunch), would put this place on my top-10 list if it weren't for rooms that tend to be too small (especially for the price) and the lack of a sizable gym. That said, it's a fine Union Square option, which happens to include complimentary wine and cheese tasting accompanied by shoulder and neck massages. *Tip:* If you were/are a big fan of Jefferson Airplane, inquire about their Grace Slick Shrine Suite.

501 Geary St. (at Taylor St.), San Francisco, CA 94102. ℰ **866/622-5284** or 415/ 292-0100. Fax 415/292-0111. www.monaco-sf.com. 201 units. $229–$409 double; $279–$619 suite. Rates include evening wine and cheese tasting. Call for discounted rates. AE, DC, DISC, MC, V. Valet parking $39. Bus: 2, 3, 4, 27, or 38. Pets accepted. **Amenities:** Restaurant; exercise room; spa; Jacuzzi; sauna; steam room; concierge; courtesy car; business center; room service; in-room massage; laundry service; dry cleaning. *In room:* A/C, TV, CD player, dataport, wireless high-speed Internet access, minibar, coffeemaker w/Starbucks coffee, hair dryer, iron, safe.

Prescott Hotel 𝘙𝘙 It may be small and lack common areas, but the boutique Prescott Hotel has some big things going for it. The staff treats you like royalty, rooms are attractively unfrilly and masculine, the location (just a block from Union Square) is perfect, and limited room service is provided by Wolfgang Puck's restaurant Postrio. Ralph Lauren fabrics in dark tones of green, plum, and burgundy and crisp white Italian linens blend well with the cherrywood furnishings in each of the soundproof rooms; the view, alas, isn't so pleasant. The very small bathrooms contain terry robes and Aveda products, and the suites have Jacuzzi bathtubs. Concierge-level guests are pampered with a free continental breakfast and evening cocktails and hors d'oeuvres.

545 Post St. (btw Mason and Taylor sts.), San Francisco, CA 94102. (© **866/ 271-3632** or 415/563-0303. Fax 415/563-6831. www.prescotthotel.com. 164 units. $245–$350 double; $280 concierge-level double (including breakfast and evening cocktail reception); from $365 suite. AE, DC, DISC, MC, V. Valet parking $40. Bus: 2, 3, 4, 30, 38, or 45. Cable car: Powell–Hyde or Powell–Mason lines (1 block east). **Amenities:** Restaurant; bar; small exercise room; concierge; limited courtesy car; limited room service. *In room:* TV w/pay movies, dataport, high-speed wireless Internet access, minibar, hair dryer, iron, safe video games.

Westin St. Francis 🏨🏨 *Kids*   At the turn of the 20th century, Charles T. Crocker and a few of his wealthy buddies decided that San Francisco needed a world-class hotel, and up went the St. Francis. Since then, hordes of VIPs have hung their hats and hosiery here, including Emperor Hirohito of Japan, Queen Elizabeth II of England, Mother Teresa, King Juan Carlos of Spain, the shah of Iran, and all the U.S. presidents from Taft through Clinton. In 1972, the hotel gained the 32-story Tower, doubling its capacity and adding banquet and conference centers. The older rooms of the main building vary in size and have more old-world charm than the newer rooms, but the Tower is remarkable for its great views of the city (including from the glass elevators) from above the 18th floor.

Although the St. Francis is too massive to offer the personal service you get at the smaller deluxe hotels on Nob Hill, few other hotels in San Francisco can match its majestic aura. Stroll through the vast, ornate lobby, and you can feel 100 years of history oozing from its hand-carved redwood paneling. The hotel has done massive renovations costing $185 million over the past decade, replacing the carpeting, furniture, and bedding in every main-building guest room; gussying up the lobby; restoring the facade; and adding one of the hottest downtown dining spots, the very expensive and fancy Michael Mina (p. 65).

The Westin makes kids feel right at home, too, with a goody bag upon check-in. The tower's Grandview Rooms evoke a contemporary design along the lines of the W Hotel. The historic main building accentuates its history with traditional, more elegant ambience, high ceilings, and crown molding. Alas, the venerable Compass Rose tearoom is no longer.

335 Powell St. (btw Geary and Post sts.), San Francisco, CA 94102. (© **866/ 500-0038** or 415/397-7000. Fax 415/774-0124. www.westinstfrancis.com. 1,195 units. Main building: $229–$529 double; Tower (Grand View): $219–$559 double; from $650 suite (in either building). Extra person $30. Continental breakfast

$15–$18. AE, DC, DISC, MC, V. Valet parking $42. Bus: 2, 3, 4, 30, 38, 45, or 76. Cable car: Powell–Hyde or Powell–Mason lines (direct stop). Pets under 40 lb. accepted (dog beds available on request). **Amenities:** 2 restaurants; elaborate health club and spa; concierge; car-rental desk; business center; room service. *In room:* A/C, TV, dataport, high-speed Internet access ($15), Wi-Fi ($9.95/day), minibar, fridge available upon request, hair dryer, iron, cordless phones.

EXPENSIVE

Handlery Union Square Hotel 🅖 🅚ids A mere half-block from Union Square, the Handlery was already a good deal frequented by European travelers before the 1908 building underwent a complete overhaul a few years ago. Now you'll find every amenity you could possibly need, plus lots of extras, in the extremely tasteful and modern (although sedate and a little dark) rooms. Rooms range from coral and gray in the historic building to taupe and tan in the newer club-level building. In between is a heated outdoor pool. Literally everything was replaced in the rooms: mattresses, alarm radios, refrigerators, light fixtures, paint, carpets, and furnishings. Perks include adjoining L.A.-based chain restaurant the Daily Grill (which is unfortunately not as good as its sister restaurants down south) and club-level options (all in the newer building) that include larger rooms, a complimentary morning newspaper, a bathroom scale, robes, two two-line phones, and adjoining doors that make the units great choices for families. Downsides? Not a lot of direct light, no grand feeling in the lobby, and lots of trekking if you want to go to and from the adjoining buildings that make up the hotel.

351 Geary St. (btw Mason and Powell sts.), San Francisco, CA 94102. © 800/843-4343 or 415/781-7800. Fax 415/781-0269. www.handlery.com. 377 units. $249–$269 double; Club section $249–$289 double; Owner's Suite $600. Extra person $10. AE, DC, DISC, MC, V. Parking $32. Bus: 2, 3, 4, 30, 38, or 45. Cable car: Powell–Hyde or Powell–Mason lines (direct stop). **Amenities:** Restaurant; heated outdoor swimming pool; access to nearby health club ($10/day); sauna; barbershop; room service; babysitting; same-day laundry. *In room:* Central air, TV w/Nintendo and pay movies, dataport, wireless Internet access, fridge, free coffee/tea-making facilities, hair dryer, iron, safe, voice mail.

Hotel Adagio 🅖🅖 🆅alue Our local hip-hotel company, Joie de Vivre, revamped every one of this 1929 Spanish Revival hotel's 171 large, bright guest rooms in gorgeous modern style. They're real lookers, each with a walnut brown and mocha color palette and dark wood furnishings. Other plusses include firm mattresses, double-paned windows that open, quiet surroundings, voice mail, and plenty of elbowroom. Executive floors (7–16) also come with robes, upscale amenities, makeup mirrors, and stereos with iPod ports.

Bathrooms are old but spotless, and have resurfaced tubs. Feel like splurging? Go for one of the two penthouse-level suites; one has lovely terraces with a New York vibe. Another good reason to stay here is the restaurant/bar **Cortez,** which draws a lively crowd of locals who meet here after work to nosh on small plates in the groovy lounge. *Tip:* Rooms above the eighth floor have good, but not great, views of the city.

550 Geary St., San Francisco, CA 94102. © **800/228-8830** or 415/775-5000. Fax 415/775-9388. www.thehoteladagio.com. 171 units. $189–$279 double. AE, DISC, MC, V. Valet parking $35. **Amenities:** Restaurant; bar; fitness center; concierge; business center w/free wireless Internet; room service; laundry service; dry cleaning; luggage storage room. *In room:* TV w/Nintendo and pay movies, CD player, dataport, free high-speed Internet access, minibar, fridge, hair dryer, iron, safe.

MODERATE

Hotel Frank 🏨🏨 Its location—only a block from Union Square—and chic-boutique makeover are the two main reasons this former Maxwell Hotel is the new darling amongst hip business travelers and serious shoppers. A major renovation in the fall of 2008 brought the hotel to a far more upscale, boutique-hotel standard. A clever interior makeover by one of the country's most cutting-edge designers, Thomas Schoos Design, Inc., incorporates a blend of popular design trends through the decades, from turn-of-the-century Beaux Art classicism to '40's Art Deco and retro '60s chic (yes, I know, it sounds odd, but it works). The guestrooms—each with 32" flat-screen TVs and iPod docking stations—exude a custom designer look: houndstooth-patterned carpeting, elongated emerald green headboards in crocodile-patterned leather, sleek white leather couches, vintage 1930s artwork. Even the bathrooms are outfitted in floor-to-ceiling Carrera marble. The hotel's 28 roomy junior suites offer excellent value despite the slightly audible elevator noise, but best of all are the pair of one-bedroom penthouses on the 13th floor, both of which offer separate living rooms and exceptional views of the city.

386 Geary St. (at Mason St.), San Francisco, CA 94102. © **800/553-1900** or 415/ 986-2000. www.personalityhotels.com. 153 units. $169–$399 double; $209–$469 Jr. suite; $499–$1,200 penthouse suits. AE, DC, DISC, MC, V. Valet parking $30. Bus: 2, 3, 4, 30, 38, or 45. Cable car: Powell–Hyde or Powell–Mason lines (1 block east). **Amenities:** Concierge; meeting facilities; 24-hour business center; room service; same-day dry cleaning; express check-out. *In room:* A/C, TV w/pay movies, free Wi-Fi, hair dryer, iron, safe, bathrobes, honor bar, turndown service.

Hotel Metropolis 🏨 *Kids Finds* Located just off of Market Street, a few blocks from Union Square, the Hotel Metropolis is ideal for people who dread staying at boring, corporate-frumpy McHotels. The lobby alone tells the story: Adorning the walls are more than 80 works of colorful (and curiously abstract) art created by children, yet a Zen-like feel permeates throughout the hotel, starting with the lobby's cascading slate-wall waterfall. The result is a yin/yang combo of playfulness and serenity. As with most downtown hotels, the rooms are on the small side, but all are vibrant and cheery, with vivid colors, custom African Limba-wood furnishings, and comfy beds with wave-shaped headboards with portholes. The six Executive Rooms on the 10th floor are upgraded with feather beds and pillows, IPod alarm clocks, and robes, while the three-room Urban Explorers Kids Suite, which sleeps up to six adults and three children, is filled with pint-sized furniture, bunk beds, a computer, a chalkboard wall, toys and rubber ducky decor in the bathroom. After a busy day in the city, you can relax with a bit of yoga or meditation in the hotel's "well-being room" complete with a miniature rock and sand garden, or enjoy a cup of tea and a good read in the book-filled loft/library. Additional perks include complimentary room service via the adjacent Farmer Brown's restaurant ("farm-fresh soul food"), a 24-hour business center with complimentary computers and laser printers, free high-speed wireless Internet, and a 24-hour exercise room. All this and rates starting at $99 makes the Hotel Metropolis a real find.

25 Mason St. (at Turk and Market sts.), San Francisco, CA 94102. 🅲 **800/553-1900** or 415/775-4600. www.hotelmetropolis.com. 105 units. $99–$289 double; $159–$369 suite. AE, DC, DISC, MC, V. Valet parking $30. Bus: All Market St. buses. Streetcar: Powell St. station. **Amenities:** Exercise room; business center; room service; same-day laundry service/dry cleaning. *In room:* TV w/PPV, free Wi-Fi, hair dryer, iron.

Hotel Union Square 🅐🅐   After a $5 million dollar renovation in the spring of 2008, the Hotel Union Square has achieved that rare hotel hat-trick of history, style, and location. History: It's San Francisco's first boutique hotel, built in 1913 for the 1915 Pan Pacific Exposition. Style: The renovation has juxtaposed contemporary and classic San Francisco, with original 1915 Egyptian-motif mosaic murals, signature staircases, and opulent moldings contrasted by sleek furnishings, completely remodeled bathrooms, and state-of-the-art technology. Location: It's only a half-block from Union Square, in the heart of the city with the cable cars passing by your window. The guestrooms feel more like urban apartments, each outfitted with platform beds with custom-made leather headboards, 600-thread count linens, sleek dark-wood desks, velvety chaise lounges, flat screen televisions, and custom lighting. Many have open loftlike layouts with exposed brick walls and floating white paneled ceiling installations, whereas the two rooftop penthouses are the ultimate in San Francisco chic with large living rooms, wet bars, and expansive redwood decks with city views. There's also a custom Kids Suite, a Dashiell Hammett-themed suite (the third man will cost you an extra $10), and "Sleep & Soak" rooms on each floor that feature spa-like bathrooms outfitted with corner soaking tubs and chaise longues. The hotel lacks a fitness center, but guests have complimentary use of the adjacent Hotel Diva fitness center, and there's even complimentary room delivery from the adjacent Tad's Steakhouse.

114 Powell St. (btw O'Farrell and Ellis sts.), San Francisco, CA 94102. *©* **800/ 553-1900** or 415/397-3000. www.hotelunionsquare.com. 131 units. $149–$349 double; $199–$499 suite; $229–$799 penthouse suites. Rates include morning coffee and tea and weekday wine reception. AE, DC, DISC, MC, V. Valet parking $30. Bus: 2, 3, 4, 30, 38, 45, or 76. Cable car: Powell–Hyde or Powell–Mason lines. Streetcar: Powell St. station. **Amenities:** 24-hour business center; room service; same-day laundry service/dry cleaning, on-site currency exchange. *In room:* TV w/PPV, free Wi-Fi, hair dryer, iron.

Hotel Vertigo ★★

I don't normally write reviews of hotels that haven't opened yet, but I've gotten insider info that the York Hotel, currently under renovation and scheduled to reopen in the fall of '08 as Hotel Vertigo, will be *the* hot new place to stay and play in San Francisco. Combining big-name designers with celebrity chefs is the new trend in high-end hospitality, so locally based Personality Hotels paired cutting-edge design company Thomas Schoos Design, Inc., with celebrity chef Tyler Florence (who will open his first-ever restaurant, Bar Florence, within the hotel) to create a hotel with instant celebrity status. It's a clever concept: The restaurant's salon-style seating and Florence's shared-plates menu will bring in the locals, while Schoos' stylistic design elements will attract tourists and business travelers looking for an alternative to the W Hotel. There's even some colorful history involved as well—the hotel occupies the former site of the Empire Hotel made famous in Alfred Hitchcock's Vertigo, hence the name. Guest rooms will feature playful, eclectic design features such as white tufted-leather headboards, custom wingback chairs in vibrant orange, and crocodile-patterned tiles in the bathrooms. iPod docking stations and 36-inch flat screen televisions will be standard as well. With room rates starting at $169 (half that of the W), it's a safe bet that the Vertigo will be one of the hottest new hotels in town.

940 Sutter St. (btw Leavenworth and Hyde sts.), San Francisco, CA 94109.
ⓒ 800/553-1900 or 415/885-6800. www.personalityhotels.com. 97 units.
$169–$399 double; $350–$495 suites. Rates include morning beverages in lobby
and express breakfast. AE, DISC, MC, V. Valet parking $30. Bus: 2, 3, or 4. **Ameni-
ties:** Fitness room; concierge; business center; room service; same-day dry cleaning;
turn-down service; overnight shoe shine; daily newspaper. *In room:* TV w/pay
movies, free Wi-Fi, hair dryer, iron, safe, robes.

INEXPENSIVE

The Andrews Hotel   For the location, price, and service, the
Andrews is a safe bet for an enjoyable stay in San Francisco. Two
blocks west of Union Square, the Andrews was a Turkish bath before
its conversion in 1981. As is typical in Euro-style hotels, the rooms
are small but well maintained and comfortable, with nice touches
like white lace curtains and fresh flowers. Continued upgrades help
keep things fresh, but large bathroom lovers beware—the facilities
here are tiny. A bonus is the adjoining Fino Bar and Ristorante,
which offers respectable Italian fare and free wine to hotel guests in
the evening.

624 Post St. (btw Jones and Taylor sts.), San Francisco, CA 94109. ⓒ 800/926-3739
or 415/563-6877. Fax 415/928-6919. www.andrewshotel.com. 48 units, some with
shower only. $92–$142 double; $139–$179 superior rooms. Rates include continental breakfast, coffee in lobby, and evening wine. AE, DC, MC, V. Valet parking $25.
Bus: 2, 3, 4, 30, 38, or 45. Cable car: Powell–Hyde or Powell–Mason lines (3 blocks
east). **Amenities:** Restaurant; access to nearby health club; concierge; room service
(5:30–10pm); babysitting; nearby self-service laundromat; laundry service; dry
cleaning. *In room:* TV/VCR w/video library, CD player in suites only, dataport, free Wi-
Fi, fridge, hair dryer on request, iron.

The Cornell Hotel de France   Its quirks make this small French-
style hotel more charming than many others in its price range. Pass
the office, where a few faces will glance in your direction and smile,
and embark on a ride in the old-fashioned elevator (we're talking
seriously old-school here) to get to your basic room. Each floor is
dedicated to a French painter and decorated with reproductions.
Rooms are all plain and comfortable, with desks and chairs, and are
individually and simply decorated. Smoking is not allowed. The full
American breakfast included in the rate is served in the cool cavern-
like provincial basement restaurant, Jeanne d'Arc. Union Square is
just a few blocks away.

715 Bush St. (btw Powell and Mason sts.), San Francisco, CA 94108. ⓒ 800/
232-9698 or 415/421-3154. Fax 415/399-1442. www.cornellhotel.com. 55 units.
$85–$155 double. Rates include full American breakfast. AE, DC, DISC, MC, V. Parking across the street $17. Bus: 2, 3, 4, 30, or 45. Cable car: Powell–Hyde or Pow-
ell–Mason lines. **Amenities:** Restaurant; computer w/Internet in lobby. *In room:* TV,
dataport, Wi-Fi (for a fee), hair dryer.

The Golden Gate Hotel ✮ (Value   San Francisco's stock of small hotels in historic turn-of-the-20th-century buildings includes some real gems, and The Golden Gate Hotel is one of them. It's 2 blocks north of Union Square and 2 blocks down (literally) from the crest of Nob Hill, with cable car stops at the corner for easy access to Fisherman's Wharf and Chinatown. The city's theaters and best restaurants are also within walking distance. But the best thing about the 1913 Edwardian hotel—which definitely has a B&B feel—is that it's family run: John and Renate Kenaston and daughter Gabriele are hospitable innkeepers who take obvious pleasure in making their guests comfortable. Each individually decorated room has recently been repainted and carpeted and has handsome antique furnishings (plenty of wicker) from the early 1900s, quilted bedspreads, and fresh flowers. Request a room with a claw-foot tub if you enjoy a good, hot soak. Afternoon tea is served daily from 4 to 7pm, and guests are welcome to use the house fax and computer with wireless Internet free of charge.

775 Bush St. (btw Powell and Mason sts.), San Francisco, CA 94108. ℂ 800/ 835-1118 or 415/392-3702. Fax 415/392-6202. www.goldengatehotel.com. 25 units, 14 with bathroom. $85–$105 double without bathroom; $150 double with bathroom. Rates include continental breakfast and afternoon tea. AE, DC, MC, V. Self-parking $20. Bus: 2, 4, 30, 38, or 45. Cable car: Powell–Hyde or Powell–Mason lines (1 block east). BART: Powell and Market. **Amenities:** Access to health club 1 block away; activities desk; laundry service/dry cleaning next door. *In room:* TV, dataport, free Wi-Fi, hair dryer and iron upon request.

Halcyon Hotel (Value   Inside this small, four-story brick building is a penny-pincher's dream come true, the kind of place where you'll find everything you need yet won't have to pay through the nose to get it. The small but clean studio guest rooms are equipped with microwave ovens, refrigerators, flatware and utensils, toasters, alarm clocks, coffeemakers and coffee, phones with free local calls, mail delivery, and voice mail—all the comforts of home in the heart of Union Square (you can even bring your pet!). A coin-operated washer and dryer are located in the basement, along with free laundry soap and irons. The managers are usually on hand to offer friendly, personal service, making this option all in all an unbeatable deal. Be sure to ask about special rates for weekly stays.

649 Jones St. (btw Geary and Post sts.), San Francisco, CA 94102. ℂ 800/627-2396 or 415/929-8033. Fax 415/441-8033. www.halcyonsf.com. 25 units. $79–$99 double year-round; $450–$600 weekly. AE, DC, DISC, MC, V. Parking garage nearby $14–$16 per day. Bus: 2, 3, 4, 9, 27, or 38. Pets accepted. **Amenities:** Access to nearby health club; concierge; tour desk; laundry facilities; free fax available in lobby. *In room:* TV, dataport, kitchen, fridge, coffeemaker, hair dryer, iron, voice mail.

Hotel Bijou (*Value*) Three words sum up this hotel: clean, colorful, and cheap. Although it's on the periphery of the gritty Tenderloin (just 3 blocks off Union Sq.), once inside this gussied-up 1911 hotel, all's cheery, bright, and perfect for budget travelers who want a little style with their savings. Joie de Vivre hotel group disguised the hotel's age with lively decor, a Deco theater theme, and a heck of a lot of vibrant paint. To the left of the small lobby is a "theater" where guests can watch San Francisco–based double features nightly (it has cute old-fashioned theater seating, though it's just a basic TV showing videos). Upstairs, rooms named after locally made films are small, clean, and colorful (think buttercup, burgundy, and purple), and have all the basics from clock radios, dressers, and small desks to tiny bathrooms (one of which is so small you have to close the door to access the toilet). Alas, a few mattresses could be firmer, and there's only one small and slow elevator. But considering the price, and perks like the continental breakfast and friendly service, you can't go wrong here.

111 Mason St., San Francisco, CA 94102. (©) **800/771-1022** or 415/771-1200. Fax 415/346-3196. www.hotelbijou.com. 65 units. $99–$159 double. Rates include continental breakfast. AE, DC, DISC, MC, V. Valet parking $27. Bus: All Market St. buses. Streetcar: Powell St. station. **Amenities:** Concierge; limited room service; same-day laundry service/dry cleaning; DSL access in lobby ($4/20 min). *In room:* TV, dataport, high-speed Internet, Wi-Fi ($7.95/day), hair dryer, iron.

Hotel des Arts (*Value*) While this bargain find has the same floor plan as San Francisco's numerous other Euro-style hotels—small lobby, narrow hallways, cramped rooms—the owners of the des Arts have made an obvious effort to distance themselves from the competition by including a visually stimulating dose of artistic license throughout the hotel. The lobby, for example, hosts a rotating art gallery featuring contemporary works by emerging local artists and is outfitted with groovy furnishings, while the guest rooms are soothingly situated with quality furnishings and tasteful accouterments. There's one suite that can sleep up to four persons at no additional charge. You'll love the lively location as well: right across the street from the entrance to Chinatown and 2 blocks from Union Square. There's even a French brasserie right downstairs. Considering the price (rooms with a very clean shared bathroom start at $59), quality, and location, it's quite possibly the best budget hotel in the city. *Tip:* Log onto the hotel's website to check out the "Painted Rooms" designed by local artists, then call the hotel directly to book your favorite.

447 Bush St. (at Grant St.), San Francisco, CA 94108. ✆ **800/956-4322** or 415/956-3232. Fax 415/956-0399. www.sfhoteldesarts.com. 51 units, 26 with private bathroom. $79–$159 double with bathroom; $59–$79 double without bathroom. Rates include continental breakfast. AE, DC, MC, V. Nearby parking $18. Cable car: Powell–Hyde or Powell–Mason lines. **Amenities:** 24-hr. concierge, fax, and copy services; laundry and valet service. *In room:* TV, 2-line direct-dial telephone w/dataport and voice mail, minifridge and microwave in many rooms, hair dryer, iron and board.

2 Nob Hill

VERY EXPENSIVE

The Fairmont San Francisco 🌟🌟🌟 (Kids)   The granddaddy of Nob Hill's elite cadre of ritzy hotels—and the only spot in San Francisco where each of the city's cable car lines meet—the century-old Fairmont is a must-visit if only to marvel at the incredibly glamorous lobby with its vaulted ceilings, Corinthian columns, a spectacular spiral staircase, and rococo furniture (it's easy to feel underdressed in such opulent surroundings). And yes, such decadence carries to the guest rooms where luxuries abound: oversized marble bathrooms, thick down blankets, goose-down king pillows, extra-long mattresses, and large walk-in closets. Because it's perched at the top of Nob Hill, there are spectacular city views from every guest room, but nuances such as a health club & spa, a 24-hour concierge, twice-daily maid service, babysitting services, and a business center enhance every guest's stay. Within the lobby is the ornate **Laurel Court** restaurant and lounge, which serves as the hotel's centerpiece. (It's fun to indulge in afternoon tea here, served daily 2:30–4:30pm.) A local institution that's been around since I was a kid is the hotel's **Tonga Room,** a fantastically kitsch Disneyland-like tropical bar and restaurant where happy hour hops and "rain" falls every 30 minutes.

950 Mason St. (at California St.), San Francisco, CA 94108. ✆ **866/540-4491** or 415/772-5000. Fax 415/772-5086. www.fairmont.com. 591 units. Main building $229–$349 double; from $500 suite. Tower $289–$469 double; from $750 suite. Penthouse $12,500. Extra person $30. AE, DC, DISC, MC, V. Parking $43. Cable car: California St. line (direct stop). **Amenities:** 2 restaurants/bars; health club (free for Fairmont President's Club members; $15/day or $20/2 days, non-members); concierge; tour desk; car-rental desk; business center; shopping arcade; salon; room service; massage; babysitting; same-day laundry service/dry cleaning; wireless Internet in lobby. *In room:* A/C, TV w/pay movies and video games available, dataport, high-speed Internet access, kitchenette in some units, minibar, hair dryer, iron, safe.

InterContinental Mark Hopkins 🌟🌟🌟   Built in 1926 on the spot where railroad millionaire Mark Hopkins's turreted mansion once stood, the 19-story Mark Hopkins gained global fame during

World War II when it was de rigueur for Pacific-bound servicemen to toast their goodbye to the States in the Top of the Mark cocktail lounge. Nowadays, this grand hotel caters mostly to convention-bound corporate executives, since its prices often require corporate charge accounts. Each neoclassical room is exceedingly comfortable and comes with all the fancy amenities you'd expect from a world-class hotel, including custom furniture, plush fabrics, sumptuous bathrooms, Frette bathrobes, and extraordinary views of the city. The luxury suites are twice the size of most San Francisco apartments and cost close to a month's rent per night. A minor caveat: The hotel has only three guest elevators, making a quick trip to your room difficult during busy periods.

The **Top of the Mark** (p. 166), a fantastic bar/lounge (open daily), offers dancing to live jazz or swing, Sunday brunch, and cocktails in swank, old-fashioned style. (Romantics, this place is for you, but keep in mind that there's a $10 cover fee Fri–Sat after 8:30pm for the live nightly entertainment.) The Nob Hill Restaurant offers California cuisine nightly and breakfast on Sunday.

1 Nob Hill (at California and Mason sts.), San Francisco, CA 94108. ⓒ 800/ 972-3124 or 415/392-3434. Fax 415/421-3302. www.markhopkins.net. 380 units. $399–$599 double; from $650 suite; from $3,000 luxury suite. Breakfast $17 for juice, coffee, and pastry to $23 for full buffet. AE, DC, DISC, MC, V. Valet parking $44, some oversize vehicles prohibited. Bus: 1. Cable car: California St. or Powell lines (direct stop). **Amenities:** 2 restaurants; bar; exercise room; concierge; business center; secretarial services; room service; babysitting; laundry service/dry cleaning; concierge-level floors. *In room:* A/C, TV w/pay movies, VCR/DVD in suites only, dataport, Wi-Fi in all rooms for nominal fee, minibar, coffeemaker, hair dryer, iron, safe.

The Ritz-Carlton, San Francisco 𝕬𝕬𝕬   Ranked among the top hotels in the world, The Ritz-Carlton San Francisco has been the benchmark for the city's luxury hotels since it opened in 1991. A Nob Hill landmark, the former Metropolitan Insurance headquarters stood vacant for years until The Ritz-Carlton company acquired it and embarked on a $100-million, 4-year renovation. The interior was completely gutted and restored with fine furnishings, fabrics, and artwork, including a pair of Louis XVI blue marble urns with gilt mountings, and 19th-century Waterford candelabras. And just to make sure they stay on top, the rooms were completely upgraded last year to the tune of $12.5 million, and now include 32-inch LCD TVs, DVD/CD players, Wi-Fi, and two cordless phones. The Italian marble bathrooms offer every possible amenity: double sinks, telephone, name-brand toiletries, and plush terry robes. The more expensive rooms take advantage of the hotel's location—the south slope of Nob Hill—and have good views of the city. Clubrooms, on the top floors, have a dedicated concierge, separate elevator-key access, and complimentary small plates throughout the day. No restaurant in town has more formal service than this hotel's **Dining Room,** which serves modern French cuisine with a Japanese influence. The less formal **Terrace Restaurant** offers contemporary Mediterranean cuisine and the city's best Sunday brunch. The Lobby lounge serves classic afternoon tea and cocktails with low-key live entertainment daily, and sushi Wednesday through Saturday.

600 Stockton St. (btw Pine and California sts.), San Francisco, CA 94108. © 800/241-3333 or 415/296-7465. Fax 415/986-1268. www.ritzcarlton.com. 336 units. $445–$480 double; $600–$850 club-level double; from $750–$850 executive suite. Buffet breakfast $32; Sun champagne brunch $65. Weekend discounts and packages available. AE, DC, DISC, MC, V. Parking $55. Cable car: California St. cable car line (direct stop). **Amenities:** 2 restaurants; 3 bars; indoor pool; outstanding fitness center; Jacuzzi; steam room; concierge; courtesy car; business center; secretarial services; room service; in-room massage and manicure; same-day laundry service/dry cleaning. *In room:* A/C, TV w/pay movies, dataport, high-speed Internet access and Wi-Fi ($13/day), minibar, hair dryer, iron, safe.

MODERATE

Nob Hill Hotel (*Value*)   The Nob Hill Hotel is an amazing deal for such an over-the-top Victorian inn, with rates around $130 peak season (and often less). Located in a quiet area of between the Tenderloin and Nob Hill (aka Tendernob), it was built in 1906 and fully restored in 1998, and whoever renovated the lobby did a smashing job restoring it to its original "Old San Francisco Victorian" splendor, complete with original marble flooring, high ceilings with decorative moldings, and stained-glass panels and alabaster dating from about 1892. Though the rooms are small, they are all handsomely decorated with old-fashioned furnishings such as Victorian antique armoires, rich carpeting, marble bathrooms, brass beds with comforters, and carved-wood nightstands. A pleasant oxymoron: All the rooms are equipped with a plethora of high-tech amenities such as Internet access and personal voice mail. Complimentary pastries and coffee are served each morning, and there's even free evening wine tasting. The adjacent **Il Bacio** restaurant is a good place to refuel on regional Italian cuisine before venturing down the street to Union Square. *Tip:* The hotel's website offers a Priceline-style "Name Your Own Rate" option that might save you big bucks on your hotel room.

835 Hyde St. (btw Bush and Sutter sts.), San Francisco, CA 94109. © **877/662-4455** or 415/885-2987. Fax 415/921-1648. www.nobhillhotel.com. 53 units. $130–$150 double. Rates include continental breakfast. DC, DISC, MC, V. Parking $24. Bus: 2, 3, or 4. **Amenities:** Adjoining restaurant (Italian); 24-hr. fitness passes available; copy, fax, and e-mail services; laundry service. *In room:* TV w/pay movies, CD/radio alarm clocks, dataport, microwave, hair dryer, iron, suites have Jacuzzi tubs, fax, and English-style garden.

The Nob Hill Inn ℱ   Built in 1907 as a private home, this four-story inn has been masterfully refurbished with Victorian-style antiques, expensive fabrics, reproduction artwork, and a magnificent etched-glass European-style lift. Even the low-priced Gramercy rooms receive equal attention: with good-size bathrooms (with claw-foot tubs), antique furnishings, faux-antique phones, discreetly placed televisions, and comfortable full-size beds. Granted, the cheaper rooms are quite small, but they're so utterly charming that it's tough to complain, especially when you consider that rates include continental breakfast, afternoon tea and sherry, and the distinction of staying in one of the city's most prestigious neighborhoods. *Tip:* Ideal for families of four are the inn's one-bedroom apartment-style suites, which include a stocked kitchenette, a private master bedroom, and a parlor with a sofa sleeper.

1000 Pine St. (at Taylor St.), San Francisco, CA 94109. © **415/673-6080.** Fax 415/673-6098. www.nobhillinn.com. 21 units. $125–$195 double; $245–$275 suite. Rates include continental breakfast, afternoon tea, and sherry. AE, DC, DISC, MC, V. Parking $25–$35 per day in nearby garages. Bus: 1. Cable car: California St. line. **Amenities:** Concierge. *In room:* TV, kitchenette in some, hair dryer, iron.

3 SoMa

VERY EXPENSIVE

Four Seasons Hotel San Francisco ℱℱℱ   What makes this überluxury hotel one of my favorites in the city is its perfect combination of elegance, trendiness, and modern luxury. The entrance, either off Market or through a narrow alley off Third Street, is deceptively underwhelming, although it does tip you off to the hotel's overall discreetness. Take the elevators up to the lobby and you're instantly surrounded by calm, cool, and collected hotel perfection. After all, what's not to love about dark mood lighting, comfy leather chairs, bottomless bowls of olives and spicy wasabi-covered peanuts, a tempting cocktail list, and a pianist playing jazz standards intermingled with No Doubt and Cold Play? Many of the oversize rooms (starting at 460 sq. ft. and including 46 suites) overlook Yerba Buena

Gardens. Not too trendy, not too traditional, they're just right, with custom-made mattresses and pillows that guarantee the all-time best night's sleep, beautiful works of art, and huge luxury marble bathrooms with deep tubs and L'Occitane toiletries. Hues of taupe, beige, and green are almost as soothing as the impeccable service. Adding to the perks are free access to the building's huge Sports Club L.A. (the best hotel gym in the city), round-the-clock business services, a 2-block walk to Union Square and the Moscone Convention Center, and a vibe that combines sophistication with a hipness far more refined than the W or the Clift. Its only contender in that department is the St. Regis.

757 Market St. (btw Third and Fourth sts.), San Francisco, CA 94103. ⓒ 800/ 819-5053 or 415/633-3000. Fax 415/633-3001. www.fourseasons.com/sanfrancisco. 277 units. $450–$855 double; $825 executive suite. AE, DC, DISC, MC, V. Parking $39. Bus: All Market St. buses. Streetcar: F, and all underground streetcars. BART: All trains. **Amenities:** Restaurant; bar; huge fitness center; spa; concierge; high-tech business center; secretarial services; salon; room service; in-room massage; overnight laundry service/dry cleaning, wireless Internet access in lobby. *In room:* A/C, TV w/pay movies, fax, dataport, high-speed Internet access ($13/day), minibar, hair dryer, safe.

St. Regis Hotel ⓐⓐⓐ   The latest in full-blown high-tech luxury is yours at this überchic 40-story SoMa tower, which debuted in late 2005. Strategically located near the Museum of Modern Art and Yerba Buena Gardens, this shrine to urban luxury welcomes guests (and residents willing to pay upwards of $2 million for an apartment) with a 16-foot-long gas fireplace and streamlined lobby bar that's frequented by city socialites. A "personal butler" will take you to your room and show you how to use its coolest feature: a touchscreen control panel that works everything, from the phone to the drapes to the temperature to the lights. Decor is minimalist, with dark woods, cream, taupes, and sexy touches like Barcelona benches, 42-inch plasma TVs, and leather paneling (at least in the suites). Bathrooms beckon with deep soaking tubs, 13-inch LCD TVs, rainforest showerheads, and fancy toiletries. You may want to lounge on a chaise and can peek into the happenings of downtown bustle or the green patch of grass that marks Yerba Buena Gardens, but definitely leave your room for an afternoon at the posh two-floor **Remède Spa,** the huge pool and fitness center, and restaurant **Ame,** where chef Hiro Sone, who also owns Terra in Napa Valley, presides over an Asian-influenced menu that includes delicacies such as hamachi sashimi and decadences like foie gras and unagi (eel) over mushroom risotto.

Where to Stay around Town

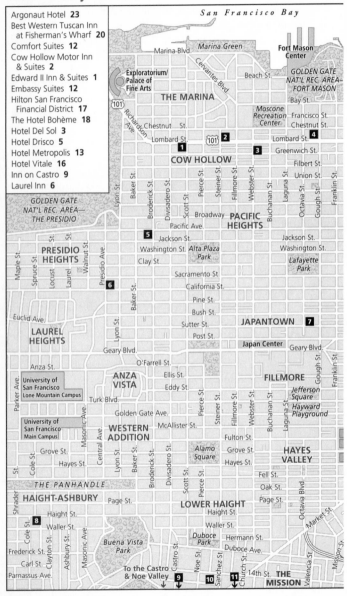

San Francisco Bay

Fort Mason Center

Marina Blvd   Marina Green

GOLDEN GATE NAT'L REC. AREA– FORT MASON

Exploratorium/ Palace of Fine Arts

Cervantes Blvd

Beach St.

Bay St.

THE MARINA

Moscone Recreation Center

Francisco St.

Richardson Ave.

Chestnut St.

Chestnut St.

Lombard St.

Lombard St.

COW HOLLOW

Greenwich St.

Filbert St.

Baker St.

Broderick St.

Divisadero St.

Scott St.

Pierce St.

Steiner St.

Fillmore St.

Webster St.

Buchanan St.

Laguna St.

Octavia St.

Gough St.

Franklin St.

Union St.

Broadway

PACIFIC HEIGHTS

Pacific Ave.

GOLDEN GATE NAT'L REC. AREA— THE PRESIDIO

Jackson St.

Jackson St.

PRESIDIO HEIGHTS

Washington St.   Alta Plaza Park

Washington St.

Maple St.

Spruce St.

Locust St.

Laurel St.

Walnut St.

Presidio Ave.

Baker St.

Lyon St.

Clay St.

Sacramento St.

Lafayette Park

California St.

Pine St.

Bush St.

LAUREL HEIGHTS

Euclid Ave.

Sutter St.

JAPANTOWN

Post St.

Geary Blvd.

Japan Center

Geary Blvd.

Anza St.

O'Farrell St.

Parker Ave.

University of San Francisco Lone Mountain Campus

ANZA VISTA

Ellis St.

FILLMORE

Eddy St.

Masonic Ave.

Turk Blvd.

Pierce St.

Steiner St.

Fillmore St.

Webster St.

Buchanan St.

Laguna St.

Gough St.

Franklin St.

Jefferson Square

Hayward Playground

University of San Francisco Main Campus

Golden Gate Ave.

WESTERN ADDITION

McAllister St.

Central Ave.

Fulton St.

Grove St.

Lyon St.

Baker St.

Broderick St.

Divisadero St.

Scott St.

Pierce St.

Alamo Square

Grove St.

HAYES VALLEY

Cole St.

Hayes St.

Hayes St.

Fell St.

THE PANHANDLE

Oak St.

Octavia Blvd.

HAIGHT-ASHBURY

Page St.

LOWER HAIGHT

Page St.

Market St.

Shrader St.

Haight St.

Haight St.

Cole St.

Waller St.

Waller St.

Clayton St.

Ashbury St.

Masonic Ave.

Frederick St.

Buena Vista Park

Duboce Park

Hermann St.

Carl St.

Duboce Ave.

Parnassus Ave.

To the Castro & Noe Valley

Castro St.

Noe St.

Sanchez St.

Church St.

14th St.   THE MISSION

Valencia St.

Mission St.

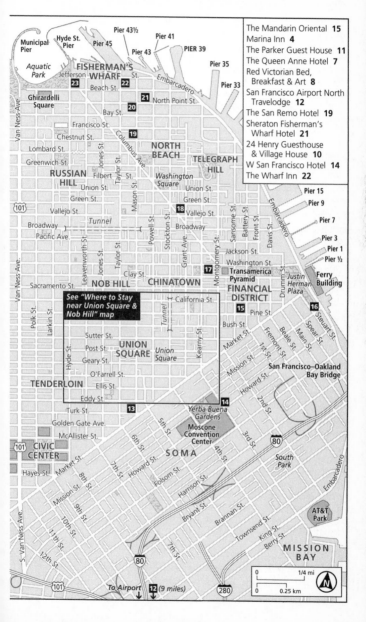

The Mandarin Oriental **15**
Marina Inn **4**
The Parker Guest House **11**
The Queen Anne Hotel **7**
Red Victorian Bed,
  Breakfast & Art **8**
San Francisco Airport North
  Travelodge **12**
The San Remo Hotel **19**
Sheraton Fisherman's
  Wharf Hotel **21**
24 Henry Guesthouse
  & Village House **10**
W San Francisco Hotel **14**
The Wharf Inn **22**

See "Where to Stay
near Union Square &
Nob Hill" map

125 Third St. (at Mission St.), San Francisco, CA 94103. *(* **877/787-3447** or 415/
284-4000. Fax 415/284-4100. www.stregis.com/sanfrancisco. 260 units. Double
from $529–$679; suites from $1,050–$8,500. AE, DC, DISC, MC, V. Parking $45 per
day. Bus: 15, 30, or 45. Streetcar: J, K, L, or M to Montgomery. **Amenities:** 2 restaurants; bar; health club w/heated lap pool; giant spa; steam room; sauna; whirlpool;
24-hr. concierge; 24-hr. business center; room service; laundry service; dry cleaning;
wireless Internet ($15/day), conference rooms. *In room:* A/C, 2 TVs w/pay movies,
fax, dataport, minibar, high-speed Internet access ($15/day), hair dryer, iron upon
request, safe, printer, scanner, copier.

W San Francisco Hotel *(((((* Starwood Hotels & Resorts' 31-
story property is as modern and hip as its fashionable clientele.
Sophisticated, slick, and stylish, it suits its neighbors, which include
the Museum of Modern Art, the Moscone Center, and the Metreon
entertainment center. The striking gray granite facade, piped with
polished black stone, complements the octagonal three-story glass
entrance and lobby. The hip, urban style extends to the guest rooms,
which have a residential feel. Each contains a feather bed with a
goose-down comforter and pillows, Waterworks linens, an oversize
dark-wood desk, an upholstered chaise longue, and louvered blinds
that open to (usually) great city views. Each room also contains a
compact media wall complete with a Sony CD/DVD player, an
extensive CD library, and a 27-inch color TV with optional high-
speed Internet service (and an infrared keyboard) at $15 per day.
Bathrooms are super-sleek and stocked with Bliss products. Further-
ing the cool vibe is a bi-level **XYZ** bar and restaurant, which serves
wonderful Californian cuisine within a beautiful modern interior. In
2005, the W welcomed a 5,000-square-foot outpost of NYC's **Bliss
Spa** to the premises. All in all, this is one of the top places to stay in
San Francisco, particularly if you enjoy the nightlife scene.

181 Third St. (btw Mission and Howard sts.), San Francisco, CA 94103. *(* **877/
WHOTELS** or 415/777-5300. Fax 415/817-7823. www.whotels.com/sanfrancisco.
410 units. From $359 double; $1,800–$2,500 suite. AE, DC, DISC, MC, V. Valet park-
ing $40. Bus: 15, 30, or 45. Streetcar: J, K, L, or M to Montgomery. **Amenities:**
Restaurant; 2 bars; heated atrium pool and Jacuzzi; fitness center; spa; concierge;
business center; secretarial services; 24-hr. room service; same-day laundry serv-
ice/dry cleaning; Wi-Fi in public spaces. *In room:* A/C, TV w/pay movies, CD/DVD
player fax (in some rooms), dataport, high-speed Internet access, minibar, coffeemaker, hair dryer, iron, safe.

EXPENSIVE

Hotel Vitale *(((((* Perched at the foot of The Embarcadero with
outstanding waterfront and Bay Bridge views from east-facing
rooms, this 199-unit hotel opened in 2005 to instant popularity. In

addition to its prime location across from the Ferry Building Marketplace (p. 106), Hotel Vitale looks pretty darned chic, from the clean-lined lobby, lounge, and decent but not destination-worthy **Americano** restaurant (with a hopping after-work bar scene), to the modern and masculine rooms awash in earth tones and armed with contemporary perks like flatscreen TVs, CD players with groovy compilations, gourmet minibars and for-sale bath products, huge bathrooms with walk-in showers, and nature-themed pop art. Despite excellent service from the well-trained staff, there are a few subtleties that separate Vitale from true luxury hotel status: For example, my fancy flatscreen TV didn't face the bed or the couch and wasn't on hinges that allowed it to be adjusted—very annoying—and the fitness room is flat-out lame with three cardio machines and a few weights. However, they're now offering complimentary access to the nearby YMCA health club, which has all the workout essentials. So, if you can live with a few quirks, it's a very attractive place to stay—my NYC friend loves this hotel—especially if you book one of the suites with 270-degree San Francisco views.

8 Mission St. (at Embarcadero), San Francisco, CA 94105. © 888/890-8868 or 415/278-3700. Fax 415/278-3750. www.hotelvitale.com. 199 units. $269–$399 double; from $699 suite. Rates include morning paper, free morning yoga, and free courtesy car to downtown locations on weekdays. AE, DC, DISC, MC, V. Valet parking $42. Bus: 2, 7, 14, 21, 71, or 71L. **Amenities:** Restaurant; exercise room; spa; concierge; business center; room service; laundry service; dry cleaning; free Internet salon; free Wi-Fi. *In room:* A/C, TV w/pay movies, CD player, dataport, high-speed Internet access, Wi-Fi, minibar, hair dryer, iron, safe.

San Francisco Marriott 🐾🐾   Some call it a masterpiece; others liken it to the world's biggest parking meter. In either case, the Marriott is one of the largest buildings in the city, making it a popular stop for convention-goers and those looking for a room with a view. Fortunately, the controversy does not extend to the rooms, which are pleasant, vibrant, and contemporary with large bathrooms and exceptional city vistas. *Tip:* Upon arrival, enter from Fourth Street, between Market and Mission, to avoid a long trek to the registration area.

55 Fourth St. (btw Market and Mission sts.), San Francisco, CA 94103. © 800/228-9290 or 415/896-1600. Fax 415/486-8101. www.Marriott.com/sfodt. 1,598 units. $199–$349 double; $499–$3,250 suite. AE, DC, DISC, MC, V. Parking $46. Bus: All Market St. buses. Streetcar: All Market St. streetcars. Cable car: Powell–Hyde or Powell–Mason lines (3 blocks west). **Amenities:** 2 restaurants; 2 bars; indoor pool; health club; tour desk; car rental; business center; dry cleaning; Wi-Fi in select areas. *In room:* A/C, TV w/pay movies, dataport, high-speed Internet ($13/day), hair dryer, iron.

MODERATE

The Mosser ✦ *Value*   "Hip on the Cheap" might best sum up The Mosser, a highly atypical budget hotel that incorporates Victorian architecture with modern interior design. It originally opened in 1913 as a luxury hotel only to be dwarfed by the far more modern sky-rise hotels that surround it. But a major multimillion-dollar renovation a few years back transformed this aging charmer into a sophisticated, stylish, and surprisingly affordable SoMa lodging. Guest rooms are replete with original Victorian flourishes—bay windows and hand-carved moldings—that juxtapose well with the contemporary custom-designed furnishings, granite showers, stainless steel fixtures, ceiling fans, Frette linens, double-paned windows, and modern electronics. The least expensive rooms are quite small and share a bathroom, but are an incredible deal for such a central location. The hotel's restaurant, Annabelle's Bar & Bistro, serves lunch and dinner, and The Mosser even houses Studio Paradiso, a state-of-the-art recording studio. The location is excellent as well—3 blocks from Union Square, 2 blocks from the MOMA and Moscone Convention Center, and half a block from the cable car turnaround. It also borders on a "sketchy" street, but then again, so do most hotels a few blocks west of Union Square.

54 Fourth St. (at Market St.), San Francisco, CA 94103. ℂ **800/227-3804** or 415/986-4400. Fax 415/495-7653. www.themosser.com. 166 units, 112 with bathroom. $169–$259 double with bathroom; $79–$99 double without bathroom. Rates include safe-deposit boxes at front desk. AE, DC, DISC, MC, V. Parking $30, plus $10 for oversize vehicles. Streetcar: F, and all underground Muni and BART. **Amenities:** Restaurant; bar; 24-hr. concierge; same-day laundry service/dry cleaning. *In room:* Ceiling fan, TV, AM/FM stereo w/CD player, dataport, Wi-Fi ($9.95/day), hair dryer, iron/ironing board, voice mail.

4 The Financial District

VERY EXPENSIVE

The Mandarin Oriental ✦✦✦   No hotel combines better ultra-luxury digs with incredible views than this gem. The only reason to pause in the lobby or mezzanine is for the traditional tea service or cocktails. Otherwise, heaven begins after a rocketing ride on the elevators to the rooms, all of which are located between the 38th and 48th floors of a high-rise. The opulent rooms also feature contemporary Asian-influenced decor, but the best details by far are the huge windows with superb city views, particularly when the fog rolls in below you. Not all rooms have tub-side views (incredible and standard with the signature rooms), but every one does have a luxurious marble bathroom stocked with terry and cotton cloth robes, a makeup mirror, and silk slippers. An added bonus: The restaurant, **Silks,** has a kitchen crew working wonders with the Asian-influenced menu. If the dining room weren't so awkwardly empty, it'd be a recommended destination. That said, even without the whole package, it's an excellent place to dine.

222 Sansome St. (btw Pine and California sts.), San Francisco, CA 94104. ⓒ **800/ 622-0404** or 415/276-9888. Fax 415/433-0289. www.mandarinoriental.com. 158 units. $375–$725 double; $645–$695 signature rooms; from $1,450 suite. Continental breakfast $21; American breakfast $32. AE, DC, DISC, MC, V. Valet parking $36. Bus: All Market St. buses. Streetcar: J, K, L, or M to Montgomery. **Amenities:** Restaurant; bar; fitness center; concierge; car rental; business center; room service; in-room massage; laundry service; same-day dry cleaning; wireless Internet access. *In room:* A/C, TV w/pay movies, CD player fax on request, dataport, Wi-Fi ($13/day), minibar, hair dryer, iron, safe.

EXPENSIVE

Hilton San Francisco Financial District ⓐ   Finally there's a good reason to stay in Chinatown. Reopened in 2006 after a $40-million renovation, this upscale hotel geared toward the needs of the business traveler is a good choice for anyone seeking a convenient downtown location perfect for forays into Chinatown, North Beach, and beyond. All of the comfortably modern rooms feature either city or bay views, so you really can't go wrong. The panoramic bay views of Coit Tower, Telegraph Hill, and Alcatraz are wholly unobstructed as you look straight down the Columbus Avenue thoroughfare to Ghirardelli Square. The in-room contemporary decor includes dark muted earth-tone carpets; warm honey-colored wood; and lush, pristine palette beds with crisp white linens and featherbeds swathed in masculine dusty blue, tan, and slate-gray pillows and accents. All units boast modern goodies such as MP3-compatible alarm clocks and flatscreen TVs. All signature-floor accommodations have balconies. The seven suites have bamboo floors, fireplaces, balconies, and large luxurious bathrooms, some with nice touches like sleek yours-and-mine sinks. For concierge-floor guests, a complimentary breakfast is served in a private lounge. A coffee bar in the lobby is perfect for getting your morning fix on the fly, and the renowned day spa, trū, offers world-class treatments, a variety of them in their one-of-a-kind rainforest room with walk-through waterfall. The restaurant, Seven Fifty, blends Mediterranean and Californian cuisine, while the high-backed *Star Trek*–esque chairs in the lounge make you feel like you are commander of the fleet.

750 Kearny St. (at Washington St.), San Francisco, CA 94108. ⓒ 800/HILTONS or 415/433-6660. Fax 415/765-7891. www.sanfranciscofinancialdistrict.hilton.com. 549 units. $199–$429 double; $989–$1,200 suite. AE, DC, DISC, MC, V. Valet parking $42. Bus: 1, 9AX, 9BX, or 15. Cable car: California. **Amenities:** Restaurant; bar; coffee bar; fitness room; spa; concierge; 24-hr. business center; secretarial services; free car service to downtown; room service; laundry service; same-day dry cleaning; foreign currency exchange; notary public. *In room:* A/C, TV w/pay movies, dataport, Wi-Fi ($9.95), minibar, hair dryer, iron, safe.

5 North Beach/Fisherman's Wharf

EXPENSIVE

Argonaut Hotel ⭐⭐ *Kids*   The Kimpton Hotel Group is behind Fisherman's Wharf's best hotel, a true boutique gem that's ideally located at San Francisco Maritime National Historical Park near Fisherman's Wharf and half a block from the bay. The four-story timber and brick landmark building was originally built in 1908 as a warehouse for the California Fruit Canners Association, and later used by William Randolph Hearst to store items that eventually ended up inside his Hearst Castle in San Simeon. Its 239 rooms and 13 suites are whimsically decorated to emulate a luxury cruise ship in cheerful nautical colors of blue, white, red, and yellow (though evidence of its modest past appears in original brick walls, large timbers, and steel warehouse doors). Along with all the standard hotel amenities are special touches such as flatscreen TVs, DVD/CD players, Aveda toiletries, and—get this—leopard-spotted bathrobes. All guests are welcome at weekday evening wine receptions and can use the lobby's two popular (and free) Internet terminals. Suites have wonderful views and come fully loaded with telescopes and spa tubs. If possible, try to book a "view" room, which overlooks the wharf or bay (some rooms offer fabulous views of Alcatraz and the Golden Gate Bridge). If you're bringing the kids, know that the Argonaut's friendly staff goes out of their way to make little ones feel at home and allows each pint-size guest to pick a new plaything from the hotel's "treasure chest." With so many offerings it's no surprise the hotel was awarded a Four Diamond rating from AAA. *Tip:* The concierge seems to be able to work wonders when you need tickets to Alcatraz—even when the trips are officially sold out.

495 Jefferson St (at Hyde St.), San Francisco, CA 94109. ⓒ 866/415-0704 or 415/563-0800. Fax 415/563-2800. www.argonauthotel.com. 252 units. $189–$389 double; $489–$1,089 suite. Rates include evening wine in the lobby, daily newspaper, and kid-friendly perks like cribs and strollers. AE, DC, DISC, MC, V. Parking $39. Bus: 10, 30, or 47. Streetcar: F. Cable car: Powell–Hyde line. **Amenities:** Restaurant;

bar; fitness center; concierge; laundry service; dry cleaning; yoga video and mats; Wi-Fi in public areas. *In room:* A/C, flatscreen TV w/Nintendo and pay movies, DVD and CD players, Web TV, free high-speed Internet access, minibar, coffeemaker, hair dryer, iron, safe.

Sheraton Fisherman's Wharf Hotel   Built in the mid-1970s, this contemporary, four-story hotel offers the reliable comforts of a Sheraton in San Francisco's most popular tourist area. In other words, the clean, modern rooms are comfortable and well equipped but nothing unique to the city. On the bright side, they have a heated outdoor pool (a rarity in San Francisco). A corporate floor caters exclusively to business travelers.

2500 Mason St. (btw Beach and North Point sts.), San Francisco, CA 94133. (© 800/325-3535 or 415/362-5500. Fax 415/956-5275. www.sheratonatthewharf.com. 529 units. $199–$299 double; $550–$1,000 suite. Extra person $20. Continental breakfast $13. AE, DC, DISC, MC, V. Valet parking $36. Bus: 10 or 49. Streetcar: F. Cable car: Powell–Mason line (1 block east, 2 blocks south). **Amenities:** Restaurant; bar; outdoor heated pool; exercise room; concierge; car-rental desk; business center; limited room service; laundry; dry cleaning. *In room:* A/C, TV, fax (in suites only), dataport, high-speed Internet ($9.95/day), coffeemaker, hair dryer.

MODERATE

Best Western Tuscan Inn at Fisherman's Wharf ★★   Like an island of respectability in a sea of touristy schlock, this boutique Best Western is one of the best midrange hotels at Fisherman's Wharf. It continues to exude a level of style and comfort far beyond that of its neighboring competitors. For example, every evening in the plush lobby warmed by a grand fireplace, a wine reception is hosted by the manager, and the adjoining **Café Pescatore** serves wonderful pizzas and grilled meats from their wood-burning oven. The rooms are a definite cut above competing Fisherman's Wharf hotels: all are handsomely decorated and have writing desks and armchairs. The only caveat is the lack of scenic views—a small price to pay for a good hotel in a great location.

425 North Point St. (at Mason St.), San Francisco, CA 94133. (© **800/648-4626** or 415/561-1100. Fax 415/561-1199. www.tuscaninn.com. 221 units. $129–$369 double. Rates include coffee, tea, and evening wine reception. AE, DC, DISC, MC, V. Parking $36. Bus: 10, 15, or 47. Cable car: Powell–Mason line. Pets welcome for $50 fee. **Amenities:** Access to nearby gym; concierge; courtesy car; secretarial services; limited room service; same-day laundry service/dry cleaning. *In room:* A/C, TV w/video games and pay movies, dataport, free Wi-Fi, minibar, coffeemaker, hair dryer, iron.

The Hotel Bohème ★★ *(Finds*   Romance awaits at the intimate Hotel Bohème. Although it's located on the busiest avenue in the neighborhood, once you climb the staircase to this narrow second-floor boutique hotel, you'll discover a style and demeanor reminiscent of a home in upscale Nob Hill. Alas, there are no common areas other than a little booth for check-in and concierge, but rooms, though small, are truly sweet, with gauze-draped canopies, stylish decor such as ornate parasols shading ceiling lights, and walls dramatically colored with lavender, sage green, black, and pumpkin. The staff is ultra-hospitable, and bonuses include sherry in the lobby each afternoon. Some fabulous cafes, restaurants, bars, and shops along Columbus Avenue are just a few steps away, and Chinatown and Union Square are within easy walking distance. *Note:* Although the bathrooms are spiffy, they're also tiny and have showers only. Also, request a room off the street side, which is quieter.

444 Columbus Ave. (btw Vallejo and Green sts.), San Francisco, CA 94133. ℂ **415/ 433-9111.** Fax 415/362-6292. www.hotelboheme.com. 15 units. $164–$184 double. Rates include afternoon sherry. AE, DC, DISC, MC, V. Parking $12–$31 at nearby public garages. Bus: 12, 15, 30, 41, 45, or 83. Cable car: Powell–Mason line. **Amenities:** Concierge. *In room:* TV, dataport, free Wi-Fi, hair dryer, iron.

INEXPENSIVE

The San Remo Hotel ⊛ (*Value*)   This small, European-style *pensione* is one of the best budget hotels in San Francisco. In a quiet North Beach neighborhood, within walking distance of Fisherman's Wharf, the Italianate Victorian structure originally served as a boardinghouse for dockworkers displaced by the great fire of 1906. As a result, the rooms are small and bathrooms are shared, but all is forgiven when it comes time to pay the bill. Rooms are decorated in cozy country style, with brass and iron beds; oak, maple, or pine armoires; and wicker furnishings. The immaculate shared bathrooms feature tubs and brass pull-chain toilets with oak tanks and brass fixtures. If the penthouse—which has its own bathroom, TV, fridge, and patio—is available, book it: You won't find a more romantic place to stay in San Francisco for so little money.

2237 Mason St. (at Chestnut St.), San Francisco, CA 94133. ℂ **800/352-7366** or 415/ 776-8688. Fax 415/776-2811. www.sanremohotel.com. 62 units, 61 with shared bathroom. $65–$90 double; $175–$185 penthouse suite. AE, DC, MC, V. Self-parking $13–$14. Bus: 10, 15, 30, or 47. Streetcar: F. Cable car: Powell–Mason line. **Amenities:** Access to nearby health club; 2 massage chairs; self-service laundry; TV room; Internet kiosk in lobby. *In room:* Ceiling fan.

The Wharf Inn ⊛ (*Value*)   My top choice for good-value/great-location lodging at Fisherman's Wharf, The Wharf Inn offers above-average accommodations at one of the most popular tourist attractions in the world. The well-stocked rooms are done in handsome tones of earth, muted greens, and burnt orange, but more importantly, they are situated smack-dab in the middle of the wharf, a mere 2 blocks from Pier 39 and the cable car turnaround, and within walking distance of The Embarcadero and North Beach. The inn is ideal for car-bound families because parking is free (that saves at least $25 a day right off the bat).

2601 Mason St. (at Beach St.), San Francisco, CA 94133. ℂ **877/275-7889** or 415/673-7411. Fax 415/776-2181. www.wharfinn.com. 51 units. $99–$209 double; $299–$439 penthouse. AE, DC, DISC, MC, V. Free parking. Bus: 10, 15, 39, or 47. Streetcar: F. Cable car: Powell–Mason or Powell–Hyde lines. **Amenities:** Access to nearby health club ($10/day); concierge; tour desk; free coffee/tea, and newspapers. *In room:* TV, dataport, free Wi-Fi, hair dryer on request, iron on request.

6 The Marina/Pacific Heights/Cow Hollow
EXPENSIVE
Hotel Drisco ⊹⊹ *(Finds* Located on one of the most sought-after blocks of residential property in all of San Francisco, the Drisco, built in 1903, is one of the city's best small hotels. Refinements by interior designer Glenn Texeira (who also did the Ritz-Carlton in Manila) are evident from the very small lobby and sitting areas to the calming atmosphere of the cream, yellow, and green guest rooms. As in the neighboring mansions, traditional antique furnishings and thick, luxurious fabrics abound here. The hotel's comfy beds will make you want to loll late into the morning before primping in the large marble bathrooms, complete with robes and slippers. Each suite has a couch that unfolds into a bed (although you would never guess from the looks of it), an additional phone and TV, and superior views. A 24-hour coffee and tea service is available on the ground floor, in the same comfy rooms where breakfast is served. If you're arriving by car, however, you may not want to stay here as there is no hotel parking.

2901 Pacific Ave. (at Broderick St.), San Francisco, CA 94115. ℂ **800/634-7277** or 415/346-2880. Fax 415/567-5537. www.hoteldrisco.com. 48 units. $249 double; $369–$399 suite. Rates include buffet breakfast and evening wine hour. AE, DC, DISC, MC, V. No parking available. Bus: 3 or 24. **Amenities:** Exercise room and free pass to YMCA; concierge; business center; limited room service; same-day laundry service/dry cleaning. *In room:* TV/VCR, CD player, dataport, free high-speed Internet access, minibar, fridge, hair dryer, iron, safe.

MODERATE
Hotel Del Sol ⊹⊹ *(Kids* *(Value* The cheeriest motel in town is located just 2 blocks off the Marina District's bustling section of Lombard. Three-level Hotel del Sol is all about festive flair and luxury touches.

The sunshine theme extends from the Miami Beach–style use of vibrant color, as in the yellow, red, orange, and blue exterior, to the heated courtyard pool, which beckons the youngish clientele as they head for their cars parked (for free!) in cabana-like spaces. This is also one of the most family-friendly places to stay, with a "Kids are VIPs" program, including a family suite (three adjoining rooms with bunks and toys); a lending library of kids' books, toys, and videos; child-proofing kits; three rooms that have been professionally baby-proofed; bonded babysitting services; evening cookies and milk; pool toys; and sunglasses and visors for the young ones. Fair-weather fun doesn't stop at the front door of the hotel, which boasts 57 spacious rooms (updated with all new bedding, paint, carpets, drapes, and sofas in 2006) with equally perky interior decor (read: loud and colorful) as well as unexpected extras like CD players, Aveda products, and tips on the town's happenings and shopping meccas. Suites also include minifridges and DVD players.

3100 Webster St. (at Greenwich St.), San Francisco, CA 94123. © **877/433-5765** or 415/921-5520. Fax 415/931-4137. www.thehoteldelsol.com. 57 units. $139–$199 double; $179–$239 suite. Rates include continental breakfast and free newspapers in the lobby. AE, DC, DISC, MC, V. Free parking. Bus: 22, 28, 41, 43, 45, or 76. **Amenities:** Heated outdoor pool; same-day dry cleaning. *In room:* TV/VCR, CD player, dataport, Wi-Fi ($7.95/day), kitchenettes in 3 units, fridge and DVD in suites only, iron.

Laurel Inn ★★ *Value*   If you don't mind being out of the downtown area, this hip hotel is one of the most tranquil and affordably high-style places to rest your head. Tucked just beyond the southernmost tip of the Presidio and Pacific Heights, the outside is nothing impressive—just another motor inn. And that's what it was until the Joie de Vivre hotel company breathed new life into the place. Now decor is *très* chic and modern, with Zen-like influences (think W Hotel at half the price). The rooms, some of which have excellent city views, are smartly designed and decorated in the style of a contemporary studio apartment. The continental breakfast is fine, but why bother when you're across the street from **Ella's,** which serves San Francisco's best breakfast? Other thoughtful touches: 24-hour coffee and tea service, pet-friendly rooms, a CD and video lending library, and indoor parking. There's also great shopping a block away at Sacramento Street; and the new and hip **G Bar,** which serves libations and a surprisingly active slice of glamorous young Pacific Heights–style revelry.

444 Presidio Ave. (at California Ave.), San Francisco, CA 94115. © **800/552-8735** or 415/567-8467. Fax 415/928-1866. www.thelaurelinn.com. 49 units. $169–$209

double. Rates include continental breakfast and afternoon lemonade and cookies. AE, DC, DISC, MC, V. Free parking. Bus: 1, 3, 4, or 43. Pets accepted. **Amenities:** Adjoining bar; access to the mind-blowing JCC gym across the street at $10 per day; concierge; same-day laundry/dry cleaning. *In room:* TV/VCR, CD player, dataport, wired and wireless Internet access ($8/day), kitchenette in some units, hair dryer, iron.

INEXPENSIVE

Cow Hollow Motor Inn & Suites *Kids*   If you're less interested in being downtown than in playing in and around the beautiful bayfront Marina, check out this modest brick hotel on busy Lombard Street. There's no fancy theme, but each room has cable TV, free local phone calls, free covered parking, and a coffeemaker. Families will appreciate the one- and two-bedroom suites, which have full kitchens and dining areas as well as antique furnishings and surprisingly tasteful decor.

2190 Lombard St. (btw Steiner and Fillmore sts.), San Francisco, CA 94123. ✆ 415/921-5800. Fax 415/922-8515. www.cowhollowmotorinn.com. 129 units. $72–$125 double. Extra person $10. AE, DC, MC, V. Free parking. Bus: 28, 30, 43, or 76. **Amenities:** Laundry and dry cleaning within a block. *In room:* A/C, TV, dataport, free high-speed DSL and Wi-Fi, full kitchens in suites only, coffeemaker, hair dryer.

Edward II Inn & Suites *✿*   This three-story "English country" inn has a room for almost anyone's budget, ranging from *pensione* units with shared bathrooms to luxuriously appointed suites and cottages with whirlpool bathtubs and fireplaces. Originally built to house guests who attended the 1915 Pan-Pacific Exposition, it's still a good place to stay in spotless and comfortably appointed rooms with cozy antique furnishings. They've recently added a small fitness center and the Café Maritime, a seafood restaurant open for dinner. Room prices even include a full continental breakfast. Nearby Chestnut and Union streets offer some of the best shopping and dining in the city. The adjoining pub serves drinks nightly. The only caveat is that the hotel's Lombard Street location is usually congested with traffic.

3155 Scott St. (at Lombard St.), San Francisco, CA 94123. ✆ 800/473-2846 or 415/922-3000. Fax 415/931-5784. www.edwardii.com. 29 units, 21 with bathroom. $69–$99 double with shared bathroom; $115–$139 double with private bathroom; $179–$199 junior suite. Extra person $25. Rates include continental breakfast and evening sherry. AE, DISC, MC, V. Self-parking $12 1 block away. Bus: 28, 30, 43, or 76. **Amenities:** Pub; fitness center ($10/day); computer station (for nominal fee). *In room:* TV, free high-speed and wireless Internet access, hair dryer and iron available on request.

Marina Inn *✿* *Value*   Marina Inn is one of the best low-priced hotels in San Francisco. How it offers so much for so little is mystifying. Each guest room in the 1924 four-story Victorian looks like something from a country furnishings catalog, complete with rustic pinewood furniture, a four-poster bed with silky-soft comforter, pretty wallpaper, and soothing tones of rose, hunter green, and pale yellow. You also get remote-control televisions discreetly hidden in pine cabinetry—all for as little as $75 a night. Combine that with continental breakfast, friendly service, a business center in the lobby with an Internet kiosk, free Wi-Fi, and an armada of shops and restaurants within easy walking distance, and there you have it: one of my top choices for best overall value. *Note:* Traffic can be a bit noisy here, so the hotel added double panes on windows facing the street. Still, if you're a light sleeper you might want to stay elsewhere.

3110 Octavia St. (at Lombard St.), San Francisco, CA 94123. © **800/274-1420** or 415/928-1000. Fax 415/928-5909. www.marinainn.com. 40 units. Nov–Feb $75–$115 double; Mar–May $85–$135 double; June–Oct $95–$145 double. Rates include continental breakfast. AE, DC, DISC, MC, V. Bus: 28, 30, 43, or 76. *In room:* TV, free Wi-Fi, hair dryer and iron on request.

7 Japantown & Environs

MODERATE

The Queen Anne Hotel 🌟🌟 *Value*   This majestic 1890 Victorian charmer was once a grooming school for upper-class young women. Restored in 1980 the four-story building recalls San Francisco's golden days. Walk under rich red draperies to the lavish "grand salon" lobby replete with English oak wainscoting and period antiques and it's not hard to imagine that you've been transported to a different era. Guest rooms also contain a profusion of antiques— armoires, marble-top dressers, and other Victorian-era pieces. Some have corner turret bay windows that look out on tree-lined streets, as well as separate parlor areas and wet bars; others have cozy reading nooks and fireplaces. All rooms have phones and nice bath amenities in their marble-tiled bathrooms. Guests can relax in the parlor, with two fireplaces, or in the hotel library. If you don't mind staying outside the downtown area, this hotel is highly recommended and very classic San Francisco.

1590 Sutter St. (btw Gough and Octavia sts.), San Francisco, CA 94109. © **800/ 227-3970** or 415/441-2828. Fax 415/775-5212. www.queenanne.com. 48 units. $110–$199 double; $169–$350 suite. Extra person $10. Rates include continental breakfast on weekday mornings, local free limousine service (weekday mornings), afternoon tea and sherry, and morning newspaper. AE, DC, DISC, MC, V. Parking $14. Bus: 2, 3, or 4. **Amenities:** Access to nearby health club for $10; 24-hr. concierge; business center; same-day dry cleaning; front desk safe. *In room:* TV, dataport, free wired Internet access in some rooms and Wi-Fi throughout, hair dryer, iron.

8 The Castro & Haight-Ashbury

MODERATE

The Parker Guest House ★★ This is the best B&B option in the Castro, and one of the best in the entire city. In fact, even some of the better hotels could learn a thing or two from this fashionable, gay-friendly, 5,000-square-foot, beautifully restored 1909 Edwardian home and adjacent annex a few blocks from the heart of the Castro's action. Within the bright, cheery urban compound, period antiques abound. But thankfully, the spacious guest rooms are wonderfully updated with smart patterned furnishings, voice mail, robes, and spotless private bathrooms (plus amenities) en suite or, in two cases, across the hall. A fire burns nightly in the cozy living room, and guests are also welcome to make themselves at home in the wood-paneled common library (with fireplace and piano), sunny breakfast room overlooking the garden, and spacious garden with fountains and a steam room. Animal lovers will appreciate the companionship of the house pugs Porter and Pasty.

520 Church St. (btw 17th and 18th sts.), San Francisco, CA 94114. © **888/520-7275** or 415/621-3222. Fax 415/621-4139. www.parkerguesthouse.com. 21 units. $129–$199 double; $219 junior suite. Rates include extended continental breakfast and evening wine and cheese. AE, DISC, MC, V. Self-parking $17. Bus: 22 or 33. Streetcar: J Church. **Amenities:** Access to nearby health club; steam room; concierge. *In room:* TV, dataport, free Wi-Fi, hair dryer, iron.

Red Victorian Bed, Breakfast & Art ★ *Finds* Still having flashbacks from the 1960s? Or want to? No problem. A room at the Red Vic, in the heart of the Haight, will throw you right back into the Summer of Love (minus, of course, the free-flowing LSD). Owner Sami Sunchild has re-created this historic hotel and "Peace Center" as a living museum honoring the bygone era. The rooms are inspired by San Francisco's sights and history, and are decorated accordingly. The Flower Child Room has a sun on the ceiling and a rainbow on the wall, while the bed sports a hand-crocheted shawl headboard. The Peacock Suite, though pricey, is one funky room, with red beads, a canopy bed, and multicolored patterns throughout. The clincher is its bedroom bathtub, which has a circular pass-through looking into the sitting area. Four guest rooms have private bathrooms; the rest share four bathrooms down the hall. In general, the rooms and bathrooms are clean and the furnishings lighthearted. Rates for longer stays are a great deal. A family-style continental breakfast is a gathering place for a worldly array of guests, and there's a gift shop called the Meditation Room and Peace Center. Be sure to check out Sami's website to get a sneak peek at the weird and wonderful guest rooms.

1665 Haight St. (btw Cole and Belvedere sts.), San Francisco, CA 94117. ✆ **415/864-1978.** Fax 415/863-3293. www.redvic.com. 18 units, 4 with private bathroom. $89–$110 double with shared bathroom, $129–$149 double with private bathroom; $229 suite. Rates include continental breakfast and afternoon tea. Lower rates for stays of 3 days or more. AE, DISC, MC, V. Guarded parking lot nearby. Metro: N line. Bus: 7, 66, 71, or 73. **Amenities:** Cafe.

INEXPENSIVE

Inn on Castro 🅰 One of the better choices in the Castro, half a block from all the action, is this Edwardian-style inn decorated with contemporary furnishings, original modern art, and fresh flowers throughout. It definitely feels more like a home than an inn, so if you like less commercial abodes, this place is for you. Most rooms share a small back patio, and the suite has a private entrance and outdoor sitting area. The inn also offers access to six individual nearby apartments ($125–$190) with complete kitchens. Note that rates include a full breakfast, and that the least expensive rooms share a bathroom.

321 Castro St. (at Market St.), San Francisco, CA 94114. ✆ **415/861-0321.** Fax 415/861-0321. www.innoncastro.com. 8 units, 2 with bathroom across the hall; 6 apts. $105–$165 double. Rates include full breakfast and evening brandy. AE, DC, MC, V. Streetcar: F, K, L, or M. **Amenities:** Hall fridges stocked w/free sodas and water. *In room:* Flatscreen TV, DVD/CD, dataport, free Wi-Fi, hair dryer.

24 Henry Guesthouse & Village House Its central Castro location is not the only thing that makes 24 Henry a good choice for gay travelers. The 24 Henry building, an 1870s Victorian on a serene side street, is quite charming, as is the Village House sister property 4 blocks away. All of the individually decorated guest rooms have high ceilings and period furniture; most have shared bathrooms. A continental breakfast is served each morning in the parlor. All rooms are nonsmoking.

24 Henry St. (near Sanchez St.), San Francisco, CA 94114. ✆ **800/900-5686** or 415/864-5686. Fax 415/864-0406. www.24henry.com. 10 units, 3 with bathroom. $75–$100 double with shared bathroom; $119–$139 double with private bathroom. Extra person $20. Rates include continental breakfast. AE, MC, V. Bus: 8, 22, 24, or 37. Streetcar: F, J, K, L, M, or N. **Amenities:** Wi-Fi throughout.

9 Near San Francisco International Airport

MODERATE

Embassy Suites 🅰 If you've stayed at an Embassy Suites before, you know the drill. But this hotel is one of the best airport options, if only for the fact that every room is a suite. But there is more: The property has an indoor pool, whirlpool, courtyard with fountain, palm trees, and bar/restaurant. Plus, each tastefully decorated two-room suite was updated in 2006 with all new linens and mattresses and has nice additions such as two TVs. The all-new lobby debuted in early 2006. Additionally, a complimentary breakfast of your choice is available before you're whisked to the airport on the free shuttle—all that and the price is still right.

250 Gateway Blvd., South San Francisco, CA 94080. ⓒ 800/EMBASSY or 650/589-3400. Fax 650/589-1183. www.embassysuites.com. 312 units. $139–$199 double. Rates include breakfast and free evening beverages. AE, DC, MC, V. **Amenities:** Restaurant; bar; indoor pool; Jacuzzi; airport shuttle. *In room:* A/C, TV, Wi-Fi ($9.95/day), fridge, microwave, coffeemaker, hair dryer, iron.

INEXPENSIVE

Comfort Suites *(Kids*   Two miles north of the airport, well outside the heart of the city, Comfort Suites is a well-appointed option for travelers on the way into or out of town. Each studio-suite has a king-size bed, queen-size sleeper sofa (great for the kids), and all the basic amenities for weary travelers. There are also enough pay cable channels to keep you glued to your TV set for an entire day. Rooms are fine, but the freebies are the most attractive part of this hotel: a deluxe breakfast of waffles, eggs, sausage, and the like; an airport shuttle; and use of the outdoor hot tub.

121 E. Grand Ave., South San Francisco, CA 94080. ⓒ 866/764-1377. Fax 650/589-7796. www.sfosuites.com. 168 units. $119 double. Rates include continental breakfast. AE, DC, DISC, MC, V. **Amenities:** Outdoor Jacuzzi; airport shuttle. *In room:* A/C, TV, free high-speed Internet access in some rooms and Wi-Fi in all rooms, fridge, microwave, coffeemaker, hair dryer, iron.

San Francisco Airport North Travelodge *(Kids*   The Travelodge is a good choice for families, mainly because of the hotel's large heated pool. The rooms are as ordinary as you'd expect from a Travelodge. Still, they're comfortable and come with plenty of perks like Showtime and free toll-free and credit card calls. Each junior suite has a microwave and refrigerator. The clincher is the 24-hour complimentary shuttle, which makes the 2-mile trip to the airport in 5 minutes.

326 S. Airport Blvd. (off Hwy. 101), South San Francisco, CA 94080. ⓒ 800/578-7878 or 650/583-9600. Fax 650/873-9392. www.sfotravelodge.com. 199 units. $89–$139 double. AE, DC, DISC, MC, V. Free parking. **Amenities:** Restaurant; heated outdoor pool; courtesy shuttle to airport; dry cleaning; fax and copier services; high-speed Internet access at computer station (for fee). *In room:* A/C, TV w/pay movies, microwave available, coffeemaker, hair dryer, iron, safe.

3

Where to Dine

For more than a decade the readers of *Bon Appétit* magazine have named San Francisco their top city for dining out. And for good reason—with more than 3,500 restaurants offering cuisines from around the globe, San Francisco has more restaurants per capita than any other city in the United States.

San Francisco also attracts some of the world's most talented chefs, drawn not only to the creative freedom that has always defined San Francisco's culinary scene, but also to the year-round access to Northern California's unparalleled abundance of organic produce, seafood, free-range meats, and wine.

Afghan, Cajun, Burmese, Moroccan, Persian, Cambodian, Basque, vegan—whatever you're in the mood for, this town has it covered, which is why more San Franciscans eat out than any other city's residents in the U.S. And all you need to join America's largest dinner party is an adventurous palate, because half the fun of visiting San Francisco is the opportunity to sample the flavors of the world in one fell swoop.

Although dining in San Francisco is almost always a hassle-free experience, you should keep a few things in mind:

- If you want a table at the restaurants with the best reputations, you probably need to book 6 to 8 weeks in advance for weekends, and a couple of weeks ahead for weekdays.
- If there's a long wait for a table, ask if you can order at the bar, which is often faster and more fun.

Pricing Categories

The restaurants listed below are classified first by area, then by price, using the following categories: **Very Expensive,** dinner from $75 per person; **Expensive,** dinner from $50 per person; **Moderate,** dinner from $35 per person; and **Inexpensive,** dinner less than $35 per person. These categories reflect prices for an appetizer, main course, dessert, and glass of wine.

Tips E-Reservations

Want to book your reservations online? Go to **www.open table.com**, where you can save seats in San Francisco and the rest of the Bay Area in real time.

- Don't leave *anything* valuable in your car while dining, particularly in or near high-crime areas such as the Mission, downtown, or—believe it or not—Fisherman's Wharf. (Thieves know tourists with nice cameras and a trunkful of mementos are headed there.) Also, it's best to give the parking valet only the key to your car, *not* your hotel room or house key.
- ***Remember:*** It is against the law to smoke in any restaurant in San Francisco, even if it has a separate bar or lounge area. You're welcome to smoke outside, however.
- This ain't New York: Plan on dining early. Most restaurants close their kitchens around 10pm.
- If you're driving to a restaurant, add extra time to your itinerary for parking, which can be an especially infuriating exercise in areas like the Mission, Downtown, the Marina, and, well, pretty much everywhere. And expect to pay at least $10 to $13 for valet service, *if* the restaurant offers it.

1 Union Square

VERY EXPENSIVE

Michael Mina 𝄞𝄞𝄞 AMERICAN   Chef Michael Mina, who became a celebrity chef while overseeing Aqua (p. 69) and was *Bon Appétit* Chef of the Year for 2005–2006, takes the small-plate dining concept to extremes at this sexy, swank spot. Previously the Compass Rose tearoom in the Westin St. Francis hotel, the cream-on-cream room, with deep leather lounge chairs and tables that are too wide for romance, sets the scene for this formal prix-fixe affair. But rather than three dishes, courses arrive as a trio of different renditions of the same theme (plus three sides to match) on custom Mina-designed modular china. That's six different preparations per dish or a total of 18 different flavors over the course of an evening. It's a bit fussy for anyone who prefers to order a few things that sound good and eat lots of bites of them, but if the idea of sampling lots of styles and flavors appeals to you, this edible food-combination case study is likely to be a culinary wonder. Take diver scallops for example. One preparation is accented with lemon Osetra caviar while the other two pair them with yellow corn and summer truffles and smoked tomato and Maine lobster—not to mention three different "chilled salads" in tiny glasses. You might also find crispy pork loin done with risotto, as pulled pork with apple ravioli, and as barbecue with a corn fritter. Some dishes hit, some miss, but in all cases this is a swank affair with an incredible wine list by Rajat Parr.

335 Powell St. (at Geary St.). *(7)* **415/397-9222.** www.michaelmina.net. Reservations recommended. 3-course tasting menu $98; seasonal classic tasting menu $135. AE, DC, DISC, MC, V. Dinner Mon–Sat 5:30–10pm; Sun 5:30–9:30pm. Valet parking $17. Bus: 2, 3, 4, 30, 38, 45, or 76.

EXPENSIVE

Grand Café *(R)* FRENCH If you aren't interested in exploring restaurants beyond those in Union Square and want a huge dose of atmosphere with your seared salmon, Grand Café is your best bet. Its claims to fame? The most grand dining room in San Francisco, an enormous 156-seat, turn-of-the-20th-century grand-ballroom-like dining oasis that's a magnificent combination of old Europe and Art Nouveau. To match the surroundings, chef Ron Boyd, a San Francisco native and Domaine Chandon alum, serves dressed-up French-inspired California dishes such as sautéed salmon with French lentils and house-cured bacon or salade niçoise. You can also drop by for a lighter meal in the more casual front room, the Petit Café, which offers a raw bar and similar dishes for about half the price. In fact, I prefer to hang out in the cafe and nosh on pizzas from the wood-burning oven or a big bowl full of mussels swimming in broth with a side of sourdough bread—it's twice the atmosphere at half the price. There's also a wonderful selection of small-batch American whiskeys and single-malt Scotches.

501 Geary St. (at Taylor St., adjacent to the Hotel Monaco). *(7)* **415/292-0101.** www.grandcafe-sf.com. Reservations recommended. Main courses $18–$28. AE, DC, DISC, MC, V. Mon–Fri 7–10:30am; Sat 8am–2:30pm; Sun 9am–2:30pm; Mon–Fri 11:30am–2:30pm; Sun–Thurs 5:30–10pm; Fri–Sat 5:30–11pm. Valet parking free at brunch, $15 for 3 hr. at dinner, $3 each additional half-hour. Bus: 2, 3, 4, 27, or 38.

MODERATE

Café Claude *(R)* FRENCH Euro transplants love Café Claude, a crowded and lively restaurant tucked into a narrow (and very European feeling) side street near Union Square. Seemingly everything—every table, spoon, saltshaker, and waiter—is imported from France. With prices topping out at about $22 on the menu featuring classics like steak tartare, steamed mussels, duck confit, escargot, steak with spinach gratin and crisp potatoes, and quail stuffed with pine nuts,

Where to Dine in Union Square & the Financial District

Aqua **10**
B44 **9**
Belden Place **9**
Cafe Bastille **9**
Café Claude **8**
Cafe Tiramisu **9**
Dottie's True Blue Café **3**
Ducca **7**
Grand Café **2**
Kokkari **12**
Michael Mina **4**
Millennium **1**
Plouf **9**
Scala's Bistro **6**
Sears Fine Foods **5**
Tadich Grill **11**
Yank Sing **13**

sausage, and wild rice, Café Claude offers an affordable slice of Paris without leaving the city. But beware: My last visit the service was rather . . . er . . . French as well. There's live jazz on Thursdays, Fridays, and Saturdays from 7:30 to 10:30pm, and atmospheric sidewalk seating is available when the weather permits.

7 Claude Lane (off Sutter St.). ℂ **415/392-3515.** www.cafeclaude.com. Reservations recommended. Main courses $8–$12 lunch, $14–$22 dinner. AE, DC, DISC, MC, V. Mon–Sat 11:30am–10:30pm; Sun 5:30–10:30pm. Bus: 30. Cable car: Powell–Mason.

Millennium ⊛⊛ VEGAN Banking on the trend toward lighter, healthier cooking, chef Eric Tucker and his band of merry waiters set out to prove that a meatless menu doesn't mean you have to sacrifice taste. In a narrow, handsome, Parisian-style dining room with checkered tile flooring, French windows, and sponge-painted walls, Millennium has had nothing but favorable reviews for its egg-, and dairy-free creations since the day it opened. Favorites include Balinese-style salt and pepper-crusted oyster mushrooms with blood orange chile jam, and main courses such as truffled potato Wellington stuffed with shiitake mushroom duxelles served with spring onion and lentil sugo, seared asparagus, blood orange, and capers; or *masala dosa,* a lentil rice crepe with South Indian chickpea and red chard curry, sweet and spicy papaya chutney, and mint raita. No need to divert from PC dining with your wine choice—all the selections here are organic.

In the Savoy Hotel, 580 Geary St. (at Jones St.). ℂ **415/345-3900.** www.millennium restaurant.com. Reservations recommended. Main courses $18–$22. AE, DC, DISC, MC, V. Sun–Thurs 5:30–9:30pm; Fri–Sat 5:30–10pm. Bus: 38. Streetcar: All Muni lines. BART: Powell St.

Scala's Bistro ⊛⊛ FRENCH/ITALIAN Firmly entrenched at the base of the refurbished Sir Francis Drake hotel, this downtown favorite blends Italian-bistro and old-world atmosphere with jovial and bustling results. With just the right balance of elegance and informality, this is a perfect place to have some fun (and apparently most people do). Of the tempting array of Italian and French dishes, it's de rigueur to start with the "Earth and Surf" calamari appetizer or grilled portobello mushrooms. Golden beet salad and garlic cream mussels are also good bets. Generous portions of moist, rich duck-leg confit will satisfy hungry appetites, but if you can order only one thing, make it Scala's signature dish: seared salmon. Resting on a bed of creamy buttermilk mashed potatoes and accented with a tomato, chive, and white-wine sauce, it's downright delicious. Finish with Bostini cream pie, a dreamy combo of vanilla custard and orange chiffon cake with a warm chocolate glaze.

In the Sir Francis Drake hotel, 432 Powell St. (at Sutter St.). ℂ **415/395-8555.** www.scalasbistro.com. Reservations recommended. Breakfast $7–$10; main courses $12–$24 lunch and dinner. AE, DC, DISC, MC, V. Daily 8–10:30am and 11:30am–midnight. Bus: 2, 3, 4, 30, 45, or 76. Cable car: Powell–Hyde line.

INEXPENSIVE

Dottie's True Blue Café ⍟ *Kids* AMERICAN/BREAKFAST
This family-owned breakfast restaurant is one of my favorite downtown diners. This is the kind of place you'd expect to see off Route 66, where most customers are on a first-name basis with the staff and everyone is welcomed with a hearty hello and steaming mug of coffee. Dottie's serves far-above-average American morning fare (big portions of French toast, pancakes, bacon and eggs, omelets, and the like), delivered to tables laminated with old movie star photos on rugged, diner-quality plates. Whatever you order arrives with delicious homemade bread, muffins, or scones, as well as house-made jelly. There are also daily specials and vegetarian dishes.

In the Pacific Bay Inn, 522 Jones St. (at O'Farrell St.). ℂ **415/885-2767.** Reservations not accepted. Breakfast $5–$11. DISC, MC, V. Wed–Mon 7:30am–3pm (lunch 11:30am–3pm). Bus: 2, 3, 4, 27, or 38. Cable car: Powell–Mason line.

Sears Fine Foods ⍟ *Kids* AMERICAN   Sears is not just another downtown diner—it's an old-fashioned institution, famous for its crispy, dark-brown waffles, light sourdough French toast served with house-made strawberry preserves, and silver dollar–size Swedish pancakes (18 per serving!). As the story goes, Ben Sears, a retired clown, founded the diner in 1938. His Swedish wife, Hilbur, was responsible for the legendary pancakes, which, although the restaurant is under new ownership, are still whipped up according to her family's secret recipe. Sears also offers classic lunch and dinner fare—try the Reuben for lunch and cod fish and chips for dinner, followed by a big slice of pie for dessert. Breakfast is served until 3pm every day, and plan on a brief wait to be seated on weekends.

439 Powell St. (btw. Post and Sutter sts.). ℂ **415/986-0700.** www.searsfine food.com. Reservations accepted for parties of 6 or more. Breakfast $3–$8; salads and soups $3–$8; main courses $6–$10. AE, DC, MC, V. Daily 6:30am–10pm (breakfast until 3pm). Cable car: Powell-Mason or Powell-Hyde lines. Bus: 2, 3, 4, or 38.

2 Financial District

VERY EXPENSIVE

Aqua ⍟⍟ SEAFOOD   At San Francisco's finest seafood restaurant, heralded chef Laurent Manrique dazzles customers with a bewildering juxtaposition of earth and sea. Under his care, the artfully composed dishes are delicately decadent: the ahi tartare with fresh herbs, Moroccan spices, and lemon confit is divine and one of the best I've ever had. Other favorites are the celery root soup with black truffle flan, frogs' legs, and rock shrimp; the Alaskan black cod wrapped in smoked bacon and accompanied by tomato and date chutney and glazed carrots; and the braised veal cheeks with smoked foie gras and beef consommé—all perfectly paired with wines chosen by the sommelier. The large dining room with high ceilings, elaborate floral displays, and oversized mirrors is pleasing to the eye if not to the ear. (It can get quite loud on busy nights.) Steep prices prevent most people from making a regular appearance, but for special occasions or billable lunches, Aqua is highly recommended.

252 California St. (near Battery). ✆ **415/956-9662**. www.aqua-sf.com. Reservations recommended. Main courses $29–$39; 3-course menu $68; 6-course tasting menu $95; vegetarian tasting menu $65. AE, DC, DISC, MC, V. Mon–Fri 11:30am–2pm; Mon–Sat 5:30–10:30pm; Sun 5:30–9:30pm. Valet parking (dinner only) $10. Bus: All Market St. buses.

EXPENSIVE

Kokkari 𝄢𝄢𝄢 GREEK/MEDITERRANEAN The funny thing is, I've been to Athens, and the food there wasn't nearly as good as what they're serving at Kokkari (Ko-*kar*-ee), one of my favorite restaurants in the city. My love affair starts with the setting: a beautifully rustic dining area with a commanding fireplace and oversize furnishings. Past the tiny bar, the other main room is pure rustic revelry with exposed wood beams, pretty standing lamps, and a view of the glass-enclosed private dining room. Then there are the wonderful, traditional Aegean dishes. A must-order appetizer is the *Marithes Tiganites,* a beautiful platter of whole crispy smelts enhanced with garlic-potato *skordalia* (a traditional Greek dip) and lemon. Other favorites are the *pikilia* (a sampling of traditional Greek spreads served with dolmades and house-made pitas) and the fabulous mesquite-grilled octopus salad. Try not to overindulge before the main courses, which include grilled whole petrale sole with lemon, olive oil, and braised greens; to-die-for moussaka (eggplant, lamb, potato, and béchamel); and lamb chops with oven-roasted lemon-oregano potatoes. Also consider the rotisserie specialties such as a rotisserie-roasted pork loin.

200 Jackson St. (at Front St.). ✆ **415/981-0983**. www.kokkari.com. Reservations recommended. Main courses $14–$23 lunch, $19–$35 dinner. AE, DC, DISC, MC, V. Lunch Mon–Fri 11:30am–2:30pm; bar menu 2:30–5:30pm; dinner Mon–Thurs 5:30–10pm, Fri 5:30–11pm, Sat 5–11pm. Valet parking (dinner only) $8. Bus: 12, 15, 41, or 83.

Finds The Sun on Your Face at Belden Place

San Francisco has always been woefully lacking in the alfresco dining department. One exception is **Belden Place,** an adorable little brick alley in the heart of the Financial District that is open only to foot traffic. When the weather is agreeable, the restaurants that line the alley break out the big umbrellas, tables, and chairs, and *voilà*—a bit of Paris just off Pine Street.

A handful of adorable cafes line Belden Place and offer a variety of cuisines all at moderate prices. There's **Cafe Bastille,** 22 Belden Place (© **415/986-5673**), a classic French bistro and fun speak-easy basement serving excellent crepes, mussels, and French onion soup; it schedules live jazz on Fridays. **Cafe Tiramisu,** 28 Belden Place (© **415/ 421-7044**), is a stylish Italian hot spot serving addictive risottos and gnocchi. **Plouf,** 40 Belden Place (© **415/986-6491**), specializes in big bowls of mussels slathered in your choice of seven sauces, as well as fresh seafood. **B44,** 44 Belden Place (© **415/986-6287**), serves up a side order of Spain alongside its revered paella and other seriously zesty Spanish dishes.

Conversely, come at night for a Euro-speak-easy vibe with your dinner.

The Slanted Door *★★* VIETNAMESE   What started in 1995 as an obscure little family-run restaurant in the Mission District has become one of the most popular and written-about restaurants in the city. Due to its meteoric rise—helped along by celebrity fans such as Mick Jagger, Keith Richards, and Quentin Tarantino—it's been relocated within a beautiful bay-inspired, custom-designed space at the Ferry Building Marketplace. What hasn't changed is a menu filled with incredibly fresh and flavorful Vietnamese dishes such as catfish clay-pot flavored with cilantro, ginger, and Thai chilies; an amazing green papaya salad with roasted peanuts; and fragrant peppercorn duck served with apples and watercress. If the cellophane noodles with fresh Dungeness crab meat are on the menu, *definitely* order them. Be sure to start the feast with a pot of tea from their eclectic collection.

1 Ferry Plaza (at The Embarcadero and Market). © **415/861-8032.** www.slanted door.com. Reservations recommended. Lunch main courses $8.50–$17; most dinner dishes $15–$27; 7-item fixed-price dinner $45 (parties of 7 or more only). AE, MC, V. Daily 11am–2:30pm; Sun–Thurs 5:30–10pm; Fri–Sat 5:30–10:30pm. Bus: All Market Street buses. Streetcar: F, N-Judah line.

MODERATE

Tadich Grill ⚔ SEAFOOD   Not that the veteran restaurant needed more reason to be beloved, but the city's ongoing loss of local institutions makes 158-year-old Tadich the last of a long-revered dying breed. This business began as a coffee stand during the 1849 gold rush and claims to be the very first to broil seafood over mesquite charcoal back in the early 1920s. An old-fashioned power-dining restaurant to its core, Tadich boasts its original mahogany bar, which extends the length of the restaurant, and seven booths for private powwows. Big plates of sourdough bread top the tables.

You won't find fancy California cuisine here. The novella-like menu features a slew of classic salads such as sliced tomato with Dungeness crab or prawn Louis, meats and fish from the charcoal broiler, and even casseroles. The seafood cioppino is a specialty, as is the baked casserole of stuffed turbot with crab and shrimp à la Newburg, and the petrale sole with butter sauce. Everything comes with a heaping side of fries, but if you crave something green, order the creamed spinach.

240 California St. (btw. Battery and Front sts.). © **415/391-1849.** Reservations not accepted. Main courses $14–$20. MC, V. Mon–Fri 11am–9:30pm; Sat 11:30am–9:30pm. Bus: All Market St. buses. Streetcar: All Market St. streetcars. BART: Embarcadero.

Yank Sing ⚔⚔ CHINESE/DIM SUM   Loosely translated as "a delight of the heart," Yank Sing is widely regarded as the best dim sum restaurant in the downtown area. The servers are good at guessing your gastric threshold as they wheel stainless steel carts carrying small plates of exotic dishes around the vast dining room; if they whiz right by your table there's probably a good reason. If you're new to dim sum (which, translated, means "to touch the heart"), stick with the safe, recognizable classics such as spareribs, stuffed crab claws, scallion pancakes, shrimp balls, pork buns, and steamed dumplings filled with delicious concoctions of pork, beef, fish, or vegetables. A second location, open Monday through Friday from 11am to 3pm, is at 49 Stevenson St., off First Street (© **415/541-4949**) in SoMa, and has outdoor seating for fair-weather dining.

101 Spear St. (at Mission St. at Rincon Center). © **415/957-9300.** www.yanksing. com. Dim sum $3.65–$9.30 for 2–6 pieces. AE, DC, MC, V. Mon–Fri 11am–3pm; Sat–Sun and holidays 10am–4pm. Validated parking in Rincon Center Garage. Bus: 1, 12, 14, or 41. Streetcar: F. Cable car: California St. line. BART: Embarcadero.

3 SoMa

For a map of restaurants in this section, see the "Where to Dine around Town" map on p. 74.

VERY EXPENSIVE

Boulevard &&& AMERICAN   Master restaurant designer Pat Kuleto and chef Nancy Oakes are behind one of San Francisco's most beloved restaurants. Inside, the dramatically artistic Belle Epoque interior, with vaulted brick ceilings, floral banquettes, a mosaic floor, and tulip-shaped lamps, is the setting for Oakes's equally impressive sculptural and mouthwatering dishes. Starters alone could make a perfect meal, especially if you indulge in pan-seared day boat sea scallops with sautéed fresh hearts of palm, pomelo, basil, toasted shallots, and macadamia nuts, or the pan-seared foie gras with rhubarb syrup on whole grain toast. The nine or so main courses are equally creative and might include grilled Pacific sea bass with fresh gulf prawns, grilled artichoke, spring asparagus, and green garlic purée; or fire-roasted Angus filet with crispy Yukon gold potatoes, béarnaise sauce, sautéed spinach and crimini mushrooms, and red wine *jus*. Finish with warm chocolate cake with a chocolate caramel center, caramel corn, and butterscotch ice cream. Three levels of formality—bar, open kitchen, and main dining room—keep things from getting too snobby. Although steep prices prevent most from making Boulevard a regular gig, you'd be hard-pressed to find a better place for a special, fun-filled occasion.

1 Mission St. (btw. The Embarcadero and Steuart sts.). © **415/543-6084.** www. boulevardrestaurant.com. Reservations recommended. Main courses $14–$22 lunch, $28–$39 dinner. AE, DC, DISC, MC, V. Mon–Fri 11:30am–2pm; Sun–Thurs 5:30–10pm; Fri–Sat 5:30–10:30pm. Valet parking $12 lunch, $10 dinner. Bus: 12, 15, 30, 32, or 41. BART: Embarcadero.

Ducca &&& ITALIAN   If you've never experienced what a talented chef can do with *mozzarella di bufala,* you owe it to yourself to visit Ducca. Executive Chef Richard J. Corbo learned his trade at the Apicus culinary institute in Florence, then refined it at Restaurant Gary Danko (see p. 86) before being asked to run his own kitchen at Ducca. Since then he's earned nothing but kudos for his simple, seasonal Italian dishes seasoned with a hint of California

Where to Dine Around Town

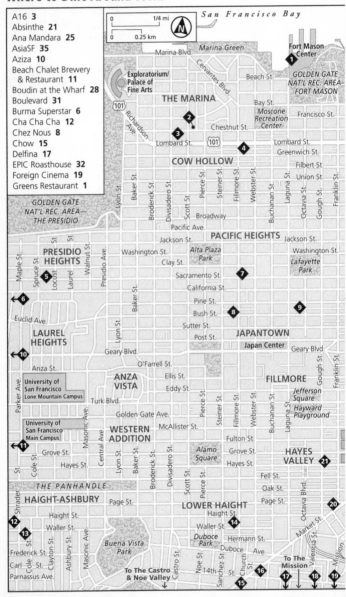

A16 **3**
Absinthe **21**
Ana Mandara **25**
AsiaSF **35**
Aziza **10**
Beach Chalet Brewery
& Restaurant **11**
Boudin at the Wharf **28**
Boulevard **31**
Burma Superstar **6**
Cha Cha Cha **12**
Chez Nous **8**
Chow **15**
Delfina **17**
EPIC Roasthouse **32**
Foreign Cinema **19**
Greens Restaurant **1**

San Francisco Bay

Fort Mason Center

GOLDEN GATE NAT'L REC. AREA—FORT MASON

Marina Blvd. Marina Green

Cervantes Blvd.

Beach St.

Marina Blvd.

Exploratorium/Palace of Fine Arts

THE MARINA

Bay St.

Moscone Recreation Center

Francisco St.

Richardson Ave.

Chestnut St.

Lombard St.

COW HOLLOW

Greenwich St.

Filbert St.

Union St.

GOLDEN GATE NAT'L REC. AREA—THE PRESIDIO

Baker St.
Broderick St.
Divisadero St.
Pierce St.
Scott St.
Steiner St.
Fillmore St.
Webster St.
Buchanan St.
Laguna St.
Octavia St.
Gough St.
Franklin St.

Broadway

Pacific Ave.

PACIFIC HEIGHTS

Jackson St.

Jackson St.

Washington St.

Alta Plaza Park

Washington St.

Lafayette Park

PRESIDIO HEIGHTS

Maple St.
Spruce St.
Locust
Laurel
Walnut St.
Presidio Ave.
Lyon St.
Baker St.

Clay St.

Sacramento St.

California St.

Pine St.

Bush St.

Sutter St.

Post St.

JAPANTOWN

Japan Center

Geary Blvd.

LAUREL HEIGHTS

Geary Blvd.

O'Farrell St.

Anza St.

Ellis St.

ANZA VISTA

Eddy St.

FILLMORE

Jefferson Square

Hayward Playground

Parker Ave.

University of San Francisco Lone Mountain Campus

Turk Blvd.

Golden Gate Ave.

University of San Francisco Main Campus

Masonic Ave.
Central Ave.
Lyon St.
Baker St.
Broderick St.
Divisadero St.
Scott St.
Pierce St.
Steiner St.
Fillmore St.
Webster St.
Buchanan St.
Laguna St.
Gough St.
Franklin St.

McAllister St.

WESTERN ADDITION

Fulton St.

Cole St.

Grove St.

Alamo Square

Grove St.

HAYES VALLEY

Hayes St.

Hayes St.

THE PANHANDLE

Fell St.

Oak St.

HAIGHT-ASHBURY

Page St.

LOWER HAIGHT

Page St.

Haight St.

Haight St.

Waller St.

Waller St.

Shrader St.

Clayton St.

Ashbury St.

Masonic Ave.

Buena Vista Park

Duboce Park

Hermann St.

Duboce Ave.

Octavia Blvd.

Market St.

Frederick St.
Cole St.
Carl St.
Parnassus Ave.

Castro St.
Noe St.
Sanchez St.
14th St.
Church St.

To The Mission

Valencia St.
Mission St.

To The Castro & Noe Valley

0 1/4 mi
0 0.25 km

N

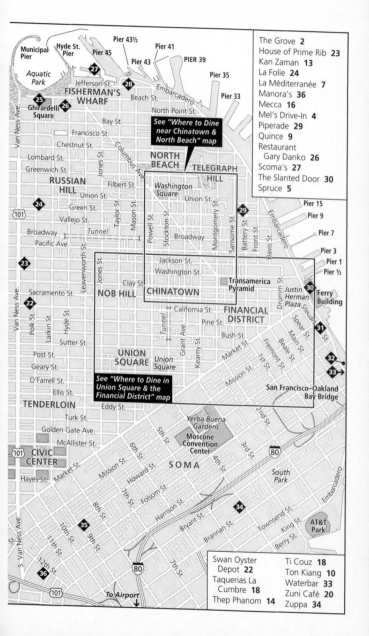

The Grove **2**
House of Prime Rib **23**
Kan Zaman **13**
La Folie **24**
La Méditerranée **7**
Manora's **36**
Mecca **16**
Mel's Drive-In **4**
Piperade **29**
Quince **9**
Restaurant
  Gary Danko **26**
Scoma's **27**
The Slanted Door **30**
Spruce **5**

Swan Oyster
  Depot **22**
Taquerias La
  Cumbre **18**
Thep Phanom **14**

Ti Couz **18**
Ton Kiang **10**
Waterbar **33**
Zuni Café **20**
Zuppa **34**

influences, such as his veal chop Milanese with a fennel pollen-breadcrumb crust and preserved lemon vinaigrette, ricotta gnocchi with fava beans and fungi, and a superb yellowtail crudo with pine nuts, currants, and mint. Corbo also offers a modest selection of *cichetti*, Italian-style bar snacks such as white anchovies, salt cod crostini, risotto fritters, et al. You'll enjoy the ambience as well, as it's smartly arranged into three inviting areas: a stylish bar and lounge, an alfresco terrace, and an airy dining room with embossed columns, cream-colored banquettes, and a bustling open kitchen. Be sure to arrive a bit early to enjoy a Compari and soda in the circular lounge or outdoors by the fireplace.

50 Third St. (btw. Market and Mission sts., adjacent to the Westin San Francisco Market Street hotel). © **415/977-0271**. www.duccasf.com. Main courses $23–$51. AE, DISC, MC, V. Breakfast 6:30–10:30am; lunch 11:30am-2pm; dinner 5:30–10:30pm. Valet parking $12. Bus: 15, 30, or 45. Streetcar: J, K, L, or M.

EPIC Roasthouse 👾👾 STEAKHOUSE   Why it took so long is a mystery, but for the first time in decades someone has finally built and opened a true destination restaurant on the Embarcadero. Two, actually. Location is everything, and the EPIC Roasthouse and its adjoining sister restaurant Waterbar (see below) were both built from the ground up on perhaps the most prime piece of real estate in the city—right on the Embarcadero with spectacular views of the Bay Bridge, Treasure Island, and city skyline. They both opened on the eve of January 29th, 2008, to such fanfare that the opening party was a debacle (everyone invited showed up). At EPIC it's all about steak. Renowned chef and co-owner Jan Birnbaum, a New Orleans man who knows his meat, runs the show within his huge exhibition kitchen, perspiring at the wood-fired heath to make sure your $76 rib eye-for-two is cooked to your specs. The restaurant's Pat Kuleto-designed interior makes for a grand entrance: Only when you're done marveling at the bold industrial elements of leather, stone, mahogany, and massive cast iron gears do you notice the phenomenal view of the Bay Bridge from the two-story-tall wall of windows. Perhaps the only thing prettier than the scenery is Birnbaum's sizzling 26 oz. bone-in porterhouse on your plate ("Every steak comes with a handle," claims Jan.). If you don't have a reservation, the upstairs Quiver Bar serves both bar and full menus, but the upstairs crowd usually consists of obnoxious businessmen and Gucci-toting gold-diggers from across the bridge. Better to call ahead and dine below. *Tip:* On sunny days beg the hostess for a table on the bay-view patio.

369 Embarcadero (at Harrison St.). © 415/369-9955. www.epicroasthousesf.com. Reservations recommended. Main courses $27–$54. AE, MC, V. Lunch Mon–Fri 11:30am–2pm; dinner Sun–Thurs 5–10:30pm and Fri–Sat 5pm–midnight; brunch Sat–Sun 10:30am–3pm. Valet parking $15 lunch, $10 dinner. Bus: 1, 12, 14, or 41. Streetcar: F. BART: Embarcadero.

Waterbar 𝕽𝕽 SEAFOOD   Built in tandem with the EPIC Roasthouse (see above), Waterbar is the surf to EPIC's turf. As with EPIC, Waterbar was built from the ground up on perhaps the most prime piece of real estate in the city along the Embarcadero. Whereas renowned restaurant designer Pat Kuleto went with a moderately conservative industrial look at the EPIC steakhouse, at Waterbar he unleashed his imagination and created the most visually playful decor since he opened Farallon in 1997. The focal point of the restaurant is a pair of radiant 19-foot floor-to-ceiling circular aquariums filled with fish and marine critters from the Pacific Ocean. The aquatic theme ebbs along on with a beautiful glass "caviar" chandelier and a horseshoe-shaped raw bar that has too few of the most coveted seats in town. Even the open kitchen is visually—and aromatically—pleasing. The menu offers a wide selection of market-driven, sustainable seafood such as Dover sole served whole (a whopping $80) and local halibut poached in milk with grilled asparagus, but more fun can be had at the raw bar noshing on oysters and small plates. Either way, be sure to start off with the superb sea scallop ceviche infused with sweet potato, smoked salt, and paprika. If the weather is agreeable, ask the hostess for a table on the patio

399 Embarcadero (at Harrison St.). © 415/284-9922. www.waterbarsf.com. Reservations recommended. Main courses $28–$36. AE, DISC, MC, V. Daily 11:30am–2pm and 5:30–10:00pm. Valet parking $15 lunch, $10 dinner. Bus: 1, 12, 14, or 41. Streetcar: F. BART: Embarcadero.

MODERATE

Zuppa 𝕽𝕽 ITALIAN   If you're looking for a casual-chic dinner spot with good affordable food, lively ambience, and a somewhat hip crowd, Zuppa is it. Located among the warehouses of SoMa, this warmed industrial room awash with dark wood tables features a back-wall bar orchestrated by on-site owners Joseph and Mary (yes, really). Joe, whose career launched from Spago Hollywood more than 2 decades ago, oversees the menu while Mary works the front of the house. With a menu of items that don't top $20, this is the way San Francisco dining used to be—if you can't decide between the antipasti of lemon-cured tuna with veggies, pizza with clams and garlic, or bone-in rib-eye, you can order all of them and not break the bank. A selection of cured meats, pizzas, and antipasti make it easy to snack

through a meal, but don't. The pastas—particularly the pork ragu—
are fantastic and shouldn't be missed, and the entrees are great as
well—especially when paired with an Italian wine. **Take note:** Parking
in local lots around here costs more on game days (the Giants ballpark
is nearby)—expect to pay around $15. Otherwise, it's very affordable.

564 Fourth St. (btw. Brannan and Bryant sts.). ✆ 415/777-5900. www.zuppa-sf.
com. Reservations recommended. Main courses $16–$19. AE, DC, DISC, MC, V.
Lunch Mon–Fri 11:30am–2:30pm; dinner Mon–Thurs 5:30–10pm, Fri–Sat
5:30–11pm, Sun 5–9pm. Street parking or pay at nearby lots. Bus: 9X, 12, 30, 45,
or 76.

INEXPENSIVE

AsiaSF ✿ ASIAN/CALIFORNIA Part restaurant, part gender-
illusionist musical revue, AsiaSF manages to be both entertaining
and satisfying. As you're entertained by mostly Asian men dressed as
women (who lip-sync show tunes when they're not waiting on
tables), you can nibble on superb grilled shrimp and herb salad; baby
back pork ribs with honey tamarind glaze, pickled carrots, and
sweet-potato crisps; or filet mignon with Korean dipping sauce, miso
eggplant, and fried potato stars. The full bar, *Wine Spectator*
award–winning wine list, and sake list add to the festivities. Fortunately, the food and the atmosphere are as colorful as the staff, which
means a night here is more than a meal—it's a very happening event.

201 Ninth St. (at Howard St.). ✆ 415/255-2742. www.asiasf.com. Reservations
recommended. Main courses $9–$20. AE, DISC, MC, V (Mon–Wed $25 minimum).
Sun–Thurs 6–10pm; Fri 6:45–10pm; Sat 5–10pm; cocktails and dancing until 2am on
weekends. Bus: 9, 12, or 47. Streetcar: Civic Center on underground streetcar. BART:
Civic Center.

Manora's ✿ THAI Manora's cranks out some of the best Thai
food in town and is well worth a jaunt to SoMa. But this is no
relaxed affair: It's perpetually packed (unless you come early), and
you'll be seated sardinelike at one of the cramped but well-appointed
tables. During the dinner rush, the noise level can make conversa-
tion among larger parties almost impossible, but the food is so
darned good, you'll probably prefer to turn toward your plate and
stuff your face anyway. Start with a Thai iced tea or coffee and tangy
soup or chicken satay, which comes with decadent peanut sauce. Follow these with any of the wonderful dinner dishes—which should be
shared—and a side of rice. There are endless options, including a
vast array of vegetarian plates. Every remarkably flavorful dish arrives
seemingly seconds after you order it, which is great if you're hungry,
a bummer if you were planning a long, leisurely dinner. **Tip:** Come
before 7pm or after 9pm if you don't want a loud, rushed meal.

1600 Folsom St. (at 12th St.). ℰ **415/861-6224**. www.manorathai.com. Reservations recommended for 4 or more. Main courses $7–$12. MC, V. Mon–Fri 11:30am–2:30pm; Mon–Sat 5:30–10:30pm; Sun 5–10pm. Bus: 9, 12, or 47.

4 Nob Hill/Russian Hill

For a map of restaurants in this section, see the "Where to Dine around Town" map on p. 74.

VERY EXPENSIVE

La Folie 🏵🏵🏵 *(Finds* FRENCH   I call this unintimidating, cozy, intimate French restaurant "the house of foie gras." Why? Because on my first visit, virtually every dish overflowed with the ultrarich delicacy. Subsequent visits proved that foie gras still reigns here, but more than that, it reconfirmed La Folie's long-standing reputation as one of the city's very best fine dining experiences—and without any stuffiness to boot. Chef/owner Roland Passot, who unlike many celebrity chefs is actually in the kitchen each night, offers melt-in-your-mouth starters such as seared foie gras with caramelized pineapple and star anise vanilla muscat broth. Generous main courses include rôti of quail and squab stuffed with wild mushrooms and wrapped in crispy potato strings; butter-poached lobster with glazed blood oranges and shiso, scallion, carrot, and toasted almond salad; and roast venison with vegetables, quince, and huckleberry sauce. The staff is extremely approachable and knowledgeable, and the new surroundings (think deep wood paneling, mirrors, long, rust-colored curtains, and gold-hued Venetian plaster) are now as elegant as the food. Best of all, the environment is relaxed, comfortable, and intimate. Finish with any of the delectable desserts. If you're not into the three-, four-, or five-course tasting menu, don't be deterred; the restaurant tells me they'll happily price out individual items.

2316 Polk St. (btw. Green and Union sts.). ℰ **415/776-5577**. www.lafolie.com. Reservations recommended. 3-course tasting menu $65; 4-course tasting menu $75; 5-course chef's tasting menu $85; vegetarian tasting menu $65. AE, DC, DISC, MC, V. Mon–Sat 5:30–10:30pm. Valet parking $15. Bus: 19, 41, 45, 47, 49, or 76.

EXPENSIVE

House of Prime Rib 🏵🏵 STEAKHOUSE   Anyone who loves a huge slab of meat and old-school–style dining will feel right at home at this shrine to prime (rib). It's a fun and ever-packed affair within the men's clublike dining rooms (fireplaces included), where drinks are stiff, waiters are loose, and all the beef is roasted in rock salt, sliced tableside, and served with salad dramatically tossed tableside followed by creamed spinach and either mashed potatoes or a baked potato and Yorkshire pudding, which accompany the entree. To placate the occasional non-meat eater, they offer a fish-of-the-day special.

1906 Van Ness Ave. (near Washington St.). ℂ 415/885-4605. Reservations recommended. Complete dinners $28–$33. AE, MC, V. Mon–Thurs 5:30–10pm; Fri 5–10pm; Sat 4:30–10pm; Sun 4–10pm. Valet parking $7. Bus: 47 or 49.

MODERATE

Swan Oyster Depot 🐟🐟 *Finds* SEAFOOD Turning 97 years old in 2009, Swan Oyster Depot is a classic San Francisco dining experience you shouldn't miss. Opened in 1912, this tiny hole in the wall, run by the city's friendliest servers, is little more than a narrow fish market that decided to slap down some bar stools. There are only 20 or so stools here, jammed cheek-by-jowl along a long marble bar. Most patrons come for a quick cup of chowder or a plate of oysters on the half shell that arrive chilling on crushed ice. The menu is limited to fresh crab, shrimp, oyster, clam cocktails, a few types of smoked fish, Maine lobster, and Boston-style clam chowder, all of which are exceedingly fresh. *Note:* Don't let the lunchtime line dissuade you—it moves fast.

1517 Polk St. (btw. California and Sacramento sts.). ℂ 415/673-1101. Reservations not accepted. Seafood cocktails $7–$15; clams and oysters on the half-shell $7.95 per half-dozen. No credit cards. Mon–Sat 8am–5:30pm. Bus: 1, 19, 47, or 49.

5 Chinatown

For a map of restaurants in this section, see the "Where to Dine near Chinatown & North Beach" map on p. 81.

INEXPENSIVE

Gold Mountain 🐟 *Finds* *Kids* CHINESE/DIM SUM This gymnasium-size restaurant is a must-visit for anyone who's never experienced what it's like to dine with hundreds of Chinese-speaking patrons conversing loudly at enormous round tables among glittering chandeliers and gilded dragons while dozens of white-shirted waitstaff push around stainless steel carts filled with small plates of exotic-looking edible adventures (Was that sentence long enough for you?). Chicken feet, pork buns, shrimp dumplings, honey-walnut prawns (yum), the ubiquitous chicken-in-foil, and a myriad of other quasi-recognizable concoctions that range from appealing to revolting (never ate beef tripe, never will) whiz about at eye-level. I remember coming here as a little kid on late Saturday mornings and being infatuated with the entire cacophonous event. And even if you eat until you're ill, you'll never put down more than $20 worth of food, making Gold Mountain a real bargain as well, especially for

Where to Dine near Chinatown & North Beach

Bix **9**

Caffè Macaroni **8**

Capp's Corner **1**

Gold Mountain **5**

Great Eastern **6**

House of Nanking **7**

Il Pollaio **2**

L'Osteria del Forno **3**

R&G Lounge **10**

The Stinking Rose **4**

large groups. Don't even bother with the regular menu: it's the dim sum service from 8am and 3pm on weekends and 10:30am to 3pm on weekdays that you want.

664 Broadway (btw. Grant Ave. and Stockton St.). ✆ 415/296-7733. Main courses $3–$9. AE, MC, V. Mon–Fri 10:30am-3pm and 5–9:30pm; Sat–Sun 8am–3pm and 5–9:30pm. Bus: 12, 15, 30, or 83.

Great Eastern ⊀ *Finds* CHINESE   If you like seafood and Chinese food and have an adventurous palate, you're going to love Great Eastern, which is well known among serious foodies for serving hard-to-find seafood pulled straight from the myriad of tanks that line the walls. Rock cod, steelhead, sea conch, sea bass, shrimp, frogs, soft-shell turtle, abalone—if it's even remotely aquatic and edible, it's on the menu at this popular Hong Kong–style dinner house that's mostly frequented by Chinese locals (so you know it's good). The day's catch, sold by the pound, is listed on a board. Both upper- and lower-level dining rooms are stylish in a Chinatown sort of way, with shiny black and emerald furnishings. The dim sum is excellent here as well—some say it's even better than the venerable Yank Sing (p. 72)—so give it a try as well. *Tip:* Unless you can translate an authentic Hong Kong menu, order a set dinner (the crab version is fantastic) or point to another table and say, "I want that."

649 Jackson St. (btw. Kearny St. and Grant Ave.). ✆ 415/986-2500. Most main courses $8–$13. AE, MC, V. Daily 10am–1am. Bus: 15, 30, 41, or 45.

House of Nanking ⊀ CHINESE   This place would be strictly a tourist joint if it weren't for the die-hard fans who happily wait— sometimes up to an hour—for a coveted seat at this inconspicuous little restaurant serving Shanghai-style cuisine. Order the requisite pot stickers, green-onion-and-shrimp pancakes with peanut sauce, or any number of pork, rice, beef, seafood, chicken, or vegetable dishes from the menu, but I suggest you trust the waiter when he recommends a special. Even with an expansion that doubled the available space, seating is tight, so prepare to be bumped around a bit and don't expect perky or attentive service—it's all part of the Nanking experience.

919 Kearny St. (at Columbus Ave.). ✆ 415/421-1429. Reservations accepted for groups of 8 or more. Main courses $6–$12. MC, V. Mon–Fri 11am–10pm; Sat–Sun noon–10pm. Bus: 9, 12, 15, or 30.

R&G Lounge ⊀ CHINESE   It's tempting to take your chances and duck into any of the exotic restaurants in Chinatown, but if you want a sure thing, go directly to the three-story R&G Lounge. During lunch, all three floors are packed with hungry neighborhood workers who go straight for the $5.50 rice-plate specials. Even then, you can order from the dinner menu, which features legendary deep-fried salt-and-pepper crab (a little greasy for my taste); and wonderful chicken with black-bean sauce. A personal favorite is melt-in-your-mouth R&G Special Beef, which explodes with the tangy flavor of the accompanying sauce. I was less excited by the tired chicken salad, house specialty noodles, and bland spring rolls. But that was just fine since I saved room for generous and savory seafood in a clay pot and classic roast duck.

631 Kearny St. (at Clay St.). © 415/982-7877. www.rnglounge.com. Reservations recommended. Main courses $9.50–$30. AE, DC, DISC, MC, V. Daily 11am–9:30pm. Parking validated across the street at Portsmouth Sq. garage 24 hr. or Holiday Inn after 5pm. Bus: 1, 9AX, 9BX, or 15. Cable Car: California.

6 North Beach/Telegraph Hill

For a map of restaurants in this section, see the "Where to Dine near Chinatown & North Beach" map on p. 81.

EXPENSIVE

Bix *Moments* AMERICAN/CALIFORNIA   The martini lifestyle may now be *en vogue*, but it was never out of style in this glamorous retro '30s-era supper club. Bix is utterly stylish, with curving mahogany paneling, giant silver pillars, and dramatic lighting, all of which sets the stage for live music and plenty of hobnobbing. Though the sleek setting has overshadowed the food in the past, the legions of diners entranced by the Bix experience don't seem to care—and it seems as of late Bix is "on" again. Chicken hash has been a menu favorite for the past 19 years, but newer luxury comfort-food dishes—such as caviar service, marrowbones with toast and shallot confit, steak tartare, and pan-roasted seasonal fish dishes—are developing their own fan clubs. **Bargain tip:** At lunch a three-course prix-fixe menu goes for $25.

56 Gold St. (btw. Sansome and Montgomery sts.). © 415/433-6300. www.bix restaurant.com. Reservations recommended. Main courses $12–$15 lunch, $16–$32 dinner. AE, DC, DISC, MC, V. Mon–Thurs 4:30–11pm; Fri 11:30am–2pm and 5:30–midnight; Sat 5:30–midnight; Sun 6–10pm. Valet parking $10. Bus: 15, 30, 41, or 45.

MODERATE

Piperade BASQUE   Chef Gerald Hirigoyen takes diners on a Basque adventure in this charming, small restaurant. Surrounded by a low wood-beam–lined ceiling, oak floors, and soft sconce lighting, it's a casual affair where diners indulge in small and large plates of Hirigoyen's superbly flavorful West Coast Basque cuisine. Your edible odyssey starts with small plates—or plates to be shared—like my personal favorites: piquillo peppers stuffed with goat cheese; and a bright and simple salad of garbanzo beans with calamari, chorizo, and piquillo peppers. Share entrees, too. Indulge in New York steak with braised shallots and french fries or sop up every drop of the sweet and savory red-pepper sauce with the braised seafood and shellfish stew. Save room for orange blossom beignets: Light and airy with a delicate and moist web of dough within and a kiss of orange essence, the beignet is dessert at its finest. There's a communal table for drop-in diners and front patio seating during warmer weather.

1015 Battery St. (at Green St.). © 415/391-2555. www.piperade.com. Reservations recommended. Main courses $17–$24. AE, DC, DISC, MC, V. Mon–Fri 11:30am–3pm and 5:30–10:30pm; Sat 5:30–10:30pm; closed Sun. Bus: 10, 12, 30, or 82x.

The Stinking Rose ITALIAN   Garlic is the "flower" from which this restaurant gets its name. From soup to ice cream, the supposedly healthful herb is a star ingredient in almost every dish. ("We season our garlic with food," exclaims the menu.) From a gourmet point of view, The Stinking Rose is unremarkable. Pizzas, pastas, and meats smothered in simple, overpowering sauces are tasty, but they're memorable only for their singular garlicky intensity. That said, this is a fun place; the restaurant's lively atmosphere and odoriferous aroma combine for good entertainment. The best dishes include iron-skillet–roasted mussels, shrimp, and crab with garlic sauce; smoked mozzarella, garlic, and tomato pizza; salt-roasted tiger prawns with garlic parsley glaze; and 40-clove garlic chicken (served with garlic mashed potatoes, of course). *Note:* For those who are not garlic-inclined, they offer garlic-free "Vampire Fare."

325 Columbus Ave. (btw. Vallejo and Broadway). © 415/781-7673. www.the stinkingrose.com. Reservations recommended. Main courses $13–$30. AE, DC, DISC, MC, V. Daily 11am–11pm. Bus: 15, 30, 41, or 45.

INEXPENSIVE

Caffè Macaroni ★ *Finds* ITALIAN   You wouldn't know it from the looks (or name) of it, but this tiny, funky restaurant on busy Columbus Avenue is one of the best southern Italian restaurants in the city. It looks as though it can hold only two customers at a time, and if you don't duck your head when entering the upstairs dining room, you might as well ask for one lump or two. Fortunately, the kitchen also packs a wallop, dishing out a large variety of antipasti and excellent pastas. The spinach-and-cheese ravioli with wild-mushroom sauce and the gnocchi are outstanding. The owners and staff are always vivacious and friendly, and young ladies in particular will enjoy the attentions of the charming Italian men manning the counter. If you're still pondering whether you should eat here, consider that most entrees are under $15.

124 Columbus Ave. (at Jackson St.). © **415/956-9737.** www.caffemacaroni.com. Reservations accepted. Main courses $9–$15. AE, MC, V. Mon–Sat 11am–2:30pm and 5:30–11pm; Sun noon–10pm. Bus: 15 or 41.

Capp's Corner ★ (Value) ITALIAN

Capp's is a place of givens: It's a given that high-spirited regulars are hunched over the bar and that you'll be served huge portions of straightforward Italian fare at low prices in a raucous atmosphere that prevails until closing. The waitresses are usually brusque and bossy, but always with a wink. Long tables are set up for family-style dining: bread, soup, salad, and choice of around 20 classic main dishes (herb-roasted leg of lamb, spaghetti with meatballs, *osso buco* with polenta, fettuccine with prawns and white-wine sauce)—all for $15 or $17 or so per person, around $10 for kids. You might have to wait awhile for a table, but if you want fun and authentic old-school dining without pomp or huge prices, you'll find the wait worthwhile.

1600 Powell St. (at Green St.). © **415/989-2589.** www.cappscorner.com. Reservations accepted. Complete dinners $15–$17. AE, DC, MC, V. Daily 11:30am–2:30pm; Mon–Fri 4:30–10:30pm; Sat–Sun 4–11pm. Bus: 15, 30, or 41.

Il Pollaio ★ (Value) ITALIAN/ARGENTINE

Simple, affordable, and consistently good is the winning combination at Il Pollaio. When I used to live in the neighborhood I ate here at least once a week and I still can't make chicken this good. Seat yourself in the tiny, unfussy room, order, and wait expectantly for the fresh-from-the-grill lemon-infused chicken, which is so moist it practically falls off the bone. Each meal comes with a choice of salad or fries. If you're not in the mood for chicken, you can opt for rabbit, lamb, pork chop, or Italian sausage. On a sunny day, get your goods to-go and picnic across the street at Washington Square.

555 Columbus Ave. (btw. Green and Union sts.). © **415/362-7727.** Reservations not accepted. Main courses $8–$15. DISC, MC, V. Mon–Sat 11:30am–9pm. Bus: 15, 30, 39, 41, or 45. Cable car: Powell–Mason line.

L'Osteria del Forno ★★ ITALIAN

L'Osteria del Forno might be only slightly larger than a walk-in closet, but it's one of the top three authentic Italian restaurants in North Beach. Peer in the window facing Columbus Avenue, and you'll probably see two Italian women with their hair up, sweating from the heat of the oven, which cranks out the best focaccia (and focaccia sandwiches) in the city. There's no pomp or circumstance here: Locals come strictly to eat. The menu features a variety of superb pizzas, salads, soups, and fresh pastas, plus a good selection of daily specials (pray for the roast pork braised in milk), which includes a roast of the day, pasta, and ravioli. Small baskets of warm focaccia keep you going until the arrival of the entrees, which should always be accompanied by a glass of Italian red. Good news for folks on the go: You can get pizza by the slice. Note that it's cash-only here.

519 Columbus Ave. (btw. Green and Union sts.). 📞 **415/982-1124.** www.losteria delforno.com. Reservations not accepted. Sandwiches $6–$7; pizzas $10–$18; main courses $6–$14. No credit cards. Sun–Mon and Wed–Thurs 11:30am–10pm; Fri–Sat 11:30am–10:30pm. Bus: 15, 30, 41, or 45.

7 Fisherman's Wharf

For a map of restaurants in this section, see the "Where to Dine around Town" map on p. 74.

VERY EXPENSIVE

Restaurant Gary Danko ★★★ FRENCH   James Beard Award–winning chef Gary Danko presides over my top pick for fine dining. Eschewing the white-glove formality of yesteryear's fine dining, Danko offers impeccable cuisine and perfectly orchestrated service in an unstuffy environment of wooden paneling and shutters and well-spaced tables (not to mention spa-style bathrooms). The three- to five-course fixed-price seasonal menu is freestyle, so whether you want a sampling of appetizers or a flight of meat courses, you need only ask. I am a devoted fan of his trademark buttery-smooth glazed oysters with lettuce cream, salsify, and Osetra caviar; seared foie gras, which may be accompanied by peaches, caramelized onions, and *verjus* (a classic French sauce); horseradish-crusted salmon medallions with dilled cucumbers; and adventurous Moroccan spiced squab with *chermoula* (a Moroccan sauce made with cilantro) and orange-cumin carrots. Truthfully, I've never had a dish here that wasn't wonderful. And wine? The list is stellar, albeit expensive. If after dinner you have the will to pass on the glorious cheese cart or flambéed dessert of the day, a plate of petit fours reminds you that Gary Danko is one sweet and memorable meal. *Tip:* If you can't get a reservation and are set on dining here, slip in and grab a seat at the 10-stool first-come, first-served bar where you can also order a la carte.

800 North Point St. (at Hyde St.). ℂ 415/749-2060. www.garydanko.com. Reservations required except at walk-in bar. 3- to 5-course fixed-price menu $61–$89. AE, DC, DISC, MC, V. Daily 5:30–10pm; bar open 5pm. Valet parking $10. Bus: 10. Streetcar: F. Cable car: Hyde.

EXPENSIVE

Ana Mandara ⭐ VIETNAMESE   Yes, Don Johnson is part owner. But more important, this Fisherman's Wharf favorite serves fine Vietnamese food in an outstandingly beautiful setting. Amid a shuttered room with mood lighting, palm trees, and Vietnamese-inspired decor, diners (mostly tourists) splurge on crispy rolls, lobster ravioli with mango and coconut sauce, and wok-charred tournedos of beef tenderloin with sweet onions and peppercress. There is no more expensive Vietnamese dining room in town, but, along with the enjoyable fare, diners pay for the atmosphere, which, if they're in the neighborhood and want something more exotic than the standby seafood dinner, is worth the price.

891 Beach St. (at Polk St.). ℂ 415/771-6800. www.anamandara.com. Reservations recommended. Main courses $19–$32. AE, DC, DISC, MC, V. Mon–Fri 11:30am–2pm; Sun–Thurs 5:30–9:30pm; Fri–Sat 5:30–10:30pm; bar until 1am. Valet parking Tues–Sun $9. Bus: 19, 30, or 45.

Scoma's ⭐ SEAFOOD   A throwback to the dining of yesteryear, Scoma's eschews trendier trout preparations and fancy digs for good old-fashioned seafood served in huge portions amid a very casual windowed waterfront setting. Gourmands should skip this one. But if your idea of heaven is straightforward seafood classics—fried calamari, raw oysters, pesto pasta with rock shrimp, crab cioppino, lobster thermidor—served with a generous portion of old-time hospitality, then Scoma's is as good as it gets. Unfortunately, a taste of tradition will cost you big time. Prices are as steep as those at some of the finest restaurants in town. Personally, I'd rather splurge at Gary Danko. But many of my out-of-town guests insist we meet at Scoma's, which is fine by me since it's a change of pace from today's chic spots, and the parking's free.

Pier 47 and Al Scoma Way (btw. Jefferson and Jones sts.). ℂ 800/644-5852 or 415/771-4383. www.scomas.com. Reservations not accepted. Most main courses $18–$35. AE, DC, DISC, MC, V. Sun–Thurs 11:30am–10pm; Fri–Sat 11:30am–10:30pm; bar opens 30 min. prior to lunch daily. Free valet parking. Bus: 10 or 47. Streetcar: F.

INEXPENSIVE

Boudin at the Wharf DELI/AMERICAN   This industrial-chic Fisherman's Wharf shrine to the city's famous tangy French-style bread is impossible to miss. Even if you're not hungry, drop in to see bakers at work making 3,000 loaves daily or take the tour and learn about the city sourdough bread's history (Boudin is the city's oldest continually operating business). Good, strong coffee is served at **Peet's Coffee** (another Bay Area great), and at **Bakers Hall** you'll find picnic possibilities such as handcrafted cheeses, fruit spreads, and chocolates, as well as a wall map highlighting the town's best places to spread a blanket and feast. There's also a casual **self-serve cafe** serving sandwiches, clam chowder bowls, salads, and pastries, and the more formal **Bistro Boudin** restaurant, which offers Alcatraz views with its Dungeness crab Louis, pizza, crab cakes, and burgers on sourdough buns.

160 Jefferson St., near Pier 43½. ℂ **415/928-1849.** www.boudinbakery.com. Reservations recommended at bistro. Main courses cafe $6–$10, bistro $11–$33. AE, DC, DISC, MC, V. Cafe daily 8am–10pm; bistro Mon–Fri noon–10pm; Sat 11:30am–10pm; Sun 11:30am–9pm. Bus: 10, 15, or 47. Streetcar: F.

8 The Marina/Pacific Heights/Cow Hollow

For a map of restaurants in this section, see the "Where to Dine around Town" map on p. 74.

EXPENSIVE

Quince 𝔎𝔎 CALIFORNIA/ITALIAN   Its discreet location in a quiet residential neighborhood hasn't stopped this tiny and predominantly white-hued restaurant from becoming one of the city's hardest reservations to get. With only 15 tables, diners are clamoring for a seat to savor the nightly changing Italian-inspired menu by Michael Tusk, who mastered the art of pasta while working at the East Bay's famed Chez Panisse and Oliveto restaurants. Regardless, it's worth the effort—especially if you love simple food that honors a few high-quality, organic ingredients. Dining divinity might start with a pillowy spring garlic soufflé or white asparagus with a lightly fried egg and brown butter, but it really hits heavenly notes with the pasta course, be it garganelli with English peas and prosciutto, tagliatelle with veal ragout and fava beans, or artichoke ravioli. Meat and fish selections don't fall short either, with delicately prepared mixed grill plates, tender Alaskan halibut with fava beans, and juicy lamb with fennel and olives. Desserts aren't quite as celestial, but the trio of citrus sorbets make for a light, pleasant finish to a wonderful meal.

1701 Octavia St. (at Bush St.). ℂ **415/775-8500.** www.quincerestaurant.com. Reservations required. Main courses $16–$29. AE, MC, V. Mon–Thurs 5:30–10pm; Fri–Sat 5–10pm. Valet parking $8. Bus: 1, 31, or 38.

Spruce ⓖ CONTEMPORARY AMERICAN   If you haven't heard of San Francisco's Pacific Heights neighborhood, it's where most of the city's old money lives, and now the ladies-who-lunch have a new place to hang their cloches: Spruce. Housed in a beautifully restored 1930-era auto barn, Spruce consists of a restaurant, café, bar, and lounge under a single roof, making it both a destination restaurant and neighborhood hangout. As you enter there's a library nook on one side filled with newspapers, cookbooks, and more, and a café on the other side offering gourmet takeaway items. Further inside is an elegant bar to the right and 70-seat restaurant to left, both topped with a vast cathedral ceiling highlighted by a glass-and-steel skylight. With mohair couches, faux-ostrich chairs, and a black-and-chocolate décor it's all quite visually appealing, but, alas, the cuisine isn't quite as impressive. The organic, locally sourced produce is wonderfully fresh, but many of the dishes we tried—spearmint and nettle ravioli, leek and fennel soup with salt cod dumplings, honey lacquered duck breast—were lacking in flavor, and the service suffered from mysteriously long spells of absence. Spruce is still one of the exciting new restaurants in San Francisco, but it's best enjoyed from a seat at the bar while tucking into their fantastic all-natural burger & fries while pondering which wine to choose from their 70 by-the-glass selections.

3640 Sacramento Street (at Spruce St.). ⓒ **415/931-5100**. www.sprucesf.com. Reservations recommended. Main courses $25–$40. AE, DC, DISC, MC, V. Mon–Fri 11:30am–11pm, Sat–Sun 5–11pm. Valet parking $12 dinner only. Bus: 1, 2, or 4.

MODERATE

A16 ⓖⓖ ITALIAN   This sleek, casual, and wonderfully lively spot is one of San Francisco's best and busiest restaurants, featuring Neapolitan-style pizza and cuisine from the region of Campania. Named after the motorway that traverses the region, the divided space boasts a wine and beer bar up front, a larger dining area and open kitchen in the back, and a wall of wines in between. But its secret weapon is the creative menu of outstanding appetizers, pizza, and entrees, which are orchestrated by chef Nate Appleman with the same perfection as they were by opening chef Christophe Hille. Even if you must hoard the insanely good braised pork shoulder to yourself, start by sharing roasted asparagus with walnut cream and pecorino tartuffo or artichoke and tuna conserva with grilled bread and chiles. Co-owner and wine director Shelley Lindgren guides diners through one of the city's most exciting wine lists, featuring 40 wines by the half-glass, glass, and carafe. Oddly enough, their desserts are consistently mediocre, but perhaps that will change by the time you visit.

2355 Chestnut St. (btw. Divisadero and Scott sts.). ℂ **415/771-2216**. www.a16sf. com. Reservations recommended. Main courses $8–$13 lunch, $14–$20 dinner. AE, DC, MC, V. Wed–Fri 11:30am–2:30pm; Sun–Thurs 5–10pm; Fri–Sat 5–11pm. Bus: 22, 30, or 30X.

Chez Nous 🌟🌟 FRENCH   Diners get crammed into the 40-seat dining area of this bright, cheery, small, and bustling dining room, but the eclectic tapas are so delicious and affordable, no one seems to care. Indeed, this friendly and fast-paced neighborhood haunt has become a blueprint for other restaurants that understand the allure of small plates. But Chez Nous stands out as more than a petite-portion trendsetter. The clincher is that most of its Mediterranean dishes taste so clean and fresh you can't wait to come back and dine here again. Start with the soup, whatever it is; don't skip tasty french fries with *harissa* (Tunisian hot sauce) aioli; savor the lamb chops with lavender sea salt; and save room for their famed dessert, the minicustard-cakelike *canneles de Bordeaux.*

1911 Fillmore St. (btw. Pine and Bush sts.). ℂ **415/441-8044**. Reservations accepted, but walk-ins welcome. Small dishes $5–$13. AE, MC, V. Daily 11:30am–3pm and 5:30–10pm (Fri–Sat until 11pm). Bus: 22, 41, or 45.

Greens Restaurant 🌟🌟 VEGETARIAN   In an old waterfront warehouse, with enormous windows overlooking the bridge, boats, and the bay, Greens is one of the most renowned vegetarian restaurants in the country. Executive chef Annie Somerville (author of *Fields of Greens*) cooks with the seasons, using produce from local organic farms. Within the quiet dining room, a weeknight dinner might feature such appetizers as mushroom soup with Asiago cheese and tarragon; or grilled portobello and endive salad. Entrees run the gamut from pizza with wilted escarole, red onions, lemon, Asiago, and Parmesan, to Vietnamese yellow curry or risotto with black trumpet mushrooms, leeks, savory spinach, white-truffle oil, Parmesan Reggiano, and thyme. Those interested in the whole shebang should make reservations for the $48 four-course dinner served on Saturday only. Lunch and brunch are equally fresh and tasty. The adjacent Greens To Go sells sandwiches, soups, salads, and pastries.

Building A, Fort Mason Center (enter Fort Mason opposite the Safeway at Buchanan and Marina sts.). ℂ **415/771-6222**. www.greensrestaurant.com. Reservations recommended. Main courses $9.50–$14 lunch, $15–$20 dinner, fixed-price dinner $48; Sun brunch $8–$14. AE, DISC, MC, V. Tues–Sat noon–2:30pm; Sun 10:30am–9pm; Mon–Sat 5:30–9pm. Greens To Go Mon–Thurs 8am–8pm; Fri–Sat 8am–5pm; Sun 10:30am–4pm. Parking in hourly lot $4 for up to 2½ hours. Bus: 28 or 30.

INEXPENSIVE

The Grove ⭑ CAFE   The Grove is the kind of place you go just to hang out and enjoy the fact that you're in San Francisco. That the heaping salads, lasagna, pasta, sandwiches, and daily specials are predictably good is an added bonus. I like coming here on weekday mornings for the easy-going vibe, strong coffee, and friendly, fast service. Inside you can sit at one of the dark wood tables on the scuffed hardwood floor and people-watch through the large open windows, but on sunny days the most coveted seats are along the sidewalk. It's the perfect place to read the newspaper, sip an enormous mug of coffee, and be glad you're not at work right now. A second Pacific Heights location is at 2016 Fillmore St. between California and Pine Sts (② **415/474-1419**).

2250 Chestnut St. (btw. Scott and Pierce sts.). ② **415/474-4843**. Most main courses $6–$7. MC, V. Mon–Fri 7am–11pm; Sat–Sun 8am–11pm. Bus: 22, 28, 30, 30X, 43, 76, or 82X.

La Méditerranée ⭑ *Value* MEDITERRANEAN   With an upscale-cafe ambience and quality food, La Méditerranée has long warranted its reputation as one of most appealing inexpensive restaurants on upper Fillmore. Here you'll find freshly prepared traditional Mediterranean food that's worlds apart from the Euro-eclectic fare many restaurants now call "Mediterranean." Baba ghanouj, tabbouleh, dolmas, and hummus start out the menu. My favorite dish here is the chicken Cilicia, a phyllo-dough dish that's hand-rolled and baked with cinnamony spices, almonds, chickpeas, and raisins. Also recommended are the zesty chicken pomegranate drumsticks on a bed of rice. Both come with green salad, potato salad, or soup for around $9.50. Ground lamb dishes, quiches, and Middle Eastern combo plates round out the affordable menu, and wine comes by the glass and in half- or full liters. A second location is at 288 Noe St., at Market Street (② **415/431-7210**).

2210 Fillmore St. (at Sacramento St.). ② **415/921-2956**. www.cafelamed.com. Main courses $7–$10 lunch, $8–$12 dinner. AE, MC, V. Sun–Thurs 11am–10pm; Fri–Sat 11am–11pm. Bus: 1, 3, or 22.

Mel's Drive-In ⭑ *Kids* AMERICAN   Sure, it's contrived, touristy, and nowhere near healthy, but when you get that urge for a chocolate shake and banana cream pie at the stroke of midnight—or when you want to entertain the kids—no other place in the city comes through like Mel's Drive-In. Modeled after a classic 1950s diner, right down to the jukebox at each table, Mel's harkens back to the halcyon days when cholesterol and fried foods didn't jab your guilty conscience with every greasy, wonderful bite. Too bad the prices don't reflect the '50s; a burger with fries and a Coke costs about $12.

Another Mel's at 3355 Geary St., at Stanyan Street (© **415/387-2244**), is open from 6am to 1am Sunday through Thursday and 6am to 3am Friday and Saturday. Additional locations are: 1050 Van Ness (© **415/292-6357**), open Sunday through Thursday 6am to 3am and Friday through Sunday 6am to 4am; and 801 Mission St. (© **415/227-4477**), open Sunday through Wednesday 6am to 1am, Thursday 6am to 2am, and Friday and Saturday 24 hours.

2165 Lombard St. (at Fillmore St.). © **415/921-3039.** www.melsdrive-in.com. Main courses $6.50–$12 breakfast, $7–$10 lunch, $8–$15 dinner. MC, V. Sun–Wed 6am–1am; Thurs 6am–2am; Fri–Sat 24 hr. Bus: 22, 30, or 43.

9 Civic Center & Hayes Valley

For a map of restaurants in this section, see the "Where to Dine around Town" map on p. 74.

MODERATE

Absinthe ⊛ FRENCH   This Hayes Valley hot spot is sexy, fun, reasonably priced, and frequented by everyone from the theatergoing crowd to the young and chic. Decor is all brasserie, with French rattan cafe chairs, copper-topped tables, a pressed-tin ceiling, soft lighting, period art, and a rich use of color and fabric, including leather and mohair banquettes. It's always a pleasure to unwind at the bar with a Ginger Rogers—gin, mint, lemon juice, ginger ale, and a squeeze of lime. The lengthy lunch menu offers everything from oysters and caviar to Caesar salad and a respectable burger, but I always end up getting the same thing: their outstanding open-faced smoked-trout sandwich on grilled Italian bread. In the divided dining room, main courses are equally satisfying, from coq au vin and steak frites to roasted whole Dungeness crab with poached leeks in mustard vinaigrette, salt roasted potatoes, and aioli. The best item on the weekend brunch menu is the creamy polenta with mascarpone, maple syrup, bananas, and toasted walnuts.

398 Hayes St. (at Gough St.). © **415/551-1590.** www.absinthe.com. Reservations recommended. Brunch $8–$14; most main courses $12–$22 lunch, $18–$28 dinner. AE, DC, DISC, MC, V. Tues–Fri 11:30am–midnight (bar until 2am Fri); Sat 11am–midnight (bar until 2am); Sun 11am–10pm (bar until midnight). Valet parking (Tues–Sat after 5pm) $10. Bus: 21.

Zuni Café ⊛⊛ _Finds_ MEDITERRANEAN   Zuni Café embodies the best of San Francisco dining: Its clientele spans young hipsters to hunky gays, the cuisine is consistently terrific, and the atmosphere is electric. Its expanse of windows overlooking Market Street gives the place a sense of space despite the fact that it's always packed. For the full effect, stand at the bustling, copper-topped bar and order a glass of wine and a few oysters from the oyster menu (a dozen or so varieties are on hand at all times). Then, because *of course* you made advance reservations, take your seat in the stylish exposed-brick two-level maze of little dining rooms or on the outdoor patio. Then do what we all do: Splurge on chef Judy Rodgers' Mediterranean-influenced menu. Although the ever-changing menu always includes meat (such as hanger steak), fish (grilled or braised on the kitchen's wood grill), and pasta (tagliatelle with nettles, applewood-smoked bacon, butter, and Parmesan), it's almost sinful not to order her brick-oven roasted chicken for two with Tuscan-style bread salad. I rarely pass up the polenta with mascarpone and a proper Caesar salad. But then again, if you're there for lunch or after 10pm, the hamburger on grilled rosemary focaccia bread is a strong contender for the city's best. Whatever you decide, be sure to order a stack of shoestring potatoes.

1658 Market St. (at Franklin St.). ⓒ **415/552-2522.** www.zunicafe.com. Reservations recommended. Main courses $10–$19 lunch, $15–$29 dinner. AE, MC, V. Tues–Sat 11:30am–midnight; Sun 11am–11pm. Valet parking $10. Bus: 6, 7, or 71. Streetcar: All Market St. streetcars.

10 Mission District

For a map of restaurants in this section, see the "Where to Dine around Town" map on p. 74.

MODERATE

Delfina ⏣⏣ ITALIAN Unpretentious warehouse-chic atmosphere, reasonable prices, and chef/co-owner Craig Stoll's superb seasonal Italian cuisine have made this family-owned restaurant one of the city's most cherished. Stoll, who was one of *Food & Wine*'s Best New Chefs in 2001 and a 2005 James Beard Award nominee, changes the menu daily, while his wife Annie works the front of the house (when she's not being a mom). Standards include Niman Ranch flatiron steak with french fries, and roasted chicken with Yukon Gold mashed potatoes and royal trumpet mushrooms. The winter menu might include slow-roasted pork shoulder or gnocchi with squash and chestnuts, while spring indulgences can include sand dabs with frisée, fingerling potatoes, and lemon-caper butter; or lamb with polenta and sweet peas. Trust me—order the buttermilk *panna cotta* (custard) if it's available. *A plus:* A few tables and counter seating are reserved for walk-in diners. Delfina also has a heated and covered patio that's used mid-March through November.

3621 18th St. (btw. Dolores and Guerrero sts.). ℂ 415/552-4055. www.delfinasf. com. Reservations recommended. Main courses $13–$22. MC, V. Sun–Thurs 5:30–10pm; Fri–Sat 5:30–11pm. Parking lot at 18th and Valencia sts, $8. Bus: 26 or 33. Streetcar: J.

Foreign Cinema 🕸🕸 MEDITERRANEAN This place is so chic and well-hidden that it eludes me every time I drive past it on Mission Street (**hint:** look for the valet stand). The "cinema" here is a bit of a gimmick: It's an outdoor dining area (partially covered and heated, but still chilly) where mostly foreign films are projected onto the side of an adjoining building without any audio. What's definitely not a gimmick, however, is the superb Mediterranean-inspired menu created by husband-and-wife team John Clark and Gayle Pirie. Snackers like me find solace at the oyster bar with a half-dozen locally harvested Miyagi oysters and a devilishly good *brandade* (fish purée) gratin. Heartier eaters can opt for grilled halibut with chanterelles and roasted figs in a fig vinaigrette; fried Madras curry-spiced chicken with gypsy peppers; or grilled natural rib-eye with Tuscan-style beans and rosemary-fried peppercorn sauce—all made from seasonal, sustainably farmed, organic ingredients when possible. Truth be told, even if the food weren't so good, I'd still come here—it's just that cool. If you have to wait for your table, consider stepping into their adjoining bar, Laszlo.

2534 Mission St. (btw. 21st and 22nd sts.). ℂ 415/648-7600. www.foreign cinema.com. Reservations recommended. Main courses $17–$26. AE, MC, V. Mon–Thurs 6–10pm; Fri–Sat 6–11pm; Sun 5–10pm; brunch Sat–Sun 11am–3pm. Valet parking $10. Bus: 14, 14L, or 49.

INEXPENSIVE

Taquerias La Cumbre MEXICAN If San Francisco commissioned a flag honoring its favorite food, we'd probably all be waving a banner of the Golden Gate Bridge bolstering a giant burrito—that's how much we love the mammoth tortilla-wrapped meals. Taquerias La Cumbre has been around forever and still retains its "Best Burrito" title, each deftly constructed using fresh pork, steak, chicken, or vegetables, plus cheese, beans, rice, salsa, and maybe a dash of guacamole or sour cream. The fact that it's served in a cafeteria-like brick-lined room with overly shellacked tables featuring a woman with overflowing cleavage makes it taste even better.

515 Valencia St. (btw. 16th and 17th sts.). ℂ 415/863-8205. Reservations not accepted. Tacos and burritos $3.50–$6.50; dinner plates $5–$7. No credit cards. Mon–Sat 11am–9pm; Sun noon–9pm. Bus: 14, 22, 33, 49, or 53. BART: Mission.

Ti Couz ⍟ CREPES   At Ti Couz (pronounced "Tee Cooz"), one of the most architecturally stylish and popular restaurants in the Mission, the headliner is simple: the delicate, paper-thin crepe. More than 30 choices of fillings make for infinite expertly executed combinations. The menu advises you how to enjoy these wraps: Order a light crepe as an appetizer, a heftier one as a main course, and a drippingly sweet one for dessert. Recommended combinations are listed, but you can build your own from the 15 main-course selections (such as smoked salmon, mushrooms, sausage, ham, scallops, and onions) and over 15 dessert options (caramel, fruit, chocolate, Nutella, and more). Soups and salads are equally stellar; the seafood salad, for example, is a delicious and generous compilation of shrimp, scallops, and ahi tuna with veggies and five kinds of lettuce.

3108 16th St. (at Valencia St.). ☎ **415/252-7373.** Reservations not accepted. Crepes $2–$12. MC, V. Mon and Fri 11am–11pm; Tues–Thurs 5–10pm; Sat–Sun 10am–11pm. Bus: 14, 22, 26, 33, 49, or 53. BART: 16th or Mission.

11 The Castro

Although you see gay and lesbian singles and couples at almost any restaurant in San Francisco, the following spots cater particularly to the gay community—but being gay is certainly not a requirement for enjoying them. For a map of restaurants in this section, see the "Where to Dine around Town" map on p. 74.

EXPENSIVE

Mecca ⍟ NEW AMERICAN   In 1996, Mecca entered the San Francisco dining scene in a decadent swirl of chocolate-brown velvet, stainless steel, cement, and brown leather. It's an industrial-chic supper club that makes you want to order a martini just so you'll match the ambience. The eclectic city clientele (with a heavy dash of same-sex couples) mingles at the oval centerpiece bar. A night here promises a live DJ spinning hot grooves, and a globally inspired New American meal prepared by chef Randy Lewis and served at tables tucked into several nooks. Lewis's menu items are as varied and interesting as his clientele: Moroccan-spiced lamb meatballs; "Last-Night's-Red-Wine-by-the-Glass Braised Short Ribs"; pan-seared Scottish salmon served with gnocchi, mustard seed vinaigrette, and pecan-apple relish; and a wickedly good Angus cheeseburger with tomato marmalade and garlic aioli on a brioche bun. When the place is jumping on a weekend night it's a great opportunity for tourists to experience an only-in-San Francisco vibe.

2029 Market St. (by 14th and Church sts.). ℭ **415/621-7000.** www.sfmecca.com. Reservations recommended. Main courses $22–$34. AE, DC, MC, V. Tues–Thurs 5–10pm; Fri–Sat 5pm–midnight; Sun 4–10pm. Valet parking $10. Bus: 8, 22, 24, or 37. Streetcar: F, K, L, or M.

INEXPENSIVE

Chow ℛ *Value* AMERICAN   Chow claims to serve American cuisine, but the management must be thinking of today's America, because the menu is not exactly meatloaf and apple pie. And that's just fine for eclectic and cost-conscious diners. After all, what's not to like about starting with a Cobb salad before moving on to Thai-style noodles with steak, chicken, peanuts, and spicy lime-chile garlic broth, or cioppino? Better yet, everything except the fish of the day costs under $15, especially the budget-wise daily sandwich specials, which range from meatball with mozzarella (Sun) to grilled tuna with Asian-style slaw, pickled ginger, and a wasabi mayonnaise (Mon); both come with salad, soup, or fries. Although the food and prices alone would be a good argument for coming here, beer on tap, a great inexpensive wine selection, and the fun, tavernlike environment clinch the deal. A second location, **Park Chow,** is at 1240 Ninth Ave. (ℭ **415/665-9912**). You can't make reservations unless you have a party of eight or more, but if you're headed their way, you can call ahead to place your name on the wait list (recommended).

215 Church St. (near Market St.). ℭ **415/552-2469.** Reservations not accepted. Main courses $7–$15. DISC, MC, V. Mon–Thurs 11am–11pm; Fri 11am–midnight; Sat 10am–midnight; Sun 10am–11pm; brunch served Sat–Sun 10–2:30pm. Bus: 8, 22, or 37. Streetcar: F, J, K, L, or M.

12 Haight-Ashbury

For a map of restaurants in this section, see the "Where to Dine around Town" map on p. 74.

INEXPENSIVE

Cha Cha Cha ℛℛ *Value* CARIBBEAN   This is one of my all-time favorite places to get festive, but it's not for everybody. Dining at Cha Cha Cha is not about a meal, it's about an experience. Put your name on the waiting list, crowd into the minuscule bar, and sip sangria while you wait. When you do get seated (it can take up to two pitchers of sangria, but by then you really don't care), you'll dine in a loud—and I mean *loud*—dining room with Santería altars, banana trees, and plastic tropical-themed tablecloths. The best thing to do is order from the tapas menu and share the dishes family-style. Fried calamari, fried new potatoes, Cajun shrimp, and mussels in saffron broth are all bursting with flavor and accompanied by luscious sauces—whatever you choose, you can't go wrong. This is the kind of place where you take friends in a partying mood and make an evening of it. If you want the flavor without the festivities, come during lunch. Their second, larger location, in the Mission District, at 2327 Mission St., between 19th and 20th streets (© **415/648-0504**), is open for dinner only and has a full bar specializing in mojitos.

1801 Haight St. (at Shrader St.). © **415/386-7670.** www.cha3.com. Reservations not accepted. Tapas $5–$9; main courses $12–$15. MC, V. Daily 11:30am–4pm; Sun–Thurs 5–11pm; Fri–Sat 5–11:30pm. Bus: 6, 7, or 71. Streetcar: N.

Kan Zaman ✪ *Finds* MIDDLE EASTERN   An evening dining at Kan Zaman is one of those quintessential Haight-Ashbury experiences that you can't wait to tell your friends about back in Ohio. As you pass through glass-beaded curtains, you're led by the hostess to knee-high tables under a billowed canopy tent. Shoes removed, you sit cross-legged with your friends in cushioned comfort. The most adventurous of your group requests an *argeeleh*, a large hookah pipe filled with fruity honey or apricot tobacco. Reluctantly at first, everyone simultaneously sips the sweet smoke from the cobralike tendrils emanating from the hookah, then dinner arrives—inexpensive platters offering a variety of classic Middle Eastern cuisine: smoky baba ghanouj, kibbe (cracked wheat with spiced lamb) meat pies, Casablanca beef couscous, spicy hummus with pita bread, succulent lamb and chicken kabobs. The spiced wine starts to take effect, just in time for the beautiful, sensuous belly dancers who glide across the dining room, mesmerizing the rapt audience with their seemingly impossible gyrations. The evening ends, the bill arrives: $17 each. Perfect. *Note:* Belly dancing starts at 9pm Thursday though Saturday only.

1793 Haight St. (at Shrader St.). © **415/751-9656.** Main courses $4–$14. MC, V. Mon–Thurs 5pm–midnight; Fri 5pm–2am; Sat noon–2am; Sun noon–midnight. Metro: N. Bus: 6, 7, 66, 71, or 73.

Thep Phanom ✪ THAI   It's the combination of fresh ingredients, attractive decor, and friendly service, and that heavenly balance of salty, sweet, hot, and sour flavors, that have made Thep Phanom one of the city's most beloved Thai restaurants. Those who like to play it safe will be more than happy with standards such as pad Thai, coconut-lemon-grass soup, and prawns in red curry sauce, but consider diverting from the usual suspects for such house specialties as Thaitanic Beef (stir-fried beef and string beans in a spicy sauce), prawns with eggplant and crisped basil, and *ped sawan*—duck with a delicate honey sauce served over spinach. There's good people-watching here as well—the restaurant's reputation attracts a truly diverse San Francisco crowd. Be sure to make reservations or prepare for a long wait on weekend nights, and don't leave anything even remotely valuable in your car.

400 Waller St. (at Fillmore St.). ℂ **415/431-2526**. www.thepphanom.com. Reservations recommended. Main courses $9–$13. AE, DC, DISC, MC, V. Daily 5:30–10:30pm. Bus: 6, 7, 22, 66, or 71.

13 Richmond/Sunset Districts

For a map of restaurants in this section, see the "Where to Dine around Town" map on p. 74.

MODERATE

Aziza ℛℛ MOROCCAN If you're looking for something really different—or a festive spot for a large party—head deep into the Avenues for an exotic taste of Morocco. Chef-owner Mourad Lahlou creates an excellent dining experience through colorful and distinctly Moroccan surroundings combined with a modern yet authentic take on the cuisine of his homeland. In any of the three opulently adorned dining rooms (the front room features private booths, the middle room is more formal, and the back has lower seating and a Moroccan lounge feel), you can indulge in the seasonal five-course tasting menu ($49) or individual treats such as kumquat-enriched lamb shank; saffron guinea hen with preserved lemon and olives; or Paine Farm squab with wild mushrooms, bitter greens, and a *ras el hanout* reduction (a traditional Moroccan blend of 40 or so spices). Consider finishing off with my favorite dessert (if it's in season): rhubarb galette with rose- and geranium-scented crème fraîche, vanilla aspic, and rhubarb consommé.

5800 Geary Blvd. (at 22nd Ave.). ℂ **415/752-2222**. www.aziza-sf.com. Reservations recommended. Main courses $10–$22; 5-course menu $39. MC, V. Wed–Mon 5:30–10:30pm. Valet parking $8 weekdays, $10 weekends. Bus: 29 or 38.

Beach Chalet Brewery & Restaurant ℛ AMERICAN While Cliff House has more historical character and better ocean views, the Beach Chalet down the road has far better food, drinks, and atmosphere (ergo, it's where the locals go). The Chalet occupies the upper floor of a historic public lounge adorned with WPA frescos that originally opened in 1900 and has been fully restored. Dinner is pricey, and the ocean view disappears with the sun, so come for lunch or an early dinner when you can eat your hamburger, buttermilk fried calamari, or grilled Atlantic salmon with one of the best vistas around. It the evening it's a more local crowd, especially on Tuesday through Sunday evenings when live bands accompany the cocktails and house-brewed ales. Breakfast is served here as well. *Note:* Be careful getting into the parking lot (accessible only from the north-bound side of the highway)—it's a quick, sandy turn.

In early 2004, owners Lara and Greg Truppelli added the adjoining **Park Chalet** restaurant to the Beach Chalet. The 3,000-square-foot glass-enclosed extension behind the original landmark building offers more casual fare—with entrees ranging from $11 to $23—including rib-eye steak, fish and chips, roasted chicken, and pizza. Other reasons to come? Retractable glass walls reveal Golden Gate Park's landmark Dutch windmill, a fireplace warms the room on chillier evenings, and live music is performed Tuesday and Thursday through Sunday evenings. Weather permitting, you can eat out back on the lawn; there's even a weekend barbecue from 11am to dusk in the summer. The restaurant opens at 11am daily in the summer (noon in winter) and, like the Beach Chalet, has varying closing times, so call ahead.

1000 Great Hwy. (at west end of Golden Gate Park, near Fulton St.). ⓒ **415/386-8439.** www.beachchalet.com. Main courses $8–$17 breakfast, $11–$27 lunch/dinner. AE, MC, V. Beach Chalet: Breakfast Mon–Fri 9–11am; lunch daily 11am–5pm; dinner Sun–Thurs 5–10pm, Fri–Sat 5–11pm; brunch Sat–Sun 9am–2pm. Park Chalet: Lunch Mon–Fri noon–9pm; dinner Sun–Thurs 5–9pm, Fri–Sat 5–11pm; brunch Sat–Sun 11am–2pm. Bus: 18, 31, or 38. Streetcar: N.

INEXPENSIVE

Burma Superstar ⓚ *Value* BURMESE Despite its gratuitous name, this basic dining room garners two-star status by offering exceptional Burmese food at rock-bottom prices. Unfortunately, the allure of the tealeaf salad, Burmese-style curry with potato, and sweet-tangy sesame beef is one of the city's worst-kept secrets. Add to that a no-reservations policy and you can count on waiting in line for up to an hour. (FYI, parties of two are seated more quickly than larger groups, and it's less crowded at lunch.) On the bright side, you can pencil your cellphone number onto the waiting list and browse the Clement Street shops until you receive a call.

309 Clement St. (at Fourth Ave.). ⓒ 415/387-2147. www.burmasuperstar.com. Reservations not accepted. Main courses $8–$16. MC, V. Sun–Thurs 11am–3:30pm and 5:30–9:30pm; Fri–Sat 11am–3:30pm and 5:30–10pm. Bus: 2, 4, 38, or 44.

Ton Kiang ⓚⓚ CHINESE/DIM SUM Ton Kiang is the number one place in the city to have dim sum (served daily), only partially due to the fact that they make all their sauces, pickles, and other delicacies in-house. The experience goes like this: Wait in line (which is out the door 11am–1:30pm on weekends), get a table on the first or second floor, and get ready to say yes to dozens of delicacies, which are brought to the table for your approval. From stuffed crab claws, roast Beijing duck, and a gazillion dumpling selections (including scallop and vegetable, shrimp, and beef) to the delicious and hard-to-find *doa miu* (snow pea sprouts flash-sautéed with garlic and peanut oil) and a mesmerizing mango pudding, every tray of morsels coming from the kitchen is an absolute delight. Though it's hard to get past the dim sum, which is served all day every day, the full menu of Hakka cuisine is worth investigation as well—fresh and flavorful soups; an array of seafood, beef, and chicken; and clay-pot specialties.

5821 Geary Blvd. (btw. 22nd and 23rd aves.). (©) **415/387-8273.** www.tonkiang. net. Reservations accepted for parties of 8 or more. Dim sum $2–$5.50; main courses $9–$25. AE, DC, DISC, MC, V. Mon–Thurs 10am–10pm; Fri 10am–10:30pm; Sat 9:30am–10:30pm; Sun 9am–10pm. Bus: 38.

4

Exploring San Francisco

San Francisco's parks, museums, tours, and landmarks are favorites for travelers the world over and offer an array of activities to suit every visitor. But no particular activity or place makes the city one of the most popular destinations in the world. It's San Francisco itself—its charm, its atmosphere, its perfect blend of big metropolis with small-town hospitality. No matter what you do while you're here—whether you spend all your time in central areas like Union Square or North Beach, or explore the outer neighborhoods—you're bound to discover the reason millions of visitors keep leaving their hearts in San Francisco.

1 Famous San Francisco Sights

Alcatraz Island ★★★ *Kids* Visible from Fisherman's Wharf, Alcatraz Island (also known as The Rock) has seen a checkered history. Juan Manuel Ayala was the first European to discover it in 1775 and named it after the many pelicans that nested on the island. From the 1850s to 1933, when the army vacated the island, it served as a military post, protecting the bay's shoreline. In 1934, the government converted the buildings of the military outpost into a maximum-security prison. Given the sheer cliffs, treacherous tides and currents, and frigid water temperatures, it was believed to be a totally escape-proof prison. Among the famous gangsters who occupied cell blocks A through D were Al Capone, Robert Stroud, the so-called Birdman of Alcatraz (because he was an expert in ornithological diseases), Machine Gun Kelly, and Alvin Karpis. It cost a fortune to keep them imprisoned here because all supplies, including water, had to be shipped in. In 1963, after an apparent escape in which no bodies were recovered, the government closed the prison. In 1969, a group of Native Americans chartered a boat to the island to symbolically reclaim the island for the Indian people. They occupied the island until 1971, the longest occupation of a federal facility by Native Americans to this day, when they were forcibly removed by the U.S. government (see www.nps.gov/archive/alcatraz/indian.html

Major San Francisco Attractions

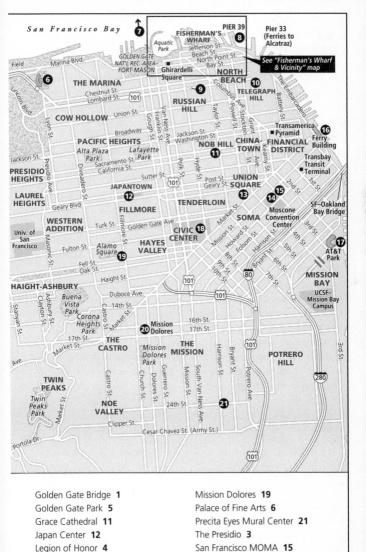

San Francisco Bay

PIER 39 8
Pier 33 (Ferries to Alcatraz)

FISHERMAN'S WHARF

Aquatic Park

Jefferson St.
Beach St.
North Point St.
Bay St.

See "Fisherman's Wharf & Vicinity" map

GOLDEN GATE NAT'L REC. AREA– FORT MASON

Ghirardelli Square

NORTH BEACH 10

Field

Marina Blvd.

THE MARINA

Chestnut St.
Lombard St. 101

6

RUSSIAN HILL 9

COW HOLLOW Union St.

TELEGRAPH HILL

Columbus Ave.

PACIFIC HEIGHTS

Broadway

Transamerica Pyramid 16

Alta Plaza Park Lafayette Park

Jackson St.
Washington St.

NOB HILL 11

CHINA-TOWN

FINANCIAL DISTRICT

Ferry Building

Sacramento St.
California St.

PRESIDIO HEIGHTS

LAUREL HEIGHTS

JAPANTOWN 12

Sutter St. 101
Post St.
Geary St.

UNION SQUARE 13

Transbay Transit Terminal

Geary Blvd.

FILLMORE

TENDERLOIN

14 15

SF–Oakland Bay Bridge

WESTERN ADDITION

Turk St.
Golden Gate Ave.

Moscone Convention Center

SOMA

Univ. of San Francisco

Fulton St.

HAYES VALLEY

CIVIC CENTER 18

Mission St.
Howard St.
Folsom St.
Harrison St.

AT&T Park 17

Alamo Square 19

Fell St.
Oak St.

Bryant St.

MISSION BAY

HAIGHT-ASHBURY

Haight St.

101

UCSF– Mission Bay Campus

Buena Vista Park

Duboce Ave.

80

Corona Heights Park

14th St.

16th St.
17th St.

Mission Dolores 20

THE CASTRO

Mission Dolores Park

THE MISSION

101

POTRERO HILL

TWIN PEAKS

Twin Peaks Park

280

NOE VALLEY

24th St.

21

Clipper St.

Cesar Chavez St. (Army St.)

Portola Dr.

101

Golden Gate Bridge **1**
Golden Gate Park **5**
Grace Cathedral **11**
Japan Center **12**
Legion of Honor **4**
Lombard Street **9**

Mission Dolores **19**
Palace of Fine Arts **6**
Precita Eyes Mural Center **21**
The Presidio **3**
San Francisco MOMA **15**
Yerba Buena Center for the Arts/Yerba Buena Gardens **14**

for more information on the Native American occupation of Alcatraz). The next year the island became part of the Golden Gate National Recreation Area. The wildlife that was driven away during the military and prison years has begun to return—the black-crested night heron and other seabirds are nesting here again—and a trail passes through the island's nature areas. Tours, including an audio tour of the prison block and a slide show, are given by the park's rangers, who entertain guests with interesting anecdotes.

Allow about 2½ hours for the round-trip boat ride and the tour. Wear comfortable shoes (the National Park Service notes that there are a lot of hills to climb on the tour) and take a heavy sweater or windbreaker, because even when the sun's out, it's cold there. You should also bring snacks and drinks with you if you think you'll want them. Although there is a beverage-and-snack bar on the ferry, the options are limited and expensive, and only water is available on the island. The excursion to Alcatraz is very popular and space is limited, so purchase tickets as far in advance as possible (up to 90 days) via the **Alcatraz Cruises** website at www.alcatrazcruises.com. You can also purchase tickets in person by visiting the Hornblower Alcatraz Landing ticket office at Pier 33. The first departure, called the "Early Bird," leaves at 9am, and ferries depart about every half-hour afterward until 2pm. Night tours (highly recommended) are also available Thursday through Monday and are a more intimate and wonderfully spooky experience.

For those who want to get a closer look at Alcatraz without going ashore, two boat-tour operators offer short circumnavigations of the island (see "Self-Guided & Organized Tours" on p. 132 for complete information).

Pier 41, near Fisherman's Wharf. ✆ **415/981-7625.** www.alcatrazcruises.com or www.nps.gov/alcatraz. Admission (includes ferry trip and audio tour) $25 adults; $23 seniors 62 and older; $15 children 5–11. Night tours cost $32 adults; $29 seniors 62 and older; $19 children 5–11. Arrive at least 20 min. before departure time.

Cable Cars ✮✮✮ *(Moments* *(Kids*   Although they may not be San Francisco's most practical means of transportation, cable cars are certainly the best loved and are a must-experience when visiting the city. Designated official historic landmarks by the National Park Service in 1964, they clank up and down the city's steep hills like mobile museum pieces, tirelessly hauling thousands of tourists each day to nowhere in particular.

London-born engineer Andrew Hallidie invented San Francisco's cable cars in 1869. He got the idea by serendipity. As the story goes, Hallidie was watching a team of overworked horses haul a heavily laden carriage up a steep San Francisco slope. As he watched, one horse slipped and the car rolled back, dragging the other tired beasts with it. At that moment, Hallidie resolved that he would invent a mechanical contraption to replace such horses, and just 4 years later, in 1873, the first cable car made its maiden run from the top of Clay Street. Promptly ridiculed as "Hallidie's Folly," the cars were slow to gain acceptance. One early onlooker voiced the general opinion by exclaiming, "I don't believe it—the damned thing works!"

Even today, many visitors have difficulty believing that these vehicles, which have no engines, actually work. The cars, each weighing about 6 tons, run along a steel cable, enclosed under the street in a center rail. You can't see the cable unless you peer straight down into the crack, but you'll hear its characteristic clickity-clanking sound whenever you're nearby. The cars move when the gripper (not the driver) pulls back a lever that closes a pincerlike "grip" on the cable. The speed of the car, therefore, is determined by the speed of the cable, which is a constant 9½ mph—never more, never less.

The two types of cable cars in use hold a maximum of 90 and 100 passengers, and the limits are rigidly enforced. The best views are from the outer running boards, where you have to hold on tightly when taking curves.

Hallidie's cable cars have been imitated and used throughout the world, but all have been replaced by more efficient means of transportation. San Francisco planned to do so, too, but the proposal met with so much opposition that the cable cars' perpetuation was actually written into the city charter in 1955. The mandate cannot be revoked without the approval of a majority of the city's voters—a distant and doubtful prospect.

San Francisco's three existing cable car lines form the world's only surviving system of cable cars, which you can experience for yourself should you choose to wait in the often long boarding lines (up to a 2-hr. wait in summer). For more information on riding them, see "Getting Around," in chapter 1, p. 20.

Powell–Hyde and Powell–Mason lines begin at the base of Powell and Market sts.; California St. line begins at the foot of Market St. $5 per ride.

Coit Tower 𝕂𝕂   In a city known for its great views and vantage points, Coit Tower is one of the best. Located atop Telegraph Hill, just east of North Beach, the round stone tower offers panoramic views of the city and the bay.

Completed in 1933, the tower is the legacy of Lillie Hitchcock Coit, a wealthy eccentric who left San Francisco a $125,000 bequest "for the purpose of adding beauty to the city I have always loved" and as a memorial to its volunteer firemen. She had been saved from a fire as a child and held the city's firefighters in particularly high esteem.

Inside the base of the tower are impressive murals titled *Life in California* and *1934*, which were completed under the WPA during the New Deal. They are the work of more than 25 artists, many of whom had studied under Mexican muralist Diego Rivera.

The only bummer: The narrow street leading to the tower is often clogged with tourist traffic. If you can, find a parking spot in North Beach and hoof it. It's actually a beautiful walk—especially if you take the Filbert Street Steps (p. 135).

Telegraph Hill. ✆ **415/362-0808**. Admission is free to enter; elevator ride to the top is $4.50 adults, $3.50 seniors, $2 children 6–12. Daily 10am–6pm. Bus: 39 (Coit).

Ferry Building Marketplace ★★★ *Finds*

There's no better way to enjoy a San Francisco morning than strolling this gourmet marketplace in the Ferry Building and snacking your way through breakfast or lunch. San Franciscans—myself included—can't get enough of this place; we're still amazed at what a fantastic job they did renovating the interior. The Marketplace is open daily and includes much of Northern California's best gourmet bounty: Cowgirl Creamery's Artisan Cheese Shop, Recchiuti Confections (amazing), Scharffen Berger Chocolate, Acme Breads, Wine Country's gourmet diner Taylor's Refresher, famed Vietnamese restaurant The Slanted Door, and myriad other restaurants, delis, gourmet coffee shops, specialty foods, and wine bars. Check out the Imperial Tea Court where you'll be taught the traditional Chinese way to steep and sip your tea; nosh on premium sturgeon roe at Tsar Nicoulai Caviar, a small Parisian-style "caviar cafe"; buy cooking items at the Sur La Table shop; grab a bite and savor the bayfront views from in- and outdoor tables; or browse the Farmers' Market on Tuesdays and Saturdays from 10am until 2pm. Trust me, you'll love this place.

The Embarcadero, at Market St. ✆ **415/693-0996**. www.ferrybuildingmarketplace. com. Most stores daily 10am–6pm; restaurant hours vary. Bus: 2, 7, 12, 14, 21, 66, or 71. Streetcar: F. BART: Embarcadero.

Fisherman's Wharf *Kids*

Few cities in America are as adept at wholesaling their historical sites as San Francisco, which has converted Fisherman's Wharf into one of the most popular tourist attractions in the world. Unless you come early in the morning to watch the few remaining fishing boats depart, you won't find many traces of the traditional waterfront life that once existed here—the only trolling going on at Fisherman's Wharf these days is for tourists' dollars. Nonetheless,

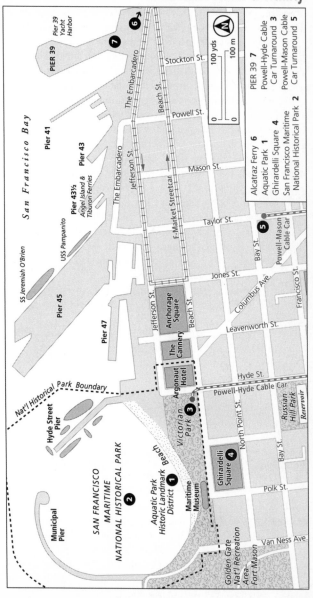

Pier 39 Yacht Harbor

PIER 39

San Francisco Bay

Pier 41

Pier 43

Pier 43½
Angel Island &
Tiburon Ferries

USS Pampanito

SS Jeremiah O'Brien

Pier 45

Pier 47

Stockton St.

The Embarcadero

Beach St.

Powell St.

The Embarcadero

Jefferson St.

Mason St.

F-Market Streetcar

Taylor St.

Jones St.

Columbus Ave.

Bay St.

Powell-Mason Cable Car

Francisco St.

Leavenworth St.

Jefferson St.

Anchorage Square

Beach St.

The Cannery

Argonaut Hotel

Hyde St.

Powell-Hyde Cable Car

North Point St.

Russian Hill Park

Reservoir

Nat'l Historical Park Boundary

Hyde Street Pier

Victorian Park

Ghirardelli Square

Bay St.

SAN FRANCISCO MARITIME NATIONAL HISTORICAL PARK

Aquatic Park Historic Landmark District

Maritime Museum

Polk St.

Municipal Pier

Van Ness Ave.

Golden Gate Nat'l Recreation Area– Fort Mason

100 yds
100 m

PIER 39 **7**
Powell-Hyde Cable
Car Turnaround **3**
Powell-Mason Cable
Car Turnaround **5**

Alcatraz Ferry **6**
Aquatic Park **1**
Ghirardelli Square **4**
San Francisco Maritime
National Historical Park **2**

107

everyone always seems to be enjoying themselves as they stroll down Pier 39 on a sunny day, especially the kids.

Originally called Meigg's Wharf, this bustling strip of waterfront got its present moniker from generations of fishermen who used to dock their boats here. A small fleet of fewer than 30 fishing boats still set out from here, but basically Fisherman's Wharf has been converted into one long shopping and entertainment mall that stretches from Ghirardelli Square at the west end to Pier 39 at the east.

Accommodating a total of 300 boats, two marinas flank Pier 39 and house the sightseeing ferry fleets, including departures to Alcatraz. In recent years, some 900 California sea lions have taken up residence on the adjacent floating docks. Until they abandon their new playground, which seems more and more unlikely, these playful, noisy (some nights you can hear them all the way from Washington Sq.) *Zalophus californianus* are one of the best free attractions on the wharf. Weather permitting, the **Marine Mammal Center** (② 415/289-SEAL) offers an educational talk at Pier 39 on weekends from 11am to 5pm that teaches visitors about the range, habitat, and adaptability of the California sea lion.

Some people love Fisherman's Wharf; others can't get far enough away from it. Most agree that, for better or for worse, it has to be seen at least once in your lifetime. There are still some traces of old-school San Francisco character here that I will always enjoy, particularly the convivial seafood street vendors who dish out piles of fresh Dungeness, clam chowder, and sourdough bread from their steaming stainless steel carts. Fisherman's Wharf is also one of the few places in the city where kids can be unleashed to roam through the aquarium, crawl through a real World War II submarine, play at the arcade, ride the carousel, and eat junk food galore. In short, there's something for everyone here, even us snobby locals.

At Taylor St. and The Embarcadero. ② **415/674-7503.** www.fishermanswharf.org. Bus: 15, 30, 32, 39, 42, or 82X. Streetcar: F-line. Cable car: Powell–Mason to the last stop and walk to the wharf. If you're arriving by car, park on adjacent streets or on the wharf btw. Taylor and Jones sts. for $16 per day, $8 with validation from participating restaurants.

Golden Gate Bridge 🅚🅚🅚 (Kids   The year 2007 marked the 70th birthday of possibly the most beautiful, and certainly the most photographed, bridge in the world. Often half-veiled by the city's trademark rolling fog, San Francisco's Golden Gate Bridge, named for the strait leading from the Pacific Ocean to the San Francisco Bay, spans tidal currents, ocean waves, and battering winds to connect The City by the Bay with the Redwood Empire to the north.

With its gracefully suspended single span, spidery bracing cables, and zooming twin towers, the bridge looks more like a work of abstract art than one of the 20th century's greatest practical engineering feats. Construction was completed in May 1937 at the then-colossal cost of $35 million (plus another $39 million in interest being financed entirely by bridge tolls).

The 1.7-mile bridge (including the approach), which reaches a height of 746 feet above the water, is awesome to cross. Although kept to a maximum of 45 miles an hour, traffic usually moves quickly, so crossing by car won't give you too much time to see the sights. If you drive from the city, take the last San Francisco exit, right before the toll plaza, park in the southeast parking lot, and make the crossing by foot. Back in your car, continue to Marin's Vista Point, at the bridge's northern end. Look back, and you'll be rewarded with one of the finest views of San Francisco.

Millions of people visit the bridge each year, gazing up at the tall orange towers, out at the vistas of San Francisco and Marin County, and down into the stacks of oceangoing liners. You can walk out onto the span from either end, but be prepared—it's usually windy and cold, and the traffic is noisy. Still, walking even a short distance is one of the best ways to experience the immense scale of the structure.

Hwy. 101 N. www.goldengatebridge.org. $5 cash toll collected when driving south. Bridge-bound Golden Gate Transit buses (© 511) depart hourly during the day for Marin County, starting from Mission and First sts. (across the street from the Transbay Terminal and stopping at Market and Seventh sts., at the Civic Center, along Van Ness Ave., at Lombard and Fillmore sts., and at Francisco and Richardson sts.).

Lombard Street ✿   Known (erroneously) as the "crookedest street in the world," this whimsically winding block of Lombard Street draws thousands of visitors each year (much to the chagrin of neighborhood residents, most of whom would prefer to block off the street to tourists). The angle of the street is so steep that the road has to snake back and forth to make a descent possible. The brick-lined street zigzags around the residences' bright flower gardens, which explode with color during warmer months. This short stretch of Lombard Street is one-way, downhill, and fun to drive. Take the curves slowly and in low gear, and expect a wait during the weekend. Save your film for the bottom where, if you're lucky, you can find a parking space and take a few snapshots of the silly spectacle. You can also take staircases (without curves) up or down on either side of the street. In truth, most locals don't understand what the fuss is all about. I'm guessing the draw is the combination of seeing such a famous landmark, the challenge of negotiating so many steep curves, and a classic photo op. *FYI:* Vermont Street, between 20th and 22nd streets in Potrero Hill, is even more crooked, but not nearly as picturesque.

Btw.Hyde and Leavenworth sts.

Pier 39 *(Overrated)*   Pier 39 is a multilevel waterfront complex a few blocks east of Fisherman's Wharf. Constructed on an abandoned cargo pier, it is, ostensibly, a re-creation of a turn-of-the-20th-century street scene, but don't expect a slice of old-time maritime life here: Today, Pier 39 is a busy mall welcoming millions of visitors per year. It has more than 110 stores, 13 bay-view restaurants, a two-tiered Venetian carousel, a Hard Rock Cafe, the Riptide Arcade, and the Aquarium of the Bay for the kids. And everything here is slanted toward helping you part with your travel dollars. This is *the* place that locals love to hate, but kids adore it here. That said, it does have a few perks: absolutely beautiful natural surroundings and bay views, fresh sea air, and hundreds of sunbathing sea lions (about 900 in peak season) lounging along its neighboring docks. (See p. 108 for info about the free weekend talks.)

On the waterfront at The Embarcadero and Beach St. ℂ **415/705-5500.** www. pier39.com. Shops daily 10am–8:30pm, with extended weekend hours during summer.

2 Museums

For information on museums in Golden Gate Park, see the "Golden Gate Park" section, beginning on p. 122.

Asian Art Museum *(★)*   Previously in Golden Gate Park and reopened in what was once the Civic Center's Beaux Arts–style central library, San Francisco's Asian Art Museum is one of the Western world's largest museums devoted to Asian art. Its collection boasts more than 15,000 art objects, such as world-class sculptures, paintings, bronzes, ceramics, and jade items, spanning 6,000 years of history and regions of south Asia, west Asia, Southeast Asia, the Himalayas, China, Korea, and Japan. Inside you'll find 40,000 square feet of gallery space showcasing 2,500 objects at any given time. Add temporary exhibitions, live demonstrations, learning activities, Cafe Asia, and a store, and you've got one very good reason to head to the Civic Center.

200 Larkin St. (btw. Fulton and McAllister sts.). ℂ **415/581-3500.** www.asianart. org. Admission $12 adults, $8 seniors 65 and over, $7 youths 13–17 and college students with ID, free for children 12 and under, $5 flat rate for all (except children under 12 who are free) after 5pm Thurs. Free 1st Sun of the month. Tues–Wed and Fri–Sun 10am–5pm; Thurs 10am–9pm. Bus: All Market St. buses. Streetcar: Civic Center.

Cable Car Museum ⭐ *Value* *Kids*   If you've ever wondered how cable cars work, this nifty museum explains (and demonstrates) it all. Yes, this is a museum, but the Cable Car Museum is no stuffed shirt. It's the living powerhouse, repair shop, and storage place of the cable car system and is in full operation. Built for the Ferries and Cliff House Railway in 1887, the building underwent an $18-million reconstruction to restore its original gaslight-era look, install an amazing spectators' gallery, and add a museum of San Francisco transit history.

The exposed machinery, which pulls the cables under San Francisco's streets, looks like a Rube Goldberg invention. Stand in the mezzanine gallery and become mesmerized by the massive groaning and vibrating winches as they thread the cable that hauls the cars through a huge figure-eight and back into the system using slack-absorbing tension wheels. For a better view, move to the lower-level viewing room, where you can see the massive pulleys and gears operating underground.

Also on display here is one of the first grip cars developed by Andrew S. Hallidie, operated for the first time on Clay Street on August 2, 1873. Other displays include an antique grip car and trailer that operated on Pacific Avenue until 1929, and dozens of exact-scale models of cars used on the various city lines. There's also a shop where you can buy a variety of cable car gifts. You can see the whole museum in about 45 minutes.

1201 Mason St. (at Washington St.). © **415/474-1887**. www.cablecarmuseum.org. Free admission. Apr–Sept daily 10am–6pm; Oct–Mar daily 10am–5pm. Closed Thanksgiving, Christmas, and New Year's Day. Cable car: Both Powell St. lines.

California Academy of Sciences ⭐⭐⭐ *Kids*   San Francisco's California Academy of Sciences has been entertaining locals and tourists for more than 150 years, and with the grand opening of the all-new Academy on September 27, 2008, it's now going stronger than ever. Four years and $500 million in the making, it's the only institution in the world to combine an aquarium, planetarium, natural history museum, and scientific research program under one roof, and so vastly entertaining that the entire family could easily spend a whole day here. In fact, the spectacular new complex has literally reinvented the role of science museums in the 21st century, where visitors interact with animals, educators, and biologists at hands-on exhibits such as a four-story living rainforest dome and the world's deepest living coral reef display. Even the Academy's 2.5-acre undulating garden roof is an exhibit, planted with 1.7 million native

California plants, including thousands of flowers (all that's missing are the Teletubbies).

More than 38,000 live animals fill the new Academy's aquarium and natural history exhibits, making it one of the most diverse collections of live animals at any museum or aquarium in the world. Highlights include the **Morrison Planetarium,** the world's largest all-digital planetarium that takes you on a guided tour of the solar system and beyond using current data from NASA to produce the most accurate and interactive digital universe ever created; the **Philippine Coral Reef,** the world's deepest living coral reef tank where 4,000 sharks, rays, sea turtles, giant clams, and other aquatic creatures live in a Technicolor forest of coral; and the **Rainforests of the World,** a living rainforest filled with mahogany and palm trees, croaking frogs, chirping birds, leaf cutter ants, bat caves, chameleons, and hundreds of tropical butterflies. You can climb into the tree-tops of Costa Rica, descend in a glass elevator into the Amazonian flooded forest, and walk along an acrylic tunnel beneath the Amazonian river fish that swim overhead. Pretty cool, eh?

Even the dining options here are first-rate, as both the **Academy Café** and **Moss Room** restaurant are run by two of the city's top chefs, Charles Phan and Loretta Keller, and feature local, organic, sustainable foods. The only thing you won't enjoy here is the entrance fee—a whopping $25 per adult—but it includes access to the all the Academy exhibits *and* the Planetarium shows, and if you arrive by public transportation they'll knock $3 off the fee (how very green). Combined with a visit to the spectacular de Young museum across the Concourse, it makes for a very entertaining and educational day in Golden Gate Park.

55 Concourse Dr., Golden Gate Park. ⓒ **415/379-8000.** www.calacademy.org. Admission $25 adults, $20 seniors 65 and over, $20 youths 12–17, $15 children 7–11, free for children 6 and under. Free to all 3rd Wed of each month. Mon–Sat 9:30am–5pm; Sun 11am–5pm. Closed Thanksgiving and Christmas. Bus: 5, 16AX, 16BX, 21, 44, or 71.

de Young Museum ⓡⓡⓡ   After closing for several years, San Francisco's oldest museum (founded in 1895) reopened in late 2005 in a state-of-the-art Golden Gate Park facility. Its vast holdings include one of the finest collections of American paintings in the United States from Colonial times through the 20th century, as well as decorative arts and crafts; western and non-western textiles; and arts from Africa, Oceania, and the Americas. Along with superb revolving exhibitions, the de Young has long been beloved for its educational arts programs for both children and adults, and now it's equally enjoyed for its stunning architecture and sculpture-graced surroundings. The striking facade consists of 950,000 pounds of textured and perforated copper that's intended to patinate with age, while the northeast corner of the building features a 144-foot tower that slowly spirals from the ground floor and culminates with an observation floor offering panoramic views of the entire Bay Area (from a distance it has the surreal look of a rusty aircraft carrier cruising through the park). Surrounding sculpture gardens and lush, grassy expanses are perfect for picnicking. Adding to the allure is surprisingly good and healthy organic fare at the grab-and-go or order-and-wait cafe/restaurant. You'll enjoy browsing through the museum's interesting gift shop as well. *Note:* Underground parking is accessed at 10th Avenue and Fulton Street. Also, admission tickets to the de Young may be used on the same day for free entrance to The Legion of Honor (see below).

50 Hagiwara Tea Garden Dr. (inside Golden Gate Park, 2 blocks from the park entrance at Eighth Ave. and Fulton). © 415/863-3330. www.thinker.org. Adults $10, seniors $7, youths 13–17 and college students with ID $6, children 12 and under free. Free 1st Tues of the month. $2 discount for Muni riders with Fast Pass or transfer receipt. AE, MC, V. Tues–Sun 9:30am–5:15pm. Closed Jan 1, Thanksgiving Day, and Dec 25. Bus: 5, 16AX, 16BX, 21, 44, or 71.

The Exploratorium *Kids* *Scientific American* magazine rated The Exploratorium "the best science museum in the world"— and I couldn't agree more. Inside you'll find hundreds of exhibits that explore everything from giant-bubble blowing to Einstein's theory of relativity. It's like a mad scientist's penny arcade, an educational fun house, and an experimental laboratory all rolled into one. Touch a tornado, shape a glowing electrical current, or take a sensory journey in total darkness in the **Tactile Dome** ($3 extra, and call © 415/561-0362 to make advance reservations)—even if you spent all day here you couldn't experience everything. Every exhibit at The Exploratorium is designed to be interactive, educational, safe and, most importantly, fun. And don't think it's just for kids; parents inevitably end up being the most reluctant to leave. I went here recently and spent 3 hours in just one small section of the museum, marveling like a little kid at all the mind-blowing hands-on exhibits related to light and eyesight. On the way out, be sure to stop in the wonderful gift store, which is chock-full of affordable brain candy.

The museum is in the Marina District at the beautiful **Palace of Fine Arts**, the only building left standing from the Panama-Pacific Exposition of 1915. The adjoining park with lagoon—the perfect place for an afternoon picnic—is home to ducks, swans, seagulls, and grouchy geese, so bring bread.

3601 Lyon St., in the Palace of Fine Arts (at Marina Blvd.). ℰ **415/397-5673,** or 415/561-0360 (recorded information). www.exploratorium.edu. Admission $14 adults; $11 seniors, youth 13–17, visitors with disabilities, and college students with ID; $9 children 4–12; free for children 3 and under. AE, MC, V. Tues–Sun 10am–5pm. Closed Mon except MLK, Jr., Day, Presidents' Day, Memorial Day, and Labor Day. Free parking. Bus: 28, 30, or Golden Gate Transit.

The Legion of Honor 𝒢𝒢   Designed as a memorial to California's World War I casualties, this neoclassical structure is an exact replica of The Legion of Honor Palace in Paris, right down to the inscription HONNEUR ET PATRIE above the portal. The exterior's grassy expanses, cliff-side paths, and incredible view of the Golden Gate and downtown make this an absolute must-visit attraction before you even get in the door. The inside is equally impressive: the museum's permanent collection covers 4,000 years of art and includes paintings, sculpture, and decorative arts from Europe, as well as international tapestries, prints, and drawings. The chronological display of 4,000 years of ancient and European art includes one of the world's finest collections of Rodin sculptures. The sunlit Legion Cafe offers indoor and outdoor seating at moderate prices. Plan to spend 2 or 3 hours here.

In Lincoln Park (34th Ave. and Clement St.). ℰ **415/750-3600,** or 415/863-3330 (recorded information). www.thinker.org. Admission $10 adults, $7 seniors 65 and over, $6 youths 13–17 and college students with ID, free for children 12 and under. Fees may be higher for special exhibitions. Free 1st Tues of each month. Tues–Sun 9:30am–5:15pm. Bus: 18.

Metreon Entertainment Center 𝒦𝒾𝒹𝓈   This 350,000-square-foot hi-tech complex houses great movie theaters, an IMAX theater, the only Sony store in the country devoted to PlayStation, the one-of-a-kind Walk of Game (à la Hollywood's stars in the sidewalk, these steel stars honor the icons of the video game industry), a luxurious arcade (think big screens and a pub), a "Taste of San Francisco" food court with decent "international" fare, and lots more shops, many of which are gaming related. The whole place is wired for Wi-Fi, so if you're a true techie and want to hang out with other techies, grab some lunch, find a comfy spot, and log on.

101 Fourth St. (at the corner of Mission St.) ℰ **415/369-6000.** www.metreon.com. Building 10am–10pm daily; individual businesses may have different hours. Bus: 5, 9, 14, 15, 30, or 45. Streetcar: Powell or Montgomery.

San Francisco Museum of Modern Art (SFMOMA) 𝒢   Swiss architect Mario Botta, in association with Hellmuth, Obata, and

Kassabaum, designed this $65-million museum, which has made SoMa one of the more popular areas to visit for tourists and residents alike. The museum's permanent collection houses the West Coast's most comprehensive collection of 20th-century art, including painting, sculpture, photography, architecture, design, and media arts. The collection features master works by Ansel Adams, Bruce Conner, Joseph Cornell, Salvador Dalí, Richard Diebenkorn, Eva Hesse, Frida Kahlo, Ellsworth Kelly, Yves Klein, Sherrie Levine, Gordon Matta-Clark, Henri Matisse, Piet Mondrian, Pablo Picasso, Robert Rauschenberg, Diego Rivera, Cindy Sherman, Alfred Stieglitz, Clyfford Still, and Edward Weston, among many others, as well as an ever-changing program of special exhibits. Unfortunately, few works are on display at one time, and for the money the experience can be disappointing—especially compared to the finer museums of New York. However, this is about as good as it gets in our boutique city, so take it or leave it. Docent-led tours take place daily. Times are posted at the admission desk. Phone or check SFMOMA's website for current details of upcoming special events and exhibitions.

The **Caffè Museo,** to the right of the museum entrance, offers very good-quality fresh soups, sandwiches, and salads. Be sure to visit the **MuseumStore,** which carries a wonderful array of modern and contemporary art books, innovative design objects and furniture, jewelry and apparel, educational children's books and toys, posters, and stationery: It's one of the best shops in town and always carries their famed "FogDome"—a snowglobe with a mini MOMA that gets foggy rather than snowy when you shake it.

151 Third St. (2 blocks south of Market St., across from Yerba Buena Gardens). ✆ 415/357-4000. www.sfmoma.org. Admission $13 adults, $8 seniors, $7 students over 12 with ID, free for children 12 and under. Half-price for all Thurs 6–9pm; free to all 1st Tues of each month. Thurs 11am–8:45pm; Fri–Tues 11am–5:45pm. Closed Wed and major holidays. Bus: 15, 30, or 45. Streetcar: J, K, L, or M to Montgomery.

Yerba Buena Center for the Arts ✫ *Finds* *Kids*   The **YBCA,** which opened in 1993, is part of the large outdoor complex that takes up a few city blocks across the street from SFMOMA, and sits atop the underground Moscone Convention Center. It's the city's cultural facility, similar to New York's Lincoln Center but far more fun on the outside. The Center's two buildings offer music, theater, dance, and visual arts programs and shows. James Stewart Polshek designed the 755-seat theater, and Fumihiko Maki designed the Galleries and Arts Forum, which features three galleries and a space designed especially for dance. Cutting-edge computer art, multimedia shows, contemporary exhibitions, and performances occupy the center's high-tech galleries.

701 Mission St. ✆ **415/978-2787** (box office). www.ybca.org. Admission for gallery $6 adults, $3 seniors, teachers, and students. Free to all 1st Tues of each month. Free for seniors and students with ID every Thurs. Tues–Wed and Sun noon–5pm; Thurs–Sat noon–8pm. Contact YBCA for times and admission to theater. Bus: 5, 9, 14, 15, 30, or 45. Streetcar: Powell or Montgomery.

Yerba Buena Gardens 😤 Unless you're at Yerba Buena to catch a performance, you're more likely to visit the 5-acre gardens, a great place to relax in the grass on a sunny day and check out several artworks. The most dramatic outdoor piece is an emotional mixed-media memorial to Martin Luther King, Jr. Created by sculptor Houston Conwill, poet Estella Majozo, and architect Joseph de Pace, it features 12 panels, each inscribed with quotations from King, sheltered behind a 50-foot-high waterfall. There are also several actual garden areas here, including a Butterfly Garden, the Sister Cities Garden (highlighting flowers from the city's 13 sister cities), and The East Garden, blending Eastern and Western styles. May through October, Yerba Buena Arts & Events puts on a series of free outdoor festivals featuring dance, music, poetry, and more by the San Francisco Ballet, Opera, Symphony, and others.

Located on 2 square city blocks bounded by Mission, Folsom, Third, and Fourth sts. www.yerbabuenagardens.com. Daily 6am–10pm. No admission fee. Contact Yerba Buena Arts & Events: ✆ **415/543-1718** or www.ybgf.org for details about the free outdoor festivals. Bus: 5, 9, 14, 15, 30, or 45. Streetcar: Powell or Montgomery.

Zeum/The Yerba Buena Ice Skating and Bowling Center 😤 *Kids* Also in Yerba Buena Gardens you'll find **Zeum,** an innovative, hands-on multimedia, arts and technology museum for kids of all ages. Zeum also features the fabulous 1906 carousel that once graced the city's bygone Oceanside amusement park, Playland-at-the-Beach; the Children's Garden; a cafe; and a fun store. Right behind Zeum, you'll find **The Yerba Buena Ice Skating and Bowling Center,** a great stopover if you're looking for fun indoor activities, including a 12-lane bowling alley and an ice-skating rink with public sessions daily.

Zeum: 221 Fourth St. (at Howard St.) ✆ **415/820-3320.** www.zeum.com. Adults $8, seniors and students $7, youth 3–18 $6, free for children 2 and under. Summer Tues–Sun 11am–5pm; hours during the school year Wed–Sun 11am–5pm. Carousel $3 per person, each ticket good for 2 rides. Daily 11am–6pm. **The Yerba Buena Ice Skating and Bowling Center:** 750 Folsom St. ✆ **415/820-3521.** www.skate bowl.com. Bowling alley: $20–$30 per lane/per hour; Sun–Thurs 10am–10pm, Fri–Sat 10am–midnight. Skating rink: call for hours and admission. Bus: 5, 9, 14, 15, 30, or 45. Streetcar: Powell or Montgomery.

3 Neighborhoods Worth a Visit

To really get to know San Francisco, break out of the downtown and Fisherman's Wharf areas to explore the ethnically and culturally diverse neighborhoods. Walk the streets, browse the shops, grab a bite at a local restaurant—you'll find that San Francisco's beauty and charm are around every corner, not just at the popular tourist destinations.

Note: For information on Fisherman's Wharf, see its entry under "Famous San Francisco Sights," on p. 106. For information on San Francisco neighborhoods and districts that aren't discussed here, see "Neighborhoods in Brief," in chapter 1, beginning on p. 17.

NOB HILL

When the cable car started operating in 1873, this hill became the city's exclusive residential area. Newly wealthy residents who had struck it rich in the gold rush (and were known by names such as the "Big Four" and the "Comstock Bonanza kings") built their mansions here, but they were almost all destroyed by the 1906 earthquake and fire. The only two surviving buildings are the Flood Mansion, which serves today as the **Pacific Union Club,** and **The Fairmont Hotel,** which was under construction when the earthquake struck and was damaged but not destroyed. Today, the burned-out sites of former mansions hold the city's luxury hotels—the **Inter-Continental Mark Hopkins,** the **Stanford Court,** the **Huntington Hotel,** and the spectacular **Grace Cathedral,** which stands on the Crocker mansion site. Nob Hill is worth a visit if only to stroll around **Huntington Park,** attend a Sunday service at the cathedral, or ooh and aah your way around the Fairmont's spectacular lobby.

SOUTH OF MARKET (SoMa)

From Market Street to Townsend Street and The Embarcadero to Division Street, SoMa has become the city's newest cultural and multimedia center. The process started when alternative clubs began opening in the old warehouses in the area nearly a decade ago. A wave of entrepreneurs followed, seeking to start new businesses in what was once an extremely low-rent area compared to the neighboring Financial District. Today, gentrification and high rents hold sway, spurred by a building boom that started with the **Moscone Convention Center** and continued with the **Yerba Buena Center for the Arts** and **Yerba Buena Gardens,** the **San Francisco Museum of Modern Art, Four Seasons Hotel, W Hotel, St. Regis Hotel,** and the **Metreon Entertainment Center.** Other institutions, businesses, and museums move into the area on an ongoing basis. A substantial portion of the city's nightlife takes place in warehouse spaces throughout the district.

NORTH BEACH 𝒜𝒜𝒜

In the late 1800s, an enormous influx of Italian immigrants to North Beach firmly established this aromatic area as San Francisco's "Little Italy." Dozens of Italian restaurants and coffeehouses continue to flourish in what is still the center of the city's Italian community. Walk down **Columbus Avenue** on any given morning, and you're bound to be bombarded by the wonderful aromas of roasting coffee and savory pasta sauces. Although there are some interesting shops and bookstores in the area, it's the dozens of eclectic little cafes, delis, bakeries, and coffee shops that give North Beach its Italian-bohemian character.

CHINATOWN 𝒜𝒜

The first of the Chinese immigrants came to San Francisco in the early 1800s to work as servants. By 1851, 25,000 Chinese people were working in California, and most had settled in San Francisco's Chinatown. Fleeing famine and the Opium Wars, they had come seeking the good fortune promised by the "Gold Mountain" of California, and hoped to return with wealth to their families in China. For the majority, the reality of life in California did not live up to the promise. First employed as workers in the gold mines during the gold rush, they later built the railroads, working as little more than slaves and facing constant prejudice. Yet the community, segregated in the Chinatown ghetto, thrived. Growing prejudice led to the Chinese Exclusion Act of 1882, which halted all Chinese immigration for 10 years and severely limited it thereafter (the Chinese Exclusion Act was not repealed until 1943). Chinese people were also denied the opportunity to buy homes outside the Chinatown ghetto until the 1950s.

Today, San Francisco has one of the largest communities of Chinese people in the United States. More than 80,000 people live in Chinatown, but the majority of Chinese people have moved out into newer areas like the Richmond and Sunset districts. Although frequented by tourists, the area continues to cater to Chinese shoppers, who crowd the vegetable and herb markets, restaurants, and shops. Tradition runs deep here, and if you're lucky, through an open window you might hear women mixing mah-jongg tiles as they play the centuries-old game. (***Be warned:*** You're likely to hear lots of spitting around here, too—it's part of local tradition.)

The gateway at Grant Avenue and Bush Street marks the entry to Chinatown. The heart of the neighborhood is Portsmouth Square, where you'll find locals playing board games (often gambling) or just sitting quietly.

On the newly beautified and renovated Waverly Place, a street where the Chinese celebratory colors of red, yellow, and green are much in evidence, you'll find three **Chinese temples:** Jeng Sen (Buddhist and Taoist) at no. 146, Tien Hou (Buddhist) at no. 125, and Norras (Buddhist) at no. 109. If you enter, do so quietly so that you do not disturb those in prayer.

A block west of Grant Avenue, **Stockton Street,** from 1000 to 1200, is the community's main shopping street, lined with grocers, fishmongers, tea sellers, herbalists, noodle parlors, and restaurants. Here, too, is the Buddhist Kong Chow Temple, at no. 855, above the Chinatown post office. Explore at your leisure.

JAPANTOWN

More than 12,000 citizens of Japanese descent (1.4% of the city's population) live in San Francisco, or Soko, as the Japanese who first emigrated here often called it. Initially, they settled in Chinatown and south of Market along Stevenson and Jessie streets from Fourth to Seventh streets. After the earthquake in 1906, SoMa became a light industrial and warehouse area, and the largest Japanese concentration took root in the Western Addition between Van Ness Avenue and Fillmore Street, the site of today's Japantown, now 100 years old. By 1940, it covered 30 blocks.

In 1913, the Alien Land Law was passed, depriving Japanese Americans of the right to buy land. From 1924 to 1952, the United States banned Japanese immigration. During World War II, the U.S. government froze Japanese bank accounts, interned community leaders, and removed 112,000 Japanese Americans—two-thirds of them citizens—to camps in California, Utah, and Idaho. Japantown was emptied of Japanese people, and war workers took their place. Upon their release in 1945, the Japanese found their old neighborhood occupied. Most of them resettled in the Richmond and Sunset districts; some returned to Japantown, but it had shrunk to a mere 6 or so blocks. Today, the community's notable sights include the **Buddhist Church of San Francisco,** 1881 Pine St. (at Octavia St.), www.bcsfweb.org; the **Konko Church of San Francisco,** 1909 Bush St. (at Laguna St.); the **Sokoji–Soto Zen Buddhist Temple,** 1691 Laguna St. (at Sutter St.); **Nihonmachi Mall,** 1700 block of Buchanan Street between Sutter and Post streets, which contains two steel fountains by Ruth Asawa; and the **Japan Center,** an Asian-oriented shopping mall occupying 3 square blocks bounded by Post,

Geary, Laguna, and Fillmore streets. At its center stands the five-tiered **Peace Pagoda,** designed by world-famous Japanese architect Yoshiro Taniguchi "to convey the friendship and goodwill of the Japanese to the people of the United States." Surrounding the pagoda, through a network of arcades, squares, and bridges, you can explore dozens of shops and showrooms featuring everything from TVs and tansu chests to pearls, bonsai, and kimonos. **Kabuki Springs & Spa** is the center's most famous tenant. But locals also head to its numerous restaurants, teahouses, shops, and multiplex movie theater.

There is often live entertainment in this neighborhood on summer weekends, including Japanese music and dance performances, tea ceremonies, flower-arranging demonstrations, martial-arts presentations, and other cultural events. **The Japan Center** (✆ **415/ 922-6776**) is open daily from 10am to midnight, although most shops close much earlier. To get there, take bus nos. 2, 3, or 4 (exit at Buchanan and Sutter sts.) or nos. 22 or 38 (exit at the northeast corner of Geary Blvd. and Fillmore St.).

HAIGHT-ASHBURY

Few of San Francisco's neighborhoods are as varied—or as famous—as Haight-Ashbury. Walk along Haight Street, and you'll encounter everything from drug-dazed drifters begging for change to an armada of the city's funky-trendy shops, clubs, and cafes. Turn anywhere off Haight, and instantly you're among the clean-cut, young urban professionals who can afford the steep rents in this hip 'hood. The result is an interesting mix of well-to-do and well-screw-you aging flower children, former Dead-heads, homeless people, and throngs of tourists who try not to stare as they wander through this most human of zoos. Some find it depressing, others find it fascinating, but everyone agrees that it ain't what it was in the free-lovin' psychedelic Summer of Love. Is it still worth a visit? Not if you are here for a day or two, but it's certainly worth an excursion on longer trips, if only to enjoy a cone of Cherry Garcia at the now-famous Ben & Jerry's Ice Cream Store on the corner of Haight and Ashbury streets, and then to wander and gawk at the area's intentional freaks.

THE CASTRO

Castro Street, between Market and 18th streets, is the center of the city's gay community as well as a lovely neighborhood teeming with shops, restaurants, bars, and other institutions that cater to the area's colorful residents. Among the landmarks are **Harvey Milk Plaza** and the **Castro Theatre** (www.castrotheatre.com), a 1930s movie palace with a Wurlitzer. The gay community began to move here in the late 1960s and early 1970s from a neighborhood called Polk Gulch, which still has a number of gay-oriented bars and stores. Castro is one of the liveliest streets in the city and the perfect place to shop for gifts and revel in free-spiritedness. Check www.castroonline.com for more info.

THE MISSION DISTRICT

Once inhabited almost entirely by Irish immigrants, The Mission District is now the center of the city's Latino community as well as a mecca for young, hip residents. It's an oblong area stretching roughly from 14th to 30th streets between Potrero Avenue on the east and Dolores on the west. In the outer areas, many of the city's finest Victorians still stand, although many seem strangely out of place in the mostly lower-income neighborhoods. The heart of the community lies along 24th Street between Van Ness and Potrero, where dozens of excellent ethnic restaurants, bakeries, bars, and specialty stores attract people from all over the city. The area surrounding 16th Street and Valencia is a hotbed for impressive—and often impressively cheap—restaurants and bars catering to the city's hip crowd. The Mission District at night doesn't feel like the safest place (although in terms of creepiness, the Tenderloin, a few blocks off Union Square, beats The Mission by far), and walking around the area should be done with caution, but it's usually quite safe during the day and is highly recommended.

For an even better insight into the community, go to the **Precita Eyes Mural Arts Center,** 2981 24th St., between Harrison and Alabama streets (© **415/285-2287;** www.precitaeyes.org), and take one of the 1½- to 2-hour tours conducted on Saturdays and Sundays at 11am and 1:30pm, where you'll see 60 murals in an 8-block walk. Group tours are available during the week by appointment. The 11am tour costs $10 for adults, $8 for students with ID, $5 for seniors, and $2 for children 17 and under; the 1:30pm tour, which is half an hour longer and includes a slide show, costs $12 for adults, $8 for students with ID, and $5 for seniors and children 17 and under. All but the Saturday-morning tour (which leaves from 3325 24th St. at the Café Venice) leave from the center's 24th Street location.

Other signs of cultural life in the neighborhood are progressive theaters such as Theatre Rhinoceros (www.therhino.org) and Theater Artaud (www.artaud.org). At 16th Street and Dolores is the Mission San Francisco de Asís, better known as **Mission Dolores** (p. 130). It's the city's oldest surviving building and the district's namesake.

4 Golden Gate Park ★★★

Everybody loves **Golden Gate Park**—people, dogs, birds, frogs, turtles, bison, trees, bushes, and flowers. Literally, everything feels uni-
fied here in San Francisco's enormous arboreal front yard. Conceived
in the 1860s and 1870s, this great 1,017-acre landmark, which
stretches inland from the Pacific coast, took shape in the 1880s and
1890s thanks to the skill and effort of John McLaren, a Scot who
arrived in 1887 and began landscaping the park.

When he embarked on the project, sand dunes and wind pre-
sented enormous challenges. But McLaren had developed a new
strain of grass called "sea bent," which he planted to hold the sandy
soil along the Firth of Forth back home, and he used it to anchor the
soil here, too. Every year the ocean eroded the western fringe of the
park, and ultimately he solved this problem, too, though it took him
40 years to build a natural wall, putting out bundles of sticks that the
tides covered with sand. He also built the two windmills that stand
on the western edge of the park to pump water for irrigation. Under
his brilliant eye, the park took shape.

Today the park consists of hundreds of gardens and attractions
connected by wooded paths and paved roads. While many worthy
sites are clearly visible, there are infinite hidden treasures, so pick up
information at **McLaren Lodge and Park Headquarters** (at Stanyan
and Fell sts.; ☎ **415/831-2700**) if you want to find the more hidden
spots. It's open daily and offers park maps for $3. Of the dozens of
special gardens in the park, most recognized are **McLaren Memorial
Rhododendron Dell,** the **Rose Garden, Strybing Arboretum,** and,
at the western edge of the park, a springtime array of thousands of
tulips and daffodils around the **Dutch windmill.**

In addition to the highlights described in this section, the park contains lots of recreational facilities: tennis courts; baseball, soccer, and
polo fields; a golf course; riding stables; and fly-casting pools. The
Strawberry Hill boathouse handles boat rentals. The park is also the
home of the **M. H. de Young Memorial Museum,** which recently
relocated to its spectacular new home at 50 Tea Garden Dr. (☎ **415/
750-3600** or 415/863-3330). For more information see p. 112.

For further information, call the San Francisco Visitor Information Center at ☎ **415/283-0177.** Enter the park at Kezar Drive, an
extension of Fell Street; bus riders can take no. 5, 6, 7, 16AX, 16BX,
66, or 71.

PARK HIGHLIGHTS

CONSERVATORY OF FLOWERS ★★   Opened to the public in 1879, this glorious Victorian glass structure is the oldest existing public conservatory in the Western Hemisphere. After a bad storm in 1995 and delayed renovations, the conservatory was closed and visitors were only able to imagine what wondrous displays existed within the striking glass assemblage. Thankfully, a $25-million renovation, including a $4-million exhibit upgrade, was completed a few years ago, and now the Conservatory is a cutting-edge horticultural destination with over 1,700 species of plants. Here you can check out the rare tropical flora of the Congo, Philippines, and beyond within the stunning structure. As one of only four public institutions in the U.S. to house a highland tropics exhibit, its five galleries also include the lowland tropics, aquatic plants, the largest Dracula orchid collection in the world, and special exhibits. It doesn't take long to visit, but make a point of staying a while; outside there are good sunny spots for people-watching as well as paths leading to impressive gardens begging to be explored. If you're around during summer and fall, don't miss the Dahlia Garden to the right of the entrance in the center of what was once a carriage roundabout—it's an explosion of colorful Dr. Seuss–like blooms. The conservatory is open Tuesday through Sunday from 9am to 5pm, closed Mondays. Admission is $5 for adults; $3 for youth 12 to 17 years of age, seniors, and students with ID; $1.50 for children 5 to 11; and free for children 4 and under and for all visitors the first Tuesday of the month. For more information, visit www.conservatoryofflowers. org or call ☎ **415/666-7001.**

JAPANESE TEA GARDEN   John McLaren, the man who began landscaping Golden Gate Park, hired Makoto Hagiwara, a wealthy Japanese landscape designer, to further develop this garden originally created for the 1894 Midwinter Exposition. It's a quiet place with cherry trees, shrubs, and bonsai crisscrossed by winding paths and high-arched bridges over pools of water. Focal points and places for contemplation include the massive bronze Buddha (cast in Japan in 1790 and donated by the Gump family), the Buddhist wooden pagoda, and the Drum Bridge, which, reflected in the water, looks as though it completes a circle. The garden is open daily November through February from 8:30am to 5pm (teahouse 10am–4:30pm), March through October from 8:30am to 6pm (teahouse 10am–5:30pm). For information on admission, call ☎ **415/752-4227.** For the **teahouse,** call ☎ **415/ 752-1171.**

Golden Gate Park

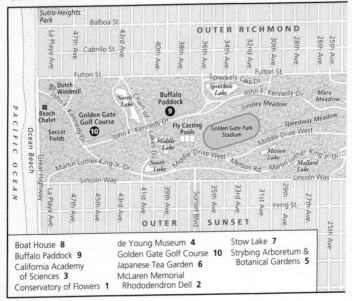

Boat House **8**	de Young Museum **4**	Stow Lake **7**
Buffalo Paddock **9**	Golden Gate Golf Course **10**	Strybing Arboretum &
California Academy	Japanese Tea Garden **6**	Botanical Gardens **5**
of Sciences **3**	McLaren Memorial	
Conservatory of Flowers **1**	Rhododendron Dell **2**	

STRAWBERRY HILL/STOW LAKE   Rent a paddle boat or rowboat and cruise around the circular Stow Lake as painters create still lifes, joggers pass along the grassy shoreline, ducks waddle around waiting to be fed, and turtles sunbathe on rocks and logs. Strawberry Hill, the 430-foot-high artificial island and highest point in the park that lies at the center of Stow Lake, is a perfect picnic spot; it boasts a bird's-eye view of San Francisco and the bay. It also has a waterfall and peace pagoda. For the **boathouse,** call ℘ **415/752-0347.** Boat rentals are available daily from 10am to 4pm, weather permitting; four-passenger rowboats go for $13 per hour, and four-person paddle boats run $17 per hour; fees are cash-only.

STRYBING ARBORETUM & BOTANICAL GARDENS   More than 7,000 plant species grow here, among them some ancient plants in a special "primitive garden," rare species, and a grove of California redwoods. Docent tours begin at 1:30pm daily, with an additional 10:20am tour on weekends. Strybing is open Monday through Friday from 8am to 4:30pm, and Saturday, Sunday, and holidays from 10am to 5pm. Admission is free. For more information, call ℘ **415/661-1316** or visit www.strybing.org.

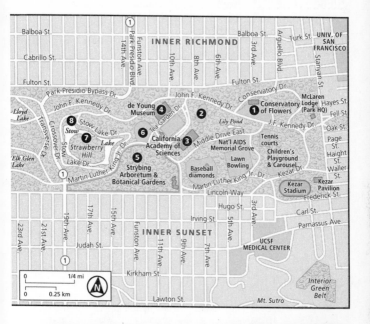

5 The Presidio & Golden Gate National Recreation Area

THE PRESIDIO

In October 1994, the Presidio passed from the U.S. Army to the National Park Service and became one of a handful of urban national parks that combines historical, architectural, and natural elements in one giant arboreal expanse. (It also contains a previously private golf course and a home for George Lucas's production company.) The 1,491-acre area incorporates a variety of terrain—coastal scrub, dunes, and prairie grasslands—that shelter many rare plants and more than 200 species of birds, some of which nest here.

This military outpost has a 220-year history, from its founding in September 1776 by the Spanish under José Joaquin Moraga to its closure in 1994. From 1822 to 1846, the property was in Mexican hands.

During the war with Mexico, U.S. forces occupied the fort, and in 1848, when California became part of the Union, it was formally transferred to the United States. When San Francisco suddenly became an important urban area during the gold rush, the U.S. government

Golden Gate National Recreation Area

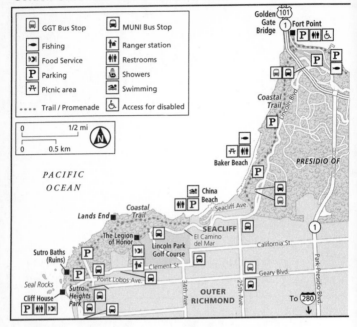

installed battalions of soldiers and built Fort Point to protect the entry to the harbor. It expanded the post during the Civil War and during the Indian Wars of the 1870s and 1880s. By the 1890s, the Presidio was no longer a frontier post but a major base for U.S. expansion into the Pacific. During the war with Spain in 1898, thousands of troops camped here in tent cities awaiting shipment to the Philippines, and the Army General Hospital treated the sick and wounded. By 1905, 12 coastal defense batteries were built along the headlands. In 1914, troops under the command of Gen. John Pershing left here to pursue Pancho Villa and his men. The Presidio expanded during the 1920s, when Crissy Army Airfield (the first airfield on the West Coast) was established, but the major action was seen during World War II, after the attack on Pearl Harbor. Soldiers dug foxholes along nearby beaches, and the Presidio became the headquarters for the Western Defense Command. Some 1.75 million men were shipped out from nearby Fort Mason to fight in the Pacific; many returned to the Presidio's hospital, whose capacity peaked one year at 72,000 patients. In the 1950s, the Presidio served as the headquarters for the Sixth U.S. Army and a missile defense post, but its role slowly shrank. In 1972, it was included in

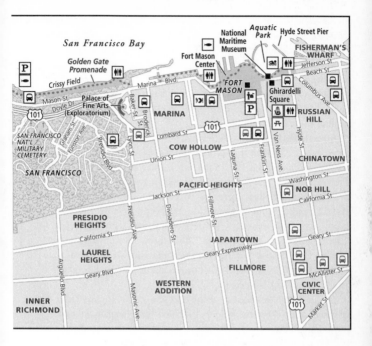

new legislation establishing the Golden Gate National Recreation Area; in 1989, the Pentagon decided to close the post and transfer it to the National Park Service.

Today, the area encompasses more than 470 historic buildings, a scenic golf course, a national cemetery, 22 hiking trails (to be doubled over the next decade), and a variety of terrain and natural habitats. The National Park Service offers walking and biking tours around the Presidio (reservations are suggested) as well as a free shuttle "PresidioGo." For more information, call the **Presidio Visitors Center** at © **415/561-4323;** www.nps.gov/prsf or www.presidio. gov. Take bus no. 28, 45, 76, or 82X to get there.

GOLDEN GATE NATIONAL RECREATION AREA

The largest urban park in the world, GGNRA makes New York's Central Park look like a putting green, covering three counties along 28 miles of stunning, condo-free shoreline. Run by the National Park Service, the Recreation Area wraps around the northern and western edges of the city, and just about all of it is open to the public with no access fees. The Muni bus system provides transportation to the more popular sites, including Aquatic Park, Cliff House, Fort Mason, and Ocean Beach. For more information, contact the **National Park Service** (© 415/561-4700; www.nps.gov/goga). For more detailed information on particular sites, see the "Getting Outside" section, later in this chapter.

Here is a brief rundown of the salient features of the park's peninsula section, starting at the northern section and moving westward around the coastline:

Aquatic Park, adjacent to the Hyde Street Pier, has a small swimming beach, although it's not that appealing (and darned cold). Far more entertaining is a visit to the San Francisco Maritime National Historical Park's Visitor Center a few blocks away.

Fort Mason Center, from Bay Street to the shoreline, consists of several buildings and piers used during World War II. Today they hold a variety of museums, theaters, shops, and organizations, and Greens vegetarian restaurant (p. 90), which affords views of the Golden Gate Bridge. For information about Fort Mason events, call © 415/441-3400 or visit www.fortmason.org. The park headquarters is also at Fort Mason.

Farther west along the bay at the northern end of Laguna Street is **Marina Green,** a favorite local spot for kite-flying, jogging, and walking along the Promenade. The St. Francis Yacht Club is also here.

Next comes the 3½-mile paved **Golden Gate Promenade** ☝, San Francisco's best and most scenic biking, jogging, and walking path. It runs along the shore past **Crissy Field** (www.crissyfield.org) and ends at Fort Point under the Golden Gate Bridge (be sure to stop and watch the gonzo windsurfers and kite surfers, who catch major wind here, and admire the newly restored marshlands). The Crissy Field Café and Bookstore is open from 9am to 5pm Wednesday through Sunday and offers yummy, organic soups, salads, sandwiches, coffee drinks, and a decent selection of outdoor-themed books and cards.

Fort Point ☝ (© 415/556-1693; www.nps.gov/fopo) was built from 1853 to 1861 to protect the narrow entrance to the harbor. It was designed to house 500 soldiers manning 126 muzzle-loading cannons. By 1900, the fort's soldiers and obsolete guns had been removed, but the formidable brick edifice remains. Fort Point is open Friday through Sunday only from 10am to 5pm, and guided tours and cannon demonstrations are given at the site once or twice a day on open days, depending on the time of year.

Lincoln Boulevard sweeps around the western edge of the bay to **Baker Beach,** where the waves roll ashore—a fine spot for sunbathing, walking, or fishing. Hikers can follow the **Coastal Trail** (www.californiacoastaltrail.org) from Fort Point along this part of the coastline all the way to Lands End.

A short distance from Baker Beach, **China Beach** is a small cove where swimming is permitted. Changing rooms, showers, a sun deck, and restrooms are available.

A little farther around the coast is **Lands End** ★, looking out to Pyramid Rock. A lower and an upper trail offer hiking amid windswept cypresses and pines on the cliffs above the Pacific.

Still farther along the coast lie **Point Lobos,** the **Sutro Baths** (www.sutrobaths.com), and **Cliff House** ★. Cliff House (www.cliffhouse.com), which recently underwent major renovations, has been serving refreshments to visitors since 1863. It's famed for its views of Seal Rocks (a colony of sea lions and many marine birds) and the Pacific Ocean. Immediately northeast of Cliff House you'll find traces of the once-grand Sutro Baths, a swimming facility that was a major summer attraction accommodating up to 24,000 people until it burned down in 1966. (Alas, my favorite Cliff House attraction, the **Musée Mécanique** ★★, an arcade featuring antique games, moved to digs at Pier 45; for more information, call ✆ **415/346-2000** or visit www.museemecanique.org.)

A little farther inland at the western end of California Street is **Lincoln Park,** which contains a golf course and the spectacular Legion of Honor museum (p. 114).

At the southern end of Ocean Beach, 4 miles down the coast, is another area of the park around Fort Funston (✆ **415/561-4700**), where there's an easy loop trail across the cliffs. Here you can watch hang gliders take advantage of the high cliffs and strong winds.

Farther south along Route 280, **Sweeney Ridge** affords sweeping views of the coastline from the many trails that crisscross its 1,000 acres. From here the expedition led by Don Gaspar de Portolá first saw San Francisco Bay in 1769. It's in Pacifica; take Sneath Lane off Route 35 (Skyline Blvd.) in San Bruno.

The GGNRA extends into Marin County, where it encompasses the Marin Headlands, Muir Woods National Monument, and Olema Valley behind the Point Reyes National Seashore.

6 Religious Buildings Worth Checking Out

Glide Memorial United Methodist Church ★★ *Moments* The best way to spend a Sunday morning in San Francisco is to visit this Tenderloin-area church to witness the exhilarating and lively sermons accompanied by an amazing gospel choir. Reverend Cecil Williams's enthusiastic and uplifting preaching and singing with the homeless and poor of the neighborhood has attracted nationwide fame over the past 40-plus years. In 1994, during the pastor's 30th-anniversary celebration, singers Angela Bofill and Bobby McFerrin joined comedian Robin Williams, author Maya Angelou, and talk-show queen Oprah Winfrey to honor him publicly. Even former President Clinton has joined the crowd. Cecil Williams now shares pastor duties with Douglas Fitch and alternates presiding over the roof-raising Sunday services in front of a diverse audience that crosses all socioeconomic boundaries. Go for an uplifting experience and some hand-clapping, shoulder-swaying gospel choir music—it's an experience you'll never forget. *Tip:* Arrive about 20 minutes early to make sure you get a seat; otherwise it's SRO.

330 Ellis St. (west of Union Sq.). © **415/674-6000.** www.glide.org. Services Sun at 9 and 11am. Bus: 27. Streetcar: Powell. BART: Powell.

Grace Cathedral   Although this Nob Hill cathedral, designed by architect Lewis P. Hobart, appears to be made of stone, it is in fact constructed of reinforced concrete beaten to achieve a stonelike effect. Construction began on the site of the Crocker mansion in 1928 but was not completed until 1964. Among the more interesting features of the building are its stained-glass windows, particularly those by the French Loire studios and Charles Counick, depicting such modern figures as Thurgood Marshall, Robert Frost, and Albert Einstein; the replicas of Ghiberti's bronze *Doors of Paradise* at the east end; the series of religious murals completed in the 1940s by Polish artist John de Rosen; and the 44-bell carillon. Along with its magical ambience, Grace lifts spirits with services, musical performances (including organ recitals on many Sundays), and its weekly Forum (Sun 9:30–10:30am except during summer and major holidays), where guests lead discussions about spirituality in modern times and have community dialogues on social issues.

1100 California St. (btw. Taylor and Jones sts.). © **415/749-6300.** www.grace cathedral.org.

Mission Dolores   San Francisco's oldest standing structure, the Mission San Francisco de Asís (also known as Mission Dolores), has withstood the test of time, as well as two major earthquakes, relatively intact. In 1776, at the behest of Franciscan missionary Junípero Serra, Father Francisco Palou came to the Bay Area to found the sixth in a series of missions that dotted the California coastline. From these humble beginnings grew what was to become the city of San Francisco. The mission's small, simple chapel, built solidly by Native Americans who were converted to Christianity, is a curious mixture of native construction methods and Spanish-colonial style. A statue of Father Serra stands in the mission garden, although the portrait looks somewhat more contemplative, and less energetic, than he must have been in real life. A 45-minute self-guided tour costs $5; otherwise, admission is $3 for adults and $2 for children.

16th St. (at Dolores St.). ✆ 415/621-8203. www.missiondolores.org. Admission $3 adults, $2 children. Daily 9am–5pm summer; 9am–4pm winter; 9am–4:30pm spring; 9am–noon Good Friday. Closed Thanksgiving, Easter, and Dec 25. Bus: 14, 26, or 33 to Church and 16th sts. Streetcar: J.

7 Architectural Highlights

ALAMO SQUARE HISTORIC DISTRICT San Francisco's collection of Victorian houses, known as **Painted Ladies,** is one of the city's most famous assets. Most of the 14,000 extant structures date from the second half of the 19th century and are private residences. Spread throughout the city, many have been beautifully restored and ornately painted. The small area bordered by Divisadero Street on the west, Golden Gate Avenue on the north, Webster Street on the east, and Fell Street on the south—about 10 blocks west of the Civic Center—has one of the city's greatest concentrations of Painted Ladies. One of the most famous views of San Francisco—seen on postcards and posters all around the city—depicts sharp-edged Financial District skyscrapers behind a row of Victorians. This fantastic juxtaposition can be seen from Alamo Square, in the center of the historic district, at Fulton and Steiner streets.

CITY HALL & CIVIC CENTER Built between 1913 and 1915, City Hall, located in the Civic Center District, is part of this "City Beautiful" complex done in the Beaux Arts style. The dome rises to a height of 306 feet on the exterior and is ornamented with oculi and topped by a lantern. The interior rotunda soars 112 feet and is finished in oak, marble, and limestone, with a monumental marble staircase leading to the second floor. With a major renovation completed in the late 1990s, the building was returned to its former splendor. No doubt you saw it on TV during early 2004, when much of the hoopla surrounding the short-lived and controversial gay marriage proceedings was depicted on the front steps. (Remember Rosie O'Donnell emerging from this very building after getting married to her girlfriend?) Public tours are given Monday through Friday at 10am, noon, and 2pm. Call ✆ **415/554-4933** for details.

8 Self-Guided & Organized Tours

THE 49-MILE SCENIC DRIVE 🐦🐦

The self-guided, 49-mile drive is an easy way to orient yourself and to grasp the beauty of San Francisco and its extraordinary location. It's also a flat-out stunning and very worthy excursion. Beginning in the city, it follows a rough circle around the bay and passes virtually all the best-known sights, from Chinatown to the Golden Gate Bridge, Ocean Beach, Seal Rocks, Golden Gate Park, and Twin Peaks. Originally designed for the benefit of visitors to San Francisco's 1939 and 1940 Golden Gate International Exposition, the route is marked by blue-and-white seagull signs. Although it makes an excellent half-day tour, this mini-excursion can easily take longer if you decide, for example, to stop to walk across the Golden Gate Bridge or to have tea in Golden Gate Park's Japanese Tea Garden.

The San Francisco **Visitor Information Center,** at Powell and Market streets (p. 1), distributes free route maps, which are handy since a few of the Scenic Drive marker signs are missing. Try to avoid the downtown area during the weekday rush hours from 7 to 9am and 4 to 6pm.

BOAT TOURS

One of the best ways to look at San Francisco is from a boat bobbing on the bay. There are several cruises to choose from, and many of them start from Fisherman's Wharf.

Blue & Gold Fleet, Pier 39, Fisherman's Wharf (© **415/773-1188;** www.blueandgoldfleet.com), tours the bay year-round in a sleek, 350-passenger sightseeing boat, complete with food and beverage facilities. The fully narrated, 1-hour cruise passes beneath the Golden Gate Bridge and comes within yards of Alcatraz Island. Don a jacket, bring the camera, and make sure it's a clear day for the best bay cruise. Frequent daily departures from Pier 39's West Marina begin at 10:45am daily during winter and 10am daily during summer. Tickets cost $21 for adults, $17 for seniors over 62 and juniors 12 to 18, and $13 for children 5 to 11; children 4 and under are admitted free. There's a $2.25 charge for ordering tickets by phone; discounts are available on their website.

The **Red & White Fleet,** Pier 43½ (© **415/673-2900;** www.redandwhite.com), offers daily Golden Gate Bay Cruise tours that leave from Pier 43½. The hour-long cruise goes along the city waterfront, beneath the Golden Gate Bridge, past Angel Island, and around Alcatraz. The cruise includes a headset audio tour that's narrated in eight languages. Tickets are $22 for adults, $16 for youths 5 to 17, and free for kids 4 and under. From April to October they also offer a 2-hour California Sunset Cruise with appetizers and music, and from May to Sept they run a SF Explorer Cruise that sails along San Francisco's downtown skyline while relating the city's history and architecture. Discounts are available through online purchase.

BUS TOURS

Gray Line (© **888/428-6937** or 415/434-8687; www.sanfrancisco sightseeing.com) is San Francisco's largest bus-tour operator. It offers numerous itineraries daily (far too many to list here). Free pickup and return are available between centrally located hotels and departure locations. Advance reservations are required for all tours except motorized cable car and trolley tours. Day and evening tours depart from Pier 43½ at Fisherman's Wharf; motorized cable car tours depart from Pier 39 and Pier 41.

9 Getting Outside

Half the fun in San Francisco takes place outdoors. If you're not in the mood to trek it, there are other things to do that allow you to enjoy the surroundings.

BALLOONING Although you must drive an hour to get to the tour site, hot-air ballooning over the Wine Country is an ethereal experience. **Adventures Aloft,** P.O. Box 2500, Vintage 1870, Yountville, CA 94599 (© **800/944-4408** or 707/944-4408; www. nvaloft.com), is Napa Valley's oldest hot-air balloon company, staffed with full-time professional pilots. Groups are small, and each flight lasts about an hour. The cost of $210 per person includes a post-adventure champagne brunch and a framed "first-flight" certificate. Flights launch daily at sunrise (weather permitting).

BEACHES Most days it's too chilly to hang out at the beach, but when the fog evaporates and the wind dies down, one of the best ways to spend the day is oceanside in the city. On any truly hot day, thousands flock to the beach to worship the sun, build sandcastles, and throw the ball around. Without a wet suit, swimming is a fiercely cold endeavor and is not recommended. In any case, dip at your own risk—there are no lifeguards on duty and San Francisco's waters are cold and have strong undertows. On the South Bay, **Baker Beach** is ideal for picnicking, sunning, walking, or fishing against the backdrop of the Golden Gate (though pollution makes your catch not necessarily worthy of eating).

Ocean Beach, at the end of Golden Gate Park, on the westernmost side of the city, is San Francisco's largest beach—4 miles long. Just offshore, at the northern end of the beach, in front of Cliff House, are the jagged Seal Rocks, inhabited by various shorebirds and a large colony of barking sea lions (bring binoculars for a close-up view). To the left, Kelly's Cove is one of the more challenging surf spots in town. Ocean Beach is ideal for strolling or sunning, but don't swim here—tides are tricky, and each year bathers drown in the rough surf.

Stop by Ocean Beach bus terminal at the corner of Cabrillo and La Playa to learn about San Francisco's history in local artist Ray Beldner's whimsically historical sculpture garden. Then hike up the hill to explore **Cliff House** and the ruins of the **Sutro Baths.** These baths, once able to accommodate 24,000 bathers, were lost to fire in 1966.

BIKING The San Francisco Parks and Recreation Department maintains two city-designated bike routes. One winds 7.5 miles through Golden Gate Park to Lake Merced; the other traverses the city, starting in the south, and continues over the Golden Gate Bridge. These routes are not dedicated to bicyclists, who must exercise caution to avoid crashing into pedestrians. Helmets are recommended for adults and required by law for kids under 18. A bike map is available from the San Francisco Visitor Information Center, at Powell and Mason streets, for $3 (see "Visitor Information" in chapter 1), and from bicycle shops all around town.

Ocean Beach has a public walk- and bikeway that stretches along 5 waterfront blocks of the Great Highway between Noriega and Santiago streets. It's an easy ride from Cliff House or Golden Gate Park.

Avenue Cyclery, 756 Stanyan St., at Waller Street, in the Haight (© 415/387-3155), rents bikes for $7 per hour or $28 per day. It's open daily, April through September from 10am to 7pm and October through March from 10am to 6pm. For cruising Fisherman's Wharf and the Golden Gate Bridge, your best bet is **Blazing Saddles** (© 415/202-8888; www.blazingsaddles.com), which has five locations around Fisherman's Wharf. Bikes rent for $28 per day, including maps, locks, and helmets; tandem bikes are available as well.

BOATING At the **Golden Gate Park Boat House** (© 415/752-0347) on Stow Lake, the park's largest body of water, you can rent a rowboat or pedal boat by the hour and steer over to Strawberry Hill, a large, round island in the middle of the lake, for lunch. There's usually a line on weekends. The boathouse is open daily from 10am to 4pm, weather permitting.

Cass' Marina, 1702 Bridgeway, Sausalito; P.O. Box 643; Sausalito, CA 94966 (© **800/472-4595** or 415/332-6789; www.cassmarina. com), is a certified sailing school that rents sailboats measuring 22 to 38 feet. Sail to the Golden Gate Bridge on your own or with a licensed skipper. In addition, large sailing yachts leave from Sausalito on a regularly scheduled basis. Call or check the website for schedules, prices, and availability of sailboats. The marina is open Wednesday through Monday from 9am to sunset.

CITY STAIR CLIMBING 🐾🐾

Many health clubs have stair-climbing machines and step classes, but in San Francisco, you need only go outside. The following city stair climbs will give you not only a good workout, but seriously stunning neighborhood, city, and bay views as well. Check www.sisterbetty.org/stairways for more ideas.

Filbert Street Steps, between Sansome Street and Telegraph Hill, are a particular challenge. Scaling the sheer eastern face of Telegraph Hill, this 377-step climb winds through verdant flower gardens and charming 19th-century cottages. Napier Lane, a narrow, wooden plank walkway, leads to Montgomery Street. Turn right and follow the path to the end of the cul-de-sac, where another stairway continues to Telegraph's panoramic summit.

The **Lyon Street Steps,** between Green Street and Broadway, were built in 1916. This historic stairway street contains four steep sets of stairs totaling 288 steps. Begin at Green Street and climb all the way up, past manicured hedges and flower gardens, to an iron gate that opens into the Presidio. A block east, on Baker Street, another set of 369 steps descends to Green Street.

FISHING Berkeley Marina Sports Center,

225 University Ave., Berkeley (© **510/237-3474;** www.berkeleysportfishing.com), makes daily trips for ling cod, rock fish, and many other types of game fish year-round, and it makes trips for salmon runs April through October. Fishing equipment is available; the cost, including boat ride and bait, is about $95 per person. Reservations are required, as are licenses for adults. One-day licenses can be purchased for $11 before departure. Find out the latest on the season by contacting their hot line at © **510/486-8300** (press 3). Excursions run daily from 6am to 4pm. Fish are cleaned, filleted, and bagged on the return trip for a small fee (free for salmon fishing).

GOLF San Francisco has a few beautiful golf courses. One of the most lavish is the **Presidio Golf Course** (© **415/561-4661;** www.presidiogolf.com). Greens fees are $60 until 12:30pm for residents Monday through Thursday and $96 for nonresidents; rates drop to $50 until 2pm, then to $35 for the rest of the day for residents and nonresidents. Friday though Sunday, rates are $96 for residents and $108 for nonresidents from 8 to 11am; from 11am to 12:30pm, the cost is $60 for residents. After that it's $50 for everyone until 2pm and $35 for the rest of the day. Carts are included. There are also two decent municipal courses in town.

The 9-hole **Golden Gate Park Course,** 47th Avenue and Fulton Street (© **415/751-8987;** www.goldengateparkgolf.com), charges greens fees of $14 per person Monday through Thursday, $18 Friday through Sunday. The 1,357-yard course is par 27. All holes are par 3, and this course is appropriate for all levels. The course is a little weathered in spots, but it's casual, fun, and inexpensive. It's open daily from sunup to sundown.

The 18-hole **Lincoln Park Golf Course,** 34th Avenue and Clement Street (© **415/221-9911;** www.parks.sfgov.org), charges greens fees of $31 per person Monday through Thursday, $36 Friday through Sunday, with rates decreasing after 4pm in summer, 2pm in winter. It's San Francisco's prettiest municipal course, with terrific views and fairways lined with Monterey cypress and pine trees. The 5,181-yard layout plays to par 68, and the 17th hole has a glistening ocean view. This is the oldest course in the city and one of the oldest in the West. It's open daily at daybreak.

HANDBALL The city's best handball courts are in Golden Gate Park, opposite Seventh Avenue, south of Middle Drive East. Courts are available free, on a first-come, first-served basis.

PARKS In addition to **Golden Gate Park** and the **Golden Gate National Recreation Area** (p. 122 and p. 127, respectively), San Francisco boasts more than 2,000 acres of parkland, most of which is perfect for picnicking or throwing around a Frisbee.

Smaller city parks include **Buena Vista Park** (Haight St. btw. Baker and Central sts.), which affords fine views of the Golden Gate Bridge and the area around it and is also a favored lounging ground for gay lovers; **Ina Coolbrith Park** (Taylor St. btw. Vallejo and Green sts.), offering views of the Bay Bridge and Alcatraz; and **Sigmund Stern Grove** (19th Ave. and Sloat Blvd.) in the Sunset District, which is the site of a famous free summer music festival.

One of my personal favorites is **Lincoln Park,** a 270-acre green on the northwestern side of the city at Clement Street and 34th Avenue. The Legion of Honor is here (p. 114), as is a scenic 18-hole municipal golf course (see "Golf," above). But the best things about this park are the 200-foot cliffs that overlook the Golden Gate Bridge and San Francisco Bay. To get to the park, take bus no. 38 from Union Square to 33rd and Geary streets, then walk a few blocks.

RUNNING The **ING Bay to Breakers Foot Race** ✿ (© **415/ 359-2800;** www.ingbaytobreakers.com) is an annual 7½-mile run from downtown to Ocean Beach. About 80,000 entrants take part in it, one of San Francisco's trademark events. Costumed participants and hordes of spectators add to the fun. The event is held on the third Sunday of May.

The San Francisco **Marathon** takes place annually in the middle of July. For more information, visit www.runsfm.com (no phone contact).

Great **jogging paths** include the entire expanse of Golden Gate Park, the shoreline along the Marina, and The Embarcadero.

TENNIS The **San Francisco Parks and Recreation Department** (© **415/753-7001**) maintains more than 132 free courts throughout the city. Almost all are available free, on a first-come, first-served basis. An additional 21 courts are available in **Golden Gate Park,** which cost $5 for 90 minutes during weekdays and $10 on weekends. Check the website for details on rules for reserving courts (www.parks.sfgov.org).

WALKING & HIKING The **Golden Gate National Recreation Area** offers plenty of opportunities. One incredible walk (or bike ride) is along the Golden Gate Promenade, from Aquatic Park to the Golden Gate Bridge. The 3½-mile paved trail heads along the northern edge of the Presidio out to Fort Point, passing the marina, Crissy Field's new restored wetlands, a small beach, and plenty of athletic locals. You can also hike the Coastal Trail all the way from the Fort Point area to Cliff House. The park service maintains several other trails in the city. For more information or to pick up a map of the Golden Gate National Recreation Area, stop by the park service headquarters at Fort Mason; enter on Franklin Street (© **415/561-4700**).

Although most people drive to this spectacular vantage point, a more rejuvenating way to experience **Twin Peaks** is to walk up from the back roads of U.C. Medical Center (off Parnassus) or from either of the two roads that lead to the top (off Woodside or Clarendon aves.). The best time to trek is early morning, when the city is quiet, the air is crisp, and sightseers haven't crowded the parking lot. Keep an eye out for cars, however, because there's no real hiking trail, and be sure to walk beyond the lot and up to the highest vantage point.

10 Spectator Sports

The Bay Area's sports scene includes several major professional franchises. Check the local newspapers' sports sections for daily listings of local events.

MAJOR LEAGUE BASEBALL

The **San Francisco Giants** play at **AT&T Park,** Third and King streets (© **415/972-2000;** www.sfgiants.com), in the China Basin section of SoMa. From April to October, 41,503 fans fill the seats here to root for the National League Giants. Tickets are hard to come by, but you can try to obtain some through **Tickets.com** (© **800/ 225-2277;** www.tickets.com).

The American League's **Oakland Athletics** play across the bay at McAfee Coliseum, at the Hegenberger Road exit from I-880, Oakland (© **510/430-8020;** www.athletics.mlb.com). The stadium holds over 50,000 spectators and is accessible through BART's Coliseum station. Tickets are available from the Coliseum Box Office or by phone through **Tickets.com** (© **800/225-2277;** www.tickets.com).

PRO BASKETBALL

The **Golden State Warriors** of the NBA play at the ORACLE Arena, a 19,200-seat facility at 7000 Coliseum Way in Oakland (© **510/986-2200;** www.nba.com/warriors). The season runs November through April, and most games start at 7:30pm. Tickets are available at the arena, online, and by phone through **Tickets. com** (© **800/225-2277;** www.tickets.com).

PRO FOOTBALL

The **San Francisco 49ers** (www.sf49ers.com) play at Monster Park, Giants Drive and Gilman Avenue, on Sundays August through December; kickoff is usually at 1pm. Tickets sell out early in the season but are available at higher prices through ticket agents beforehand and from "scalpers" (illegal ticket-sellers who are usually at the gates). Ask your hotel concierge for the best way to track down tickets.

The 49ers' archenemies, the **Oakland Raiders** (www.raiders.com), play at McAfee Coliseum, off the I-880 freeway (Nimitz). Call © **800/RAIDERS** for ticket information.

COLLEGE FOOTBALL

The **University of California Golden Bears** play at Haas Pavilion, University of California, Berkeley (© **800/462-3277** or 510/642-3277; www.calbears.com), on the university campus across the bay. Tickets are usually available at game time. Phone for schedules and information.

HORSE RACING

Ten miles northeast of San Francisco is scenic **Golden Gate Fields,** Buchanan Street off I-80, Albany (© **510/559-7300;** www.golden gatefields.com). The racing schedule changes yearly; please call or check the website for current schedule and admission prices. The track is on the seashore.

11 The Shopping Scene

Like its population, San Francisco's shopping is both worldly and intimate. Every persuasion, style, era, and fetish is represented, not in big, tacky shopping malls, but in hundreds of quaint, dramatically different boutiques scattered throughout the city. Whether you're looking for Chanel or Chinese herbal medicine, San Francisco's got it. Just pick a neighborhood and break out your credit cards—you're sure to end up with at least a few take-home treasures

MAJOR SHOPPING AREAS

San Francisco has many shopping areas, but the following places are where you'll find most of the action.

UNION SQUARE & ENVIRONS   San Francisco's most congested and popular shopping mecca is centered on Union Square and bordered by Bush, Taylor, Market, and Montgomery streets. Most of the big department stores and many high-end specialty shops are here. Be sure to venture to Grant Avenue, Post and Sutter streets, and Maiden Lane. This area is a hub for public transportation; all Market Street and several other buses run here, as do the Powell–Hyde and Powell–Mason cable car lines. You can also take the Muni streetcar to the Powell Street station.

CHINATOWN   When you pass through the gate to Chinatown on Grant Avenue, say goodbye to the world of fashion and hello to a swarm of cheap tourist shops selling everything from linen and jade to plastic toys and $2 slippers. But that's not all Chinatown has to offer. The real gems are tucked away on side streets or are small, one-person shops selling Chinese herbs, original art, and jewelry. Grant

Avenue is the area's main thoroughfare, and the side streets between Bush Street and Columbus Avenue are full of restaurants, markets, and eclectic shops. Stockton Street is best for grocery shopping (including live fowl and fish). Walking is the way to get around, because traffic through this area is slow and parking is next to impossible. Most stores in Chinatown are open daily from 10am to 10pm. Take bus no. 1, 9X, 15, 30, 41, or 45.

UNION STREET Union Street, from Fillmore Street to Van Ness Avenue, caters to the upper-middle-class crowd. It's a great place to stroll, window-shop the plethora of boutiques, try the cafes and restaurants, and watch the beautiful people parade by. Take bus no. 22, 41, 45, 47, 49, or 76.

CHESTNUT STREET Parallel and a few blocks north, Chestnut is a younger version of Union Street. It holds endless shopping and dining choices, and an ever-tanned, superfit population of postgraduate singles who hang around cafes and scope each other out. Take bus no. 22, 28, 30, 43, or 76.

FILLMORE STREET Some of the best shopping in town is packed into 5 blocks of Fillmore Street in Pacific Heights. From Jackson to Sutter streets, Fillmore is the perfect place to grab a bite and peruse the high-priced boutiques, crafts shops, and incredible housewares stores. (Don't miss Zinc Details; p. 148.) Take bus no. 1, 2, 3, 4, 12, 22, or 24.

HAIGHT STREET Green hair, spiked hair, no hair, or mohair—even the hippies look conservative next to Haight Street's dramatic fashion freaks. The shopping in the 6 blocks of upper Haight Street between Central Avenue and Stanyan Street reflects its clientele. It offers everything from incense and European and American street styles to furniture and antique clothing. Bus nos. 6, 7, 66, and 71 run the length of Haight Street, and nos. 33 and 43 run through upper Haight Street. The Muni streetcar N line stops at Waller Street and Cole Street.

SOMA Although this area isn't suitable for strolling, you'll find almost all the discount shopping in warehouse spaces south of Market. You can pick up a discount-shopping guide at most major hotels. Many bus lines pass through this area.

HAYES VALLEY It's not the prettiest area in town, with some of the shadier housing projects a few blocks away. But while most neighborhoods cater to more conservative or trendy shoppers, lower Hayes Street, between Octavia and Gough streets, celebrates anything vintage,

---

Tips **Just the Facts: Hours, Taxes & Shipping**

Store hours are generally Monday through Saturday from 10am to 6pm and Sunday from noon to 5pm. Most department stores stay open later, as do shops around Fisherman's Wharf, the most heavily visited area (by tourists).

Sales tax in San Francisco is 8.5%, which is added on at the register for all goods and services purchased. If you live out of state and buy an expensive item, you might want to have the store ship it home for you. You'll have to pay for shipping, but you'll escape paying the sales tax.

Most of the city's shops can wrap your purchase and **ship** it anywhere in the world. If they can't, you can send it yourself, either through **UPS** (© 800/742-5877), **FedEx** (© 800/463-3339), or the U.S. Postal Service.

---

chic, artistic, or downright funky. With new shops opening frequently, it's definitely the most interesting new shopping area in town, with furniture and glass stores, thrift shops, trendy shoe stores, and men's and women's clothiers. You can find lots of great antiques shops south on Octavia and on nearby Market Street. Take bus no. 16AX, 16BX, or 21.

FISHERMAN'S WHARF & ENVIRONS *(Overrated* The tourist-oriented malls along Jefferson Street include hundreds of shops, restaurants, and attractions. Among them are Ghirardelli Square, PIER 39, The Cannery, and The Anchorage.

12 Shopping A to Z

ART
The San Francisco Bay Area Gallery Guide, a comprehensive, bimonthly publication listing the city's current shows, is available free by mail. Send a self-addressed, stamped envelope to San Francisco Bay Area Gallery Guide, 1369 Fulton St., San Francisco, CA 94117 (© 415/921-1600); or pick one up at the San Francisco Visitor Information Center at 900 Market St. Most of the city's major art galleries are clustered downtown in the Union Square area.

BOOKS
In addition to the listings below, there's a **Barnes & Noble** superstore at 2550 Taylor St., between Bay and North Point streets, near

San Francisco Shopping

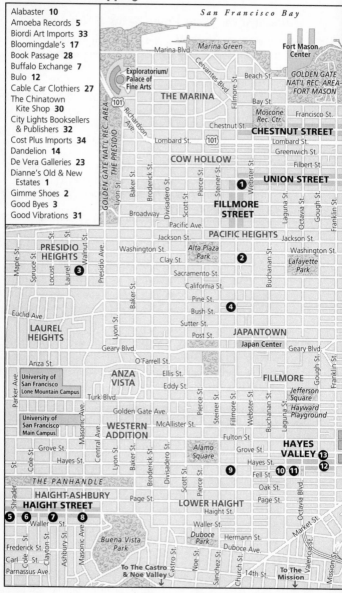

San Francisco Bay

Fort Mason Center

Marina Blvd   Marina Green

GOLDEN GATE NAT'L REC. AREA—FORT MASON

Cervantes Blvd.

Beach St.

Exploratorium/
Palace of
Fine Arts

THE MARINA

Bay St.

Moscone
Rec. Ctr.   Francisco St.

Richardson Ave.

(101)

Chestnut St.   CHESTNUT STREET

Lombard St.

Lombard St.

Greenwich St.

COW HOLLOW

Filbert St.

UNION STREET

Broadway   Pacific Ave.

FILLMORE
STREET

PACIFIC HEIGHTS   Jackson St.

PRESIDIO
HEIGHTS

Washington St.   Alta Plaza
Park

Washington St.
Lafayette
Park

Clay St.

Sacramento St.

California St.

LAUREL
HEIGHTS

Pine St.

Euclid Ave.

Bush St.

Sutter St.

Post St.   JAPANTOWN

Geary Blvd.   Japan Center   Geary Blvd.

Anza St.   O'Farrell St.

University of
San Francisco
Lone Mountain Campus

ANZA
VISTA

Ellis St.

Eddy St.

FILLMORE
Jefferson
Square

Turk Blvd.

Hayward
Playground

University of
San Francisco
Main Campus

Golden Gate Ave.

WESTERN
ADDITION

McAllister St.

Fulton St.

Grove St.   Grove St.   HAYES
VALLEY

Hayes St.

THE PANHANDLE

Alamo
Square

Hayes St.

Fell St.

Oak St.

HAIGHT-ASHBURY   Page St.   Page St.

HAIGHT STREET   LOWER HAIGHT

Waller St.   Haight St.

Waller St.

Frederick St.   Buena Vista
Park   Duboce
Park   Hermann St.

Carl St.   Duboce Ave.

Parnassus Ave.   To The Castro
& Noe Valley   14th St.   To The
Mission

Gump's **24**
H & M **19**
Jeanine Payer **18**
Jeremys **15**
La Rosa **6**
MAC **13**
Macy's **20**
Métier **26**
Neiman Marcus **22**
Niketown **25**
Nordstrom **17**
Paolo Shoes **9**
Pearl & Jade Empire **21**
Propeller **11**
Recycled Records **8**
SFMOMA
  MuseumStore **16**
Virgin Megastore **18**
Wilkes Bashford **26**
The Wok Shop **29**
Zinc Details **4**

Fisherman's Wharf (© **415/292-6762**); and a four-storied **Borders** at 400 Post St., at Union Square (© **415/399-1633**).

Book Passage If you're moseying through the Ferry Building Marketplace, drop into this cozy independent that emphasizes (for tourists and locals alike) local travel, boating on the Bay, food, cooking, sustainable agriculture and ecology, fiction, culinary and regional history and literature, and photo and gift books about the Bay Area. The store also hosts lots of author events: Check their website for details. Ferry Building Marketplace (at The Embarcadero and Market St.). © 415/835-1020. www.bookpassage.com.

The Booksmith Haight Street's best selection of new books is in this large, well-maintained shop. It carries all the top titles, along with works from smaller presses, and more than 1,000 different magazines. 1644 Haight St. (btw. Clayton and Cole sts.). © **800/493-7323** or 415/863-8688.

City Lights Booksellers & Publishers *(Finds* Brooding literary types browse this famous bookstore owned by Lawrence Ferlinghetti, the renowned Beat Generation poet. The three-level bookshop prides itself on a comprehensive collection of art, poetry, and political paperbacks, as well as more mainstream books. Open daily until midnight. 261 Columbus Ave. (at Broadway). © **415/362-8193**. www.citylights.com.

CHINA, SILVER & GLASS

Gump's *(Finds* Founded over a century ago, Gump's offers gifts and treasures ranging from Asian antiquities to contemporary art glass and exquisite jade and pearl jewelry. Many items are made specifically for the store. Gump's also has one of the city's most revered holiday window displays and is a huge wedding registry destination, though the staff can act very affected. 135 Post St. (btw. Kearny St. and Grant Ave.). © **800/766-7628** or 415/982-1616. www.gumps.com.

DEPARTMENT STORES (DOWNTOWN)

Bloomingdale's This massive 338,550-square-foot department store is the anchor of the Westfield San Francisco Centre at Fifth and Market streets (see "Major Shopping Areas" on p. 139). It's the largest Bloomies outside of New York's flagship 59th Street store, and even sports the same black-and-white polished checkerboard marble. It's owned by the same company that runs Macy's, but fashions—for both men and women—tend to be more forward. Highlights include '60s-inspired fashions by Biba, knitwear by Sonia Rykiel, handbags by Louis Vuitton, and absurdly expensive shoes by Jimmy Choo. 845 Market St. (at Fifth St.). ✆ **415/856-5300.** www.bloomingdales.com.

Macy's The seven-story Macy's West features contemporary fashions for women, juniors, and children, plus jewelry, fragrances, cosmetics, and accessories. The sixth floor offers a "hospitality suite" where visitors can leave their coats and packages, grab a cup of coffee, or find out more about the city from the concierge. The top floors contain home furnishings, and the Cellar sells kitchenware and gourmet foods. You'll even find a Boudin Cafe (though the food is not as good compared to their food at other locations) and a Wolfgang Puck Cafe on the premises. Across the street, Macy's East has five floors of men's fashions. Stockton and O'Farrell sts., Union Sq. ✆ **415/397-3333.**

Neiman Marcus Some call this Texas-based chain "Needless Mark-ups." But those who can afford the best of everything can't deny that the men's and women's clothes, precious gems, and conservative formalwear are some of the most glamorous in town. Recently renovated along with the rest of the store, the Rotunda Restaurant, on the fourth floor, is a beautiful place for lunch and afternoon tea. 150 Stockton St. (btw. Geary and O'Farrell sts.), Union Sq. ✆ **415/362-3900.**

Nordstrom Located in the newly renovated San Francisco Shopping Centre (see "Major Shopping Areas" on p. 139), Nordstrom is renowned for its personalized service. Equally devoted to women's and men's fashions, the store has one of the best shoe selections in the city and thousands of suits in stock. The Bistro, on the fourth floor, has a panoramic view and is ideal for an inexpensive lunch or light snack. Spa Nordstrom, on the fifth floor, is the perfect place to relax after a hectic day of bargain hunting. 865 Market St. (at Fifth St.). ✆ **415/243-8500.**

DISCOUNT SHOPPING

Jeremys *Value* This boutique is a serious mecca for fashion hounds thanks to the wide array of top designer fashions, from shoes to suits, at rock-bottom prices. There are no cheap knockoffs here, just good men's and women's clothes and accessories that the owner scoops up from major retailers who are either updating merchandise or discarding returns. 2 S. Park (btw. Bryant and Brannan sts. at Second St.). ✆ **415/882-4929.** www.jeremys.com.

FASHION

See also "Vintage Clothing," later in this section.

MEN'S FASHIONS

Cable Car Clothiers   Dapper men head to this fashion institution for traditional attire, such as three-button suits with natural shoulders, Aquascutum coats, McGeorge sweaters, and Atkinson ties. Closed Sundays. 200 Bush St. (at Sansome St.). ✆ **415/397-4740.** www.cable carclothiers.com.

UNISEX

H & M   This ever-trendy and cheap Swedish clothing chain opened in Union Square at the end of 2004, and had lines out the door all through the holiday season—and not just for their collection by Stella McCartney. Drop in anytime for trendy cuts and styles sure to satisfy the hip him and her along on the trip. 150 Powell St. (btw. Ellis and O'Farrell sts.). ✆ **415/986-4215.**

MAC *(Finds*   No, we're not talking cosmetics. The more-modern-than-corporate stock at this hip and hidden shop (Modern Apparel Clothing) just combined its men's and women's fashion meccas in a new space next door to pastry pit stop Citizen Cake. Drop in for men's imported tailored suits and women's separates in new and intriguing fabrics as well as gorgeous ties, vibrant sweaters, and a few choice home accouterments. Lines include Belgium's Dries Van Noten and Martin Margiela, New York's John Bartlett, and local sweater sweetheart Laurie B. The best part? Prices are more reasonable than at many of the trendy clothing stores in the area. 387 Grove St. (at Gough St.). ✆ **415/863-3011.**

Niketown   Here it's not "I can," but "I can spend." At least that's what the kings of sportswear were banking on when they opened this megastore in 1997. As you'd expect, inside the doors shoppers find themselves in a Nike world offering everything the merchandising team could create. 278 Post St. (at Stockton St.). ✆ **415/392-6453.**

Wilkes Bashford *(Finds*   Wilkes Bashford is one of the most expensive and best-known clothing stores in the city. In its 3-plus decades in business, the boutique has garnered a reputation for stocking only the finest clothes in the world (which can often be seen on ex-Mayor Willie Brown and current Mayor Gavin Newsom, who do their suit shopping here). Most fashions come from Italy and France; they include women's designer sportswear and couture and men's Kiton and Brioni suits (at $2,500 and up, they're considered the most expensive suits in the world). Closed Sundays. 375 Sutter St. (at Stockton St.). ✆ **415/986-4380.** www.wilkesbashford.com.

WOMEN'S FASHIONS

Métier *(Finds)*   Discerning and well-funded shoppers consider this the best women's clothing shop in town. Within its walls you'll find classic, sophisticated, and expensive creations, which include European ready-to-wear lines and designers: fashions by Italian designers Anna Molinari, Hache, and Blumarine and by French designer Martine Sitbon. You will also find a distinguished collection of antique-style, high-end jewelry from L.A.'s Cathy Waterman as well as ultrapopular custom-designed poetry jewelry by Jeanine Payer. Closed Sunday. 355 Sutter St. (btw. Stockton and Grant sts.). ✆ 415/989-5395. www.metiersf.com.

RAG *(Finds)*   If you want to add some truly unique San Francisco designs to your closet, head to RAG, or Residents Apparel Gallery, a co-op shop where around 55 local emerging designers showcase their latest creations. Prices are great; fashions are forward, young, and hip; and if you grab a few pieces, no one at home's going to be able to copy your look. 541 Octavia St. (at Hayes St.). ✆ 415/621-7718. www.ragsf.com.

GIFTS

Dandelion *(Finds)*   Tucked in an out-of-the-way location in SoMa is the most wonderful collection of gifts, collectibles, and furnishings. There's something for every taste and budget here, from an excellent collection of teapots, decorative dishes, and gourmet foods to silver, books, cards, and picture frames. Don't miss the Zen-like second floor, with its peaceful furnishings in Indian, Japanese, and Western styles. The store is closed Sunday and Monday except during November and December, when it's open daily. Hours are 10am to 6pm. 55 Potrero Ave. (at Alameda St.). ✆ 415/436-9500. www.tampopo.com.

Good Vibrations   A laypersons' sex-toy, book, and video emporium, Good Vibrations is a women-owned, worker-owned cooperative. Unlike most sex shops, it's not a back-alley business, but a straightforward shop with healthy, open attitudes about human sexuality. It also has a vibrator museum. 603 Valencia St. (at 17th St.). ✆ 415/522-5460 or 800/BUY-VIBE (for mail order). www.goodvibes.com. A second location is at 1620 Polk St. (at Sacramento St., ✆ 415/345-0400); and a third is at 2504 San Pablo Ave., Berkeley (✆ 510/841-8987).

SFMOMA MuseumStore *(Finds)*   With an array of artistic cards, books, jewelry, housewares, furniture, knickknacks, and creative tokens of San Francisco, it's virtually impossible not to find something here you'll consider a must-have. (Check out the FogDome!)

Aside from being one of the locals' favorite shops, it offers far more tasteful mementos than most Fisherman's Wharf options. Open late (until 9:30pm) on Thursday nights. 151 Third St. (2 blocks south of Market St., across from Yerba Buena Gardens). ✆ 415/357-4035. www.sfmoma.org.

HOUSEWARES/FURNISHINGS

Alabaster *Finds* Any interior designer who knows Biedermeier from Bauhaus knows that this Hayes Valley shop sets local home accessories trends with its collection of high-end must-haves. Their selection includes everything from lighting—antique and modern Alabaster fixtures, Fortuny silk shades, Venetian glass chandeliers—to other home accessories, like one-of-a-kind antiques, body products from Florence, and more. 597 Hayes St. (at Laguna St.). ✆ 415/558-0482. www.alabastersf.com.

Biordi Art Imports *Finds* Whether you want to decorate your dinner table, color your kitchen, or liven up the living room, Biordi's Italian majolica pottery is the most exquisite and unusual way to do it. The owner has been importing these hand-painted collectibles for 60 years, and every piece is a showstopper. Call for a catalog. They'll ship anywhere. Closed Sundays. 412 Columbus Ave. (at Vallejo St.). ✆ 415/392-8096. www.biordi.com.

Propeller *Finds* This airy skylight-lit shop is a must-stop for lovers of the latest in übermodern furniture and home accessories. Owner/designer Lorn Dittfeld handpicks pieces done by emerging designers from as far away as Sweden, Italy, and Canada as well as a plethora of national newbies. Drop in to lounge on the hippest sofas; grab pretty and practical gifts like ultracool magnetic spice racks; or adorn your home with Bev Hisey's throws and graphic pillows, diamond-cut wood tables by William Earle, or hand-tufted graphic rugs by Angela Adams. 555 Hayes St. (btw. Laguna and Octavia sts.). ✆ 415/701-7767. www.propeller-sf.com.

The Wok Shop This shop has every conceivable implement for Chinese cooking, including woks, brushes, cleavers, circular chopping blocks, dishes, oyster knives, bamboo steamers, and strainers. It also sells a wide range of kitchen utensils, baskets, handmade linens from China, and aprons. 718 Grant Ave. (at Clay St.). ✆ 415/989-3797 or 888/780-7171 for mail order. www.wokshop.com.

Zinc Details *Finds* This contemporary furniture and knickknack shop has received accolades everywhere from *Elle Decor Japan* to *Metropolitan Home* to *InStyle* for its amazing collection of glass vases, pendant lights, ceramics from all over the world, and furniture from local craftspeople. A portion of these true works of art is made specifically for the store. While you're in the 'hood, check out their new sister store around the corner at 2410 California St. (© **415/776-9002**), which showcases contemporary designer furniture. 1905 Fillmore St. (btw. Bush and Pine sts.). © **415/776-2100**. www.zincdetails.com.

JEWELRY

De Vera Galleries *(Finds)*   Don't come here unless you've got money to spend. Designer Federico de Vera's unique rough-stone jewelry collection, art glass, and vintage knickknacks are too beautiful to pass up and too expensive to be a painless purchase. Still, if you're looking for a keepsake, you'll find it here. Closed Sunday and Monday. 29 Maiden Lane (at Kearny St.). © **415/788-0828**. www.deveraobjects.com.

Dianne's Old & New Estates   Many local girls get engagement rings from this fantastic little shop featuring top-of-the-line antique jewelry—pendants, diamond rings, necklaces, bracelets, and pearls. For a special gift, check out the collection of platinum wedding and engagement rings and vintage watches. Don't worry if you can't afford it now—the shop offers 1-year interest-free layaway. And, if you buy a ring, they'll send you off with a thank-you bottle of celebration bubbly. 2181A Union St. (at Fillmore St.). © **888/346-7525** or 415/346-7525. www.diannesestatejewelry.com.

Jeanine Payer   If you want to buy a trinket that is truly San Franciscan, stop by this boutique hidden on the street level of the beautifully ornate Phelan Building where designer Jeanine Payer showcases gorgeous, handmade contemporary jewelry that she crafts in sterling silver and 18-karat gold five stories above in her studio. All of her pieces, including fabulous baby gifts, sport engraved poetry—and can even be custom done. Sound familiar? Not surprising. Celebrities such as Sheryl Crow, Debra Messing, and Ellen DeGeneres are fans. 760 Market St., Suite 533 (at O'Farrell St.). © **415/788-2414**. www.jeaninepayer.com.

Pearl & Jade Empire   The Pearl & Jade Empire has been importing jewelry from all over the world since 1957. It specializes in unusual pearls and jade and offers restringing on the premises as well as boasts a collection of amber from the Baltic Sea. 427 Post St. (btw. Powell and Mason sts.). © **415/362-0606**. www.pearlempire.com.

MUSIC

Amoeba Records   Don't be scared off by the tattooed, pierced, and fierce-looking employees (and other shoppers!) in this beloved new and used record store highlighting indie labels. They're actually more than happy to recommend some great music to you. If you're looking for the latest from Britney, this might not be the store for you (though they *do* have everything), but if you're into interesting music that's not necessarily on every station all the time, check this place out. You can buy, sell, and trade in this cavernous, loud Haight Street hot spot. 1855 Haight St. (btw. Shrader and Stanyan sts.). ☎ **415/831-1200.**

Recycled Records *(Finds)*   Easily one of the best used-record stores in the city, this loud shop in the Haight has cases of used "classic" rock LPs, sheet music, and tour programs. It's open from 10am to 8pm daily. 1377 Haight St. (btw. Central and Masonic sts.). ☎ **415/626-4075.** www.recycled-records.com.

Virgin Megastore   With thousands of CDs, including an impressive collection of imports, videos, DVDs, a multimedia department, a cafe, and related books, this enormous Union Square store can make any music-lover blow his or her entire vacation fund. It's open Sunday through Thursday from 10am to 11pm and Friday and Saturday from 10am to midnight. 2 Stockton St. (at Market St.). ☎ **415/397-4525.**

SHOES

Bulo   If you have a fetish for foot fashions, you must check out Bulo, which carries nothing but imported Italian shoes. The selection is small but styles run the gamut, from casual to dressy, reserved to wildly funky. New shipments come in every 3 to 4 weeks, so the selection is ever-changing, eternally hip, and, unfortunately, ever-expensive, with many pairs going for close to $200. Men's and women's store: 437A Hayes St. (at Gough St.). ☎ **415/864-3244.** Women's store: across the street, at 418 Hayes St. (☎ **415/255-4939**). www.buloshoes.com.

Gimme Shoes   The staff is funky-fashion snobby, the prices are steep, and the European shoes and accessories are utterly chic. 2358 Fillmore St. (at Washington St.). ☎ **415/441-3040.** Additional location at 416 Hayes St. (☎ **415/864-0691**). www.gimmeshoes.com.

Paolo Shoes   This Italian import store is run by owner Paolo Iantorno, who actually designs the shoes for his hipster shops. If gorgeous, handcrafted, colorful shoes are what you're looking for, this is the shop for you. You can get your low-heeled slip-ons here—this store features men's and women's footwear and bags—but they might be in silver python. Check out the men's perforated orange slip-ons—not for the faint of heart or fashion-modest. You might not even mind that many shoes are upwards of 200 bucks when you realize that Paolo's women's shoes are so sexy and comfortable, you won't want to take them off. 524 Hayes St. © **415/552-4580.** A second location is at 2000 Fillmore St. ((© **415/771-1944**). www.paoloshoes.com.

TOYS

The Chinatown Kite Shop   This shop's playful assortment of flying objects includes attractive fish kites, windsocks, hand-painted Chinese paper kites, wood-and-paper biplanes, pentagonal kites, and do-it-yourself kite kits, all of which make great souvenirs or decorations. Computer-designed stunt kites have two or four control lines to manipulate loops and dives. Open daily from 10am to 8pm. 717 Grant Ave. (btw. Clay and Sacramento sts.). © **415/391-8217.** www.chinatown kite.com.

VINTAGE CLOTHING

Buffalo Exchange   This large and newly expanded storefront on upper Haight Street is crammed with racks of antique and new fashions from the 1960s, 1970s, and 1980s. It stocks everything from suits and dresses to neckties, hats, handbags, and jewelry. Buffalo Exchange anticipates some of the hottest new street fashions. 1555 Haight St. (btw. Clayton and Ashbury sts.). © **415/431-7733.** A second shop is at 1210 Valencia St., at 24th St. ((© **415/647-8332**). www.buffaloexchange.com.

Good Byes *(Finds*   One of the best new- and used-clothes stores in San Francisco, Good Byes carries only high-quality clothing and accessories, including an exceptional selection of men's fashions at unbelievably low prices (for example, $350 pre-owned shoes for $35). Women's wear is in a separate boutique across the street. 3464 Sacramento St. and 3483 Sacramento St. (btw. Laurel and Walnut sts.). © **415/346-6388.** www.goodbyessf.com.

La Rosa   On a street packed with vintage-clothing shops, this is one of the more upscale options. Since 1978, it has featured a selection of high-quality, dry-cleaned secondhand goods. Formal suits and dresses are its specialty, but you'll also find sport coats, slacks, and shoes. The more moderately priced sister store, **Held Over,** is located at 1543 Haight St., near Ashbury (© **415/864-0818**); and their discount store, **Clothes Contact,** is located at 473 Valencia St., at 16th St. (© **415/621-3212**). 1711 Haight St. (at Cole St.). © **415/668-3744.**

5

San Francisco After Dark

For a city with fewer than a million inhabitants, San Francisco boasts an impressive after-dark scene. Dozens of piano bars and top-notch lounges augment a lively dance-club culture, and skyscraper lounges offer dazzling city views. The city's arts scene is also extraordinary: The opera is justifiably world renowned, the ballet is on its toes, and theaters are high in both quantity and quality. In short, there's always something going on in the city, and unlike in Los Angeles or New York you don't have to pay outrageous cover charges or be "picked" to be a part of the scene.

For up-to-date nightlife information, turn to *San Francisco Weekly* (www.sfweekly.com) and the *San Francisco Bay Guardian* (www.sfbg.com), both of which run comprehensive listings. They are available free at bars and restaurants and from street-corner boxes all around the city. *Where* (www.wheresf.com), a free tourist-oriented monthly, also lists programs and performance times; it's available in most of the city's finer hotels. The Sunday edition of the *San Francisco Chronicle* features a "Datebook" section, printed on pink paper, with information on and listings of the week's events. If you have Internet access, it's a good idea to check out www.citysearch.com or www.sfstation.com for the latest in bars, clubs, and events. And if you want to secure seats at a hot-ticket event, either buy well in advance or contact the concierge of your hotel and see if they can swing something for you.

Tix Bay Area (also known as **TIX**; ✆ **415/433-7827;** www.tixbayarea.org) sells half-price tickets on the day of performance and full-price tickets in advance to select Bay Area cultural and sporting events. TIX is also a Ticketmaster outlet and sells Gray Line tours and transportation passes. Tickets are primarily sold in person with some half-price tickets available on their website. To find out which shows have half-price tickets, call the TIX info line or check out their website. A service charge, ranging from $1.75 to $6, is levied on each ticket depending on its full price. You can pay with cash, traveler's checks, Visa, MasterCard, American Express, or Discover Card with photo ID. TIX, located on Powell Street between Geary and Post streets, is open Tuesday through Thursday from 11am to 6pm, Friday from 11am to 7pm, Saturday from 10am to 7pm, and Sunday from 10am to 3pm. *Note:* Half-price tickets go on sale at 11am.

You can also get tickets to most theater and dance events through **City Box Office,** 180 Redwood St., Suite 100, between Golden Gate and McAllister streets off Van Ness Avenue (© **415/392-4400;** www.cityboxoffice.com). MasterCard and Visa are accepted.

Tickets.com (© **800/225-2277;** www.tickets.com) sells computer-generated tickets (with a hefty service charge of $3–$19 per ticket!) to concerts, sporting events, plays, and special events. **Ticketmaster** (© **415/421-TIXS;** www.ticketmaster.com) also offers advance ticket purchases (also with a service charge).

For information on local theater, check out **www.theatrebay area.org**. For information on major league baseball, pro basketball, pro and college football, and horse racing, see the "Spectator Sports" section of chapter 4, beginning on p. 138.

And don't forget that this isn't New York: Bars close at 2am, so get an early start if you want a full night on the town in San Francisco.

1 The Performing Arts

Special concerts and performances take place in San Francisco year-round. **San Francisco Performances,** 500 Sutter St., Suite 710 (© **415/398-6449;** www.performances.org), has brought acclaimed artists to the Bay Area for 27 years. Shows run the gamut from chamber music to dance to jazz. Performances are in several venues, including the Herbst Theater and the Yerba Buena Center for the Arts. The season runs from late September to June. Tickets cost from $12 to $50 and are available through **City Box Office** (© **415/392-4400**) or through the San Francisco Performances website.

CLASSICAL MUSIC

Philharmonia Baroque Orchestra   This orchestra of baroque, classical, and "early Romantic" music performs in San Francisco and all around the Bay Area. The season lasts September through April. Performing in Herbst Theater, 401 Van Ness Ave. Tickets are sold through City Box Office, © 415/392-4400 (box office), or call 415/252-1288 (administrative offices). www.philharmonia.org. Tickets $29–$67.

San Francisco Symphony   Founded in 1911, the internationally respected San Francisco Symphony has long been an important part

San Francisco After Dark

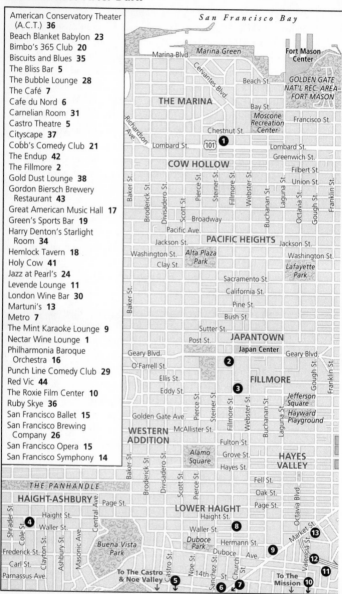

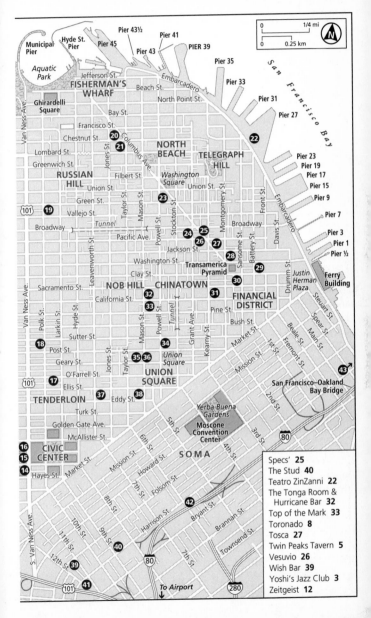

Specs' **25**
The Stud **40**
Teatro ZinZanni **22**
The Tonga Room &
   Hurricane Bar **32**
Top of the Mark **33**
Toronado **8**
Tosca **27**
Twin Peaks Tavern **5**
Vesuvio **26**
Wish Bar **39**
Yoshi's Jazz Club **3**
Zeitgeist **12**

of the city's cultural life under such legendary conductors as Pierre Monteux and Seiji Ozawa. In 1995, Michael Tilson Thomas took over from Herbert Blomstedt; he has led the orchestra to new heights and crafted an exciting repertoire of classical and modern music. The season runs September through June. Summer symphony activities include a Summer Festival and a Summer in the City series. Tickets are very hard to come by, but if you're desperate, you can usually pick up a few outside the hall the night of the concert. Also, the box office occasionally has a few last-minute tickets. Performing at Davies Symphony Hall, 201 Van Ness Ave. (at Grove St.). ℂ 415/864-6000 (box office). www.sf symphony.org. Tickets $25–$114.

OPERA

San Francisco Opera The San Francisco Opera was the second municipal opera in the United States and is one of the city's cultural icons. Brilliantly balanced casts may feature celebrated stars like Frederica Von Stade and Plácido Domingo along with promising newcomers and regular members in productions that range from traditional to avant-garde. All productions have English supertitles. The season starts in September, lasts 14 weeks, takes a break for a few months, and then picks up again in June and July. During the interim winter period, future opera stars are featured in showcases and recitals. Performances are held most evenings, except Monday, with matinees on Sunday. Tickets go on sale as early as June for subscribers and August for the general public, and the best seats sell out quickly. Unless Domingo is in town, some less coveted seats are usually available until curtain time. War Memorial Opera House, 301 Van Ness Ave. (at Grove St.). ℂ 415/864-3330 (box office). www.sfopera.com. Tickets $24–$235; standing room $10 cash only; student rush $15 cash only.

THEATER

American Conservatory Theater (A.C.T.) *Finds* The Tony Award–winning American Conservatory Theater made its debut in 1967 and quickly established itself as the city's premier resident theater group and one of the nation's best. The A.C.T. season runs September through July and features both classic and experimental works. Its home is the fabulous **Geary Theater,** a national historic landmark that is regarded as one of America's finest performance spaces. The 2006–2007 season marked A.C.T.'s 40th anniversary; they haven't been resting on their laurels. In their 4-decade history, they've reached a combined audience of seven million people. Performing at the Geary

Tips Dinner Party

Hungry for dinner and a damned good time? It ain't cheap, but Teatro ZinZanni is a rollicking ride of food, whimsy, drama, and song within a stunningly elegant 1926 spiegeltent on The Embarcadero. Part musical theater and part comedy show, the 3-hour dinner theater includes a surprisingly decent five-course meal served by dozens of performers who weave both the audience and astounding physical acts (think Cirque du Soleil) into their wacky and playful world. Anyone in need of a night of lighthearted laughter should definitely book a table here. Shows are held Wednesday through Sunday and tickets are $123 to $147 including dinner. The tent is located at Pier 29 on The Embarcadero at Battery Street. Call © 415/438-2668 or see www.zinzanni.org for more details.

Theater, 415 Geary St. (at Mason St.). © 415/749-2ACT. www.act-sf.org. Tickets $14–$82.

DANCE

San Francisco Ballet   Founded in 1933, the San Francisco Ballet is the oldest professional ballet company in the United States and is regarded as one of the country's finest. It performs an eclectic repertoire of full-length, neoclassical and contemporary ballets. The Repertory Season generally runs February through May; the company performs the *Nutcracker* in December. The San Francisco Ballet Orchestra accompanies most performances. War Memorial Opera House, 301 Van Ness Ave. (at Grove St.). © 415/865-2000 for tickets and information. www.sfballet.org. Tickets $10–$205.

2 Comedy & Cabaret

Beach Blanket Babylon *Moments*   A San Francisco tradition, *Beach Blanket Babylon* evolved from Steve Silver's Rent-a-Freak service—a group of "party guests" extraordinaire who hired themselves out as a "cast of characters" complete with fabulous costumes and sets, props, and gags. After their act caught on, it moved into the Savoy-Tivoli, a North Beach bar. By 1974, the audience had grown too large for the facility, and *Beach Blanket* has been at the 400-seat Club Fugazi ever since. The show is a comedic musical send-up that is best known for outrageous costumes and oversize headdresses. It's been playing for over 30 years, and almost every performance sells out. The show is updated often enough that locals still attend. Those under 21 are welcome at both Sunday matinees (2 and 5pm), when no alcohol is served; photo ID is required for evening performances. Write for weekend tickets at least 3 weeks in advance, or get them through their website or by calling their box office. *Note:* Only a handful of tickets per show are assigned seating; all other tickets are within specific sections depending on price, but seating is first-come, first-seated within that section. Performances are Wednesday and Thursday at 8pm, Friday and Saturday at 7 and 10pm, and Sunday at 2 and 5pm. At Club Fugazi, Beach Blanket Babylon Blvd., 678 Green St. (btw. Powell St. and Columbus Ave.). ℂ 415/421-4222. www.beachblanketbabylon. com. Tickets $25–$78.

Cobb's Comedy Club   Cobb's features such national headliners as Joe Rogan, Brian Regan, and Jake Johannsen. Comedy reigns Wednesday through Sunday, including a 15-comedian All-Pro Wednesday showcase (a 3-hr. marathon). Cobb's is open to those 18 and over, and occasionally to kids 16 and 17 when accompanied by a parent or legal guardian (call ahead). Shows are held Wednesday, Thursday, and Sunday at 8pm, Friday and Saturday at 8 and 10:15pm. 915 Columbus Ave. (at Lombard St.). ℂ 415/928-4320. www.cobbs comedy.com. Cover $13–$35. 2-beverage minimum.

Punch Line Comedy Club   Adjacent to The Embarcadero One office building, this is the largest comedy nightclub in the city. Three-person shows with top national and local talent are featured here Tuesday through Saturday. Showcase night is Sunday, when 15 comics take the mic. There's an all-star showcase or a special event on Monday. Doors always open at 7pm and shows are Sunday through Thursday at 8pm, Friday and Saturday at 8 and 10pm (18 and over; two-drink minimum). They serve a full menu Thursday through Saturday (think wings, chicken sandwiches, and curiously, ravioli), and pizzas, appetizers, and salads Sunday through Wednesday. 444 Battery St. (btw. Washington and Clay sts.), plaza level. ℂ 415/397-4337 or 415/397-7573 for recorded information. www.punchlinecomedyclub.com. Cover Sun–Mon $7.50; Tues–Thurs $13–$15, Fri and Sat $18–$20. Prices are subject to change for more popular comics, maxing out at a price of $45.

3 The Club & Music Scene

ROCK & BLUES CLUBS

In addition to the following listings, see "Dance Clubs," below, for (usually) live, danceable rock.

Bimbo's 365 Club 𝕽𝕽   Originally located on Market Street when it opened in 1931, this North Beach destination is a fabulous spot to catch outstanding live rock and jazz (think Chris Isaak and the Brian Setzer Orchestra) and dance amid glamorous surroundings. Grab tickets in advance at the box office, which is open Monday through Friday, 10am to 4pm. 1025 Columbus Ave. (at Chestnut St.). ℭ 415/474-0365. www.bimbos365club.com.

Biscuits and Blues   With a crisp, blow-your-eardrums-out sound system, New Orleans–speak-easy (albeit commercial) appeal, and a nightly lineup of live, national acts, there's no better place to muse the blues than this basement-cum-nightclub. From 7pm on, they serve drink specials, along with their signature fried chicken; namesake moist, flaky biscuits; some new small-plate entrees dubbed "Southern tapas"; and a newly expanded wine list. Menu items range from $7.95 to $17. 401 Mason (at Geary St.). ℭ 415/292-2583. www.biscuits andblues.com. Cover (during performances) $10–$20.

Cafe du Nord *(Finds*   If you like you clubs dim, sexy, and with a heavy dose of old-school ambience, boy will you dig Café du Nord. This subterranean supper club has rightfully self-proclaimed itself as the place for a "slightly lurid indie pop scene set in a beautiful old 1907 speakeasy." It's also where an eclectic crowd gathers to linger at the front room's 40-foot mahogany bar, or dine on the likes of panko-crusted prawns and blackened mahi-mahi. The small stage hosts an eclectic mix of local and visiting artists ranging from Shelby Lynne (country) to the Dickdusters (punk) and local favorite Ledisi (R&B). 2170 Market St. (at Sanchez St.). ℭ 415/861-5016. www.cafedunord. com. Cover $5–$25. Food $5–$15.

The Fillmore *(Finds*   Made famous by promoter Bill Graham in the 1960s, The Fillmore showcases big names in a moderately sized standing-room-only space. Check listings in papers, call the theater, or visit their website for information on upcoming events. And if you make it to a show, check out the fabulous collection of vintage concert posters chronicling the hall's history. 1805 Geary Blvd. (at Fillmore St.). ℭ 415/346-6000. www.thefillmore.com. Tickets $17–$45.

Great American Music Hall 𝕽𝕽   Built in 1907 as a restaurant/bordello, the Great American Music Hall is likely one of the most gorgeous rock venues you'll encounter. With ornately carved balconies, frescoed ceilings, marble columns, and huge hanging light fixtures, you won't know whether to marvel at the structure or watch the acts, which have ranged from Duke Ellington and Sarah Vaughan to Arctic Monkeys, The Radiators, and She Wants Revenge. All shows are all ages (6 and up) so you can bring your family, too. You can buy a ticket for just the show and order bar snacks (such as nachos, black bean and cheese flautas, burgers, and sandwiches); or buy a ticket that includes a complete dinner (an extra $25), which changes nightly but always includes a salad and choice of meat, fish, or veggie entree. Alas, you can't buy your ticket via telephone, but you can download a form from their website and fax it to **415/885-5075** with your Visa or MasterCard info; there is a service charge of $2 per ticket. You can also stop by the box office to purchase tickets directly ($1 service charge), or buy them at virtuous.com or Tickets.com (✆ **800/225-2277**). Valet parking is available for selects shows; check website for additional parking information. 859 O'Farrell (btw. Polk and Larkin sts.). ✆ 415/885-0750. www.musichallsf.com. Ticket prices and starting times vary; call or check website for individual show information.

JAZZ & LATIN CLUBS

Jazz at Pearl's   Touted as the city's Best Jazz Club by the *San Francisco Chronicle,* Jazz at Pearl's combines a cool 1930s vibe, great live music, and excellent seating throughout this intimate North Beach venue. With a variety of jazz, blues, and Latin recording artists playing nightly there's something for everyone at this all-ages club. However, with only 25 tables, advance purchase of tickets is highly recommended. Shows start at 8 and 10pm nightly; doors open at 7:30pm. Tickets range from $25 to $150 for VIP seating, which includes preferred seating for both shows, a bottle of champagne, and a signed CD and meet-and-greet with the artist. *Note:* There's a 2-drink minimum. 256 Columbus Ave. (at Broadway). ✆ 415/291-8255. www.jazzatpearls.com.

Yoshi's Jazz Club 🎔🎔   What started out in 1977 as a modest sushi and jazz club in Oakland has become one of the most respected jazz venues in the world: Yoshi's. For more than 3 decades SF locals had to cross the Bay Bridge to listen to Stanton Moore, Branford Marsalis, and Diana Krall in such an intimate setting. With the grand opening of Yoshi's in San Francisco's Fillmore District, now locals can take a taxi. The two-story, 28,000-square-foot, state-of-the-art jazz venue features the finest local, national, and international jazz artists, as well as first-rate Japanese cuisine at the adjoining restaurant. The elegant club is awash in gleaming dark and blond woods, big sculptural Japanese lanterns, and sensuously curved walls that envelop the intimate stage. Don't worry about the seating chart; there's not a bad seat in the house. It's the perfect place for a romantic date that starts with hamachi and ends with Harry Connick Jr., so be sure to check Yoshi's website to see who is playing while you're in town and make reservations ASAP—you'll be glad you did. 1330 Fillmore St. (at Eddy St.). ✆ 415/655-5600. www.yoshis.com.

DANCE CLUBS

Although a lot of clubs allow dancing, the following are the places to go if all you want to do is shake your groove thang.

Holy Cow   Its motto, "Never a cover, always a party" has been the case since 1987 when this industrial SoMa nightclub opened. The local clubbers rarely come here anymore, but it's still a reliable place for tourists and geezers like me who want to break a sweat on the dance floor to DJs spinning club classics and top 40. Nightly drink specials make it difficult to leave sober, so plan your transportation accordingly. *Note:* The bar's only open Thursday through Saturday form 9pm to 2am. 1535 Folsom St. (btw. 11th and 12th sts.). ✆ 415/621-6087. www.theholycow.com.

Ruby Skye   Downtown's most glamorous and colossal nightspot led a previous life as an 1890s Victorian playhouse, and many of the beautiful Art Nouveau trimmings are still in place. Mission District clubbers won't go near the place—way too disco—but for tourists it's a safe bet for a dance-filled night in the city. The light & sound system here is amazing, and on weekend nights the huge ballroom floor is packed with sweaty bodies dancing to thumping DJ beats or live music. When it's time to cool off you can chill on the mezzanine or fire up in the smoking room. Be sure to call or check the website to make sure there isn't a private event taking place. 420 Mason St. (btw. Geary and Post sts.). ✆ 415/693-0777. www.rubyskye.com. Cover $10–$25.

SUPPER CLUBS

If you can eat dinner, listen to live music, and dance (or at least wiggle in your chair) in the same room, it's a supper club—those are our criteria here.

Harry Denton's Starlight Room *(Moments*   If that new cocktail dress is burning a hole in your suitcase, get yourself dolled up tonight and say hello to Harry, our city's de facto party host. His celestial crimson-infused cocktail lounge and nightclub, perched on the top floor of the Sir Francis Drake Hotel, is a pantheon to 1930s San Francisco, a throwback to the days when red-velvet banquettes, chandeliers, and fashionable duds were de rigueur. The 360-degree view of the city is worth the cover charge alone, but what draws tourists and locals of all ages is a night of Harry Denton–style fun, which usually includes plenty of drinking, live music, and unrestrained dancing, regardless of age. The bar stocks a pricey collection of single-malt Scotches and champagnes, and you can snack from the "Lite" menu. If you make a reservation to guarantee a table, you'll also have a place to rest between songs. Early evening is more relaxed, but come the weekend this place gets loose. *Tip:* Come dressed for success (no casual jeans, open-toed shoes for men, or sneakers), or you'll be turned away at the door. Atop the Sir Francis Drake Hotel, 450 Powell St., 21st floor. ✆ 415/395-8595. www.harrydenton.com. Cover $10 Wed–Fri after 8:30pm; $15 Sat after 8:30pm.

DESTINATION BARS WITH DJ GROOVES

The Bliss Bar Surprisingly trendy for sleepy family-oriented Noe Valley, this small, stylish, and friendly bar is a great place to stop for a varied mix of locals, colorful cocktail concoctions, and a DJ spinning at the front window from 9pm to 2am every night except Sunday and Monday. If it's open, take your cocktail into the too-cool back Blue Room. And if you're on a budget, stop by from 4 to 7pm when martinis, lemon drops, cosmos, watermelon cosmos, and apple martinis are only $4. 4026 24th St. (btw. Noe and Castro sts.). ✆ 415/826-6200. www.blissbarsf.com.

Levende Lounge ✺ A fusion of fine dining, cocktailing, and DJ grooves, Levende Lounge is one of the Mission's hottest spots for young singles looking to hook up. Drop in early for happy hour Monday through Friday from 5 to 7pm, or sit down for a meal of "world-fusion" small plates (think French, Asian, and Nuevo Latino) in a more standard dinner setting amid exposed brick walls and cozy lighting. Later, tables are traded for lounge furnishings for some late-night noshing and flirting. *Tip:* Some nights have cover charges, but you can avoid the fee with a dinner reservation, and food is served until 11pm. 1710 Mission St. (at Duboce St.). ✆ 415/864-5585. www.levendesf.com.

Wish Bar Swathed in burgundy and black with exposed cinder-block walls, cement floors, and red-shaded sconces aglow with candlelight, even you will look cool at this mellow SoMa bar in the popular night crawler area around 11th and Folsom streets. With a bar in the front, DJ spinning upbeat lounge music in the back, and seating—including cushy leather couches—in between, it's often packed with a surprisingly diverse (albeit youthful) crowd. Closed Sundays. 1539 Folsom St. (btw. 11th and 12th sts.). ✆ 415/278-9474. www.wishsf.com.

4 The Bar Scene

Finding your kind of bar in San Francisco has a lot to do with which district it's in. The following is a *very* general description of what types of bars you're likely to find throughout the city:

- **Marina/Cow Hollow** bars attract a yuppie post-collegiate crowd.
- The opposite of the Marina/Cow Hollow crowd frequent the **Mission District** haunts.
- **Haight-Ashbury** caters to eclectic neighborhood cocktailers and beer-lovers.
- The **Tenderloin** is the new hotspot for serious mixologists.
- Tourists mix with conventioneers at **downtown** pubs.
- **North Beach** serves all types, mostly tourists.
- **Russian Hill's** Polk Street has become the new Marina/Cow Hollow scene.
- **The Castro** caters to gay locals and tourists.
- **SoMa** offers an eclectic mix from sports bars to DJ lounges.

The following is a list of a few of San Francisco's more interesting bars. Unless otherwise noted, these bars do not have cover charges.

Gold Dust Lounge *(Finds*   If you're staying downtown and want to head to a friendly, festive bar loaded with old-fashioned style and revelry, you needn't wander far off Union Square. This classically cheesy watering hole is all that. The red banquettes, gilded walls, dramatic chandeliers, pro bartenders, and "regulars" are the old-school real deal. Add live music and cheap drinks and you're in for a good ol' time. *Tip:* It's cash only, so come with some greenbacks. 247 Powell St. (at Geary St.). ℂ 415/397-1695.

Hemlock Tavern   This former gay dance club is now one of the most popular bars on Polk Street and always packed on weekends. There's lots of dark wood, warm colors, a line for the bathroom, and an enclosed back room that's dedicated just to smokers. The crowd is a bit younger than the Edinburgh Castle crew, but there's a similar mix of locals, hipsters, musicians, and visitors who would never think of themselves as tourists. The jukebox is sweet, and you can chow down on warm peanuts (toss the shells on the floor) and wash 'em down with a good selection of beers on tap. No cover. 1131 Polk St. (at Sutter St.). ℂ 415/923-0923. www.hemlocktavern.com.

Martuni's *(Finds*   San Francisco has plenty of bars with pianos in them, but for the real sing-along piano bar experience you'll want to head to Martuni's. After a couple of stiff martinis you'll loosen up enough to join the eclectic crowd in rousing renditions of everything from Cole Porter to Elton John. If you're not up for singing, you can cuddle with your date in the dark alcoves and watch the fun; otherwise, saddle up to the piano and let 'er rip. 4 Valencia St. (at Market St.). ⊙ 415/241-0205.

Specs' *(Finds)* The location of Spec's—look for a tiny nook on the east side of Columbus Ave. just south of Broadway—makes it a bit tough to find but well worth the search. Specs' historically eclectic decor—maritime flags hang from the ceiling while dusty posters, photos, and oddities like dried whale penises line the walls—offers plenty of visual entertainment while you toss back a cold Bud (sans glass of course). A "museum" displayed under glass contains memorabilia and items brought back by long-dead seamen who dropped in between voyages. There are plenty of salty and slightly pickled regulars to match the motif, so you may not want to order a Cosmo while doing your nails at the bar. 12 Saroyan Place (at 250 Columbus Ave.). ⊙ 415/421-4112.

The Tonga Room & Hurricane Bar *(Finds)* It's kitschy as all getout, but there's no denying the goofy Polynesian pleasures of the Fairmont Hotel's tropical oasis. Drop in and join the crowds for an umbrella drink, a simulated thunderstorm and downpour, and a heavy dose of whimsy that escapes most San Francisco establishments. If you're on a budget, you'll definitely want to stop by for the weekday happy hour from 5 to 7pm, when you can stuff your face at the all-you-can-eat bar-grub buffet (baby back ribs, chow mein, pot stickers) for $8 and the cost of one drink. Settle in and you'll catch live Top-40 music after 8pm Wednesday through Sunday, when there's a $3 to $5 cover. In the Fairmont Hotel, 950 Mason St. (at California St.). ⊙ 415/772-5278. www.tongaroom.com.

Toronado Gritty Lower Haight isn't exactly a charming street, but there's plenty of nightlife here, catering to an artistic/grungy/skateboarding 20-something crowd. While Toronado definitely draws in the young'uns, its 50-plus microbrews on tap and 100 bottled beers also entice a more eclectic clientele in search of beer heaven. The brooding atmosphere matches the surroundings: an aluminum bar, a few tall tables, minimal lighting, and a back room packed with tables and chairs. Happy hour runs 11:30am to 6pm every day for $1 off pints. 547 Haight St. (at Fillmore St.). ⊙ 415/863-2276. www.toronado.com.

Vesuvio   Situated along Jack Kerouac Alley, across from the famed City Lights bookstore, this renowned literary beatnik hangout is packed to the second-floor rafters with neighborhood writers, artists, songsters, wannabes, and everyone else ranging from longshoremen and cab drivers to businesspeople, all of whom come for the laid-back atmosphere. The convivial space consists of two stories of cocktail tables, complemented by changing exhibitions of local art. In addition to drinks, Vesuvio features an espresso machine. 255 Columbus Ave. (at Broadway). ✆ 415/362-3370. www.vesuvio.com.

Zeitgeist   The front door is black, the back door is adorned with a skeleton Playboy bunny, and inside is packed to the rafters with tattooed, pierced, and hard-core-looking partiers. But forge on. Zeitgeist is such a friendly and fun punk-rock-cum-biker-bar beer garden that even the occasional yuppie can be spotted mingling around the slammin' juke box featuring tons of local bands and huge back patio filled with picnic tables. (There tend to be cute girls here, too.) Along with fantastic dive-bar environs, you'll find 30 beers on draft, a pool table, and pinball machines. The regular crowd, mostly locals and bike messengers, come here to kick back with a pitcher, and welcome anyone else interested in the same pursuit. And if your night turns out, um, better than expected, there's a hotel upstairs. Cash only. 199 Valencia St. (at Duboce). ✆ **415/255-7505**.

BREWPUBS

Gordon Biersch Brewery Restaurant   Gordon Biersch Brewery is San Francisco's largest brew restaurant, serving decent food and tasty beer to an attractive crowd of mingling professionals. There are always several house-made beers to choose from, ranging from light to dark. Menu items run $9.50 to $26. 2 Harrison St. (on The Embarcadero). ✆ 415/243-8246. www.gordonbiersch.com.

San Francisco Brewing Company   Surprisingly low key for an alehouse, this cozy brewpub serves its creations with burgers, fries, grilled chicken breast, and the like. The bar is one of the city's few remaining old saloons (ca. 1907), aglow with stained-glass windows, tile floors, skylit ceiling, beveled glass, and mahogany bar. A massive overhead fan runs the full length of the bar—a bizarre contraption crafted from brass and palm fronds. The handmade copper brew kettle is visible from the street. Most evenings the place is packed with everyday folks enjoying music, darts, chess, backgammon, cards, dice, and, of course, beer. Menu items range from $4.15—curiously, for edamame (soybeans)—to $21 for a full rack of baby back ribs with all the fixings. The happy-hour special, an 8½-ounce microbrew beer for $1.50 (or a pint for $2.75), is offered daily from 4 to 6pm and midnight to 1am. 155 Columbus Ave. (at Pacific St.). ℭ **415/434-3344.** www.sfbrewing.com.

COCKTAILS WITH A VIEW

See "Supper Clubs," earlier, for a full review of **Harry Denton's Starlight Room.** Unless otherwise noted, these establishments have no cover charge.

Carnelian Room   On the 52nd floor of the Bank of America Building, the Carnelian Room offers uninterrupted views of the city. From a window-front table you feel as though you can reach out, pluck up the Transamerica Pyramid, and stir your martini with it. In addition to cocktails, the restaurant serves a four-course meal ($59 per person) as well as a la carte items ($24–$49 for main entrees). Jackets are required and ties are optional for men, but encouraged. *Note:* The restaurant has one of the most extensive wine lists in the city—1,600 selections, to be exact. 555 California St., in the Bank of America Building (btw. Kearny and Montgomery sts.). ℭ **415/433-7500.** www.carnelian room.com.

Cityscape   When you sit under the glass roof and sip a drink here, it's as though you're sitting out under the stars and enjoying views of the bay. Dinner, focusing on California cuisine, is available (though not destination worthy), and there's dancing to a DJ's picks nightly from 10:30pm. The mirrored columns and floor-to-ceiling windows help create an elegant and romantic ambience here. *FYI:* They also offer a live jazz champagne brunch on Sundays from 10am to 2pm. Hilton San Francisco, Tower One, 333 O'Farrell St. (at Mason St.), 46th floor. ℭ **415/923-5002.** Cover $10 Fri–Sat nights.

Top of the Mark *(Moments*   This is one of the most famous cocktail lounges in the world, and for good reason—the spectacular glass-walled room features an unparalleled 19th-floor view. During World War II, Pacific-bound servicemen toasted their goodbyes to the States here. While less dramatic today than they were back then, evenings spent here are still sentimental, thanks to the romantic atmosphere. Live bands play throughout the week; a jazz pianist on Tuesdays starts at 7pm; salsa on Wednesdays begins with dance lessons at 8pm and the band starts up at 9pm; on Thursdays Stompy Jones brings a swing vibe from 7:30pm; and a dance band playing everything from '50s hits through contemporary music keeps the joint hopping Fridays and Saturdays starting at 9pm. Drinks range from $9 to $12. A $59 three-course fixed-price sunset dinner is served Friday and Saturday at 7:30pm. Sunday brunch, served from 10am to 2pm, costs $59 for adults and includes a glass of champagne; for children 4 to 12, the brunch is $30. In the Mark Hopkins Inter-Continental, 1 Nob Hill (California and Mason sts.). © 415/616-6916. www.top ofthemark.com. Cover $5–$10.

A SPORTS BAR

Green's Sports Bar   If you think San Francisco sports fans aren't as enthusiastic as those on the East Coast, well, you're right. These days it's pretty easy to find an empty seat at Green's during a '49ers or Giants game. The city's de facto sports bar is a classic, cozy hangout with lots of dark wood, polished brass, windows that open onto the street, and an array of elevated TVs showing various sporting events via satellite. Highlights include 18 beers on tap, a pool table, and a boisterous happy hour scene every Monday through Friday from 4 to 7pm. Food isn't served, but you can place an order from the various restaurants along Polk Street and eat at the bar (they even provide a selection of menus). 2239 Polk St. (at Green St.). © 415/775-4287.

WINE & CHAMPAGNE BARS

The Bubble Lounge   This two-level champagne bar—looking ever so chic with its red velvet sofas, brick walls, and floor-to-ceiling draperies—chills more than 300 Champagnes and sparkling wines, including about 30 by the glass. As one would expect at a Financial District bubbly bar, there's a soupçon of pretentiousness emanating from the BMW-driving clientele and perpetually unshaven bartenders. If you're the type that prefers beer and free pretzels you'll hate it here, particularly if you have to wait in line for a $20 flute of something you can't even pronounce, but the pick-up scene really perks up as the bubbly flows into the night. 714 Montgomery St. (btw. Washington and Jackson sts.). © 415/434-4204. www.bubblelounge.com.

London Wine Bar   This British-style wine bar and store is a popular after-work hangout for Financial District suits. It's more of a place to drink and chat, however, than one in which to savor an array of premium wines (though they do offer a sampler). Usually 40 to 50 wines, mostly from California, are open at any given time, and about 800 are available by the bottle. It's a great venue for sampling local Napa Valley wines before you buy, and the pours are reasonably

priced. 415 Sansome St. (btw. Sacramento and Clay sts.). ✆ **415/788-4811**. www.
londonwinesf.com.

Nectar Wine Lounge   Catering to the Marina's young and beautiful, this hip place to sip pours about 50 globally diverse wines by-
the-glass (plus 800 choices by the bottle) along with creative small
plates; pairings are optional. Soothing shades of browns lend a relaxing ambience to the lounge's industrial-slick decor that includes lots
of polished woods and hexagonal highlights. 3330 Steiner St. (at Chestnut
St.). ✆ **415/345-1377**. www.nectarwinelounge.com.

5 Gay & Lesbian Bars & Clubs

Just like straight establishments, gay and lesbian bars and clubs tar-
get varied clienteles. Whether you're into leather or Lycra, business
or bondage, San Francisco has something just for you.

Check the free weeklies, the *San Francisco Bay Guardian* and *San
Francisco Weekly*, for listings of events and happenings around town.
The *Bay Area Reporter* is a gay paper with comprehensive listings,
including a weekly community calendar. All these papers are free and
distributed weekly on Wednesday or Thursday. They can be found
stacked at the corners of 18th and Castro streets and Ninth and Harrison streets, as well as in bars, bookshops, and other stores around
town. Also check out the rather homely but very informative site
titled "Queer Things to Do in the San Francisco Bay Area" at
www.sfqueer.com, or www.leatherandbears.com for a plethora of gay
happenings.

Listed below are some of the city's most established gay hangouts.

The Café *Finds*   When this place first opened it was the only predominantly lesbian dance club on Saturday nights in the city. Once
the guys found out how much fun the girls were having, they joined
the party. Today, it's a hugely popular mixed gay and lesbian scene
with three bars; two pool tables; a steamy, free-spirited dance floor;
and a small, heated patio and balcony where smoking and schmooz-
ing are allowed. A perk: They open at 4pm weekdays and 3pm weekends (2pm on Sunday). 2369 Market St. (at Castro St.). ✆ **415/861-3846**.
www.cafesf.com.

Metro   This bar provides the gay community with high-energy
music and the best view of the Castro District from its large balcony.
The bar seems to attract people of all ages who enjoy the friendliness
of the bartenders and the highly charged, cruising atmosphere.
There's a Spanish restaurant on the premises if you get hungry. 3600
16th St. (at Market St.). ✆ **415/703-9751**.

San Francisco Drag Shows

If you're out on a Friday night and looking for something to do that's definitely off the straight-laced path, head to The Cinch for its weekly **Charlie Horse** drag show, hosted by the sassy Miss Tranyshack 2005, Anna Conda. Every week is a different theme, such as "Valley of the Dolls Night" based on the scandalous Jacqueline Susann novel, or "What is Your Take on Old School," where the "ladies" of the evening masquerade as their favorite divas of the past such as Dolly Parton or Joni Mitchell. There's no cover charge, no drink minimum, and the performance is free. An added bonus: The show comes with complimentary popcorn.

If you prefer your drag queens with a slice of quiche, Harry Denton's Starlight Room (see p. 161) hosts a weekly **Sunday s a Drag** brunch performance, where divas perform female impersonation acts and lip-sync Broadway tunes. The "brunch with an attitude" has two seatings every Sunday at noon and 2:30pm. The price of brunch is $40 per person, which includes entertainment, brunch, coffee, tea, and fresh juices. For reservations call ✆ **415/395-8595** or email at reservations@harrydenton.com.

The Mint Karaoke Lounge This is a gay and lesbian karaoke bar—sprinkled with a heavy dash of straight folks on weekends—where you can get up and sing your heart out every night. Along with song, you'll encounter a mixed 20- to 40-something crowd that combines cocktails with do-it-yourself cabaret. Want to eat and listen at the same time? Feel free to bring in the Japanese food from the attached restaurant. Sashimi goes for about $7, main entrees $8, and sushi combo plates about $11. 1942 Market St. (at Laguna St.). ✆ **415/626-4726.** www.themint.net. 2-drink minimum.

The Stud The Stud, which has been around for almost 40 years, is one of the most successful gay establishments in town. The interior has an antiques-shop look. Music is a balanced mix of old and new, and nights vary from cabaret to oldies to discopunk. Check their website in advance for the evening's offerings. Drink prices range from $3.25 to $8. Happy hour runs Monday through Saturday 5 to 9pm with $1 off well drinks. 399 Ninth St. (at Harrison St.). ✆ **415/863-6623** or 415/252-STUD for event info. www.studsf.com. Cover free–$10.

6 Film

The **San Francisco International Film Festival** (© 415/561-5000; www.sffs.org), held at the end of April, is one of America's longest-running film festivals. Entries include new films by new and established directors. Call or surf ahead for a schedule or information, and check out their website for more information on purchasing tickets, which are relatively inexpensive.

If you're not here in time for the festival, don't despair. The classic, independent, and mainstream cinemas in San Francisco are every bit as good as the city's other cultural offerings.

REPERTORY CINEMAS

Castro Theatre *Finds*   Built in 1922 by renowned Bay Area architect Timothy Pflueger, and listed as a City of San Francisco registered landmark, the beautiful Castro Theatre is known for its screenings of classics and for its Wurlitzer organ, which is played before each evening show. There's a different feature almost nightly, and more often than not it's a double feature. They also play host to a number of festivals throughout the year. Bargain matinees are usually offered on Wednesday, Saturday, Sunday, and holidays. Phone or visit their website for schedules, prices, and show times. 429 Castro St. (near Market St.). © 415/621-6120. www.castrotheatre.com.

Red Vic   The worker-owned Red Vic movie collective originated in the neighboring Victorian building that gave it its name. The theater specializes in independent releases and premieres and contemporary cult hits, and situates its patrons among an array of couches. Prices are $8.50 for adults ($6.50 for matinees) and $5 for seniors and kids 12 and under. Tickets go on sale 20 minutes before each show. Phone for schedules and show times or look around the city for printouts. 1727 Haight St. (btw. Cole and Shrader sts.). © 415/668-3994. www.redvicmoviehouse.com.

The Roxie Film Center   Founded in 1909, The Roxie is the oldest continually running theater in San Francisco, and so when it almost went under in 2005, a private donor saved it with a huge donation and a great idea; the theater merged with the New College of California and is now a nonprofit film center serving both students and the general public. Management has promised that the programming will stay the same and that they will continue to screen the best new alternative films anywhere, as well as host filmmakers

FILM   171

like Akira Kurosawa and Werner Herzog. The low-budget contemporary features are largely devoid of Hollywood candy coating; many are West Coast premieres. Phone for schedules, prices, and show times. Admission is $8 adults, $4 seniors 65 plus and children 11 and under; $5 matinee is the first show on weekends. 3117 16th St. (at Valencia St.). ℂ **415/863-1087.** www.roxie.com.

Appendix: Fast Facts

American Express For travel arrangements, traveler's checks, currency exchange, and other member services, there's an office at 455 Market St., at First Street (☏ **415/536-2600**), in the Financial District, open Monday through Friday from 9am to 5:30pm and Saturday from 10am to 2pm. To report lost or stolen traveler's checks, call ☏ **800/221-7282.** For American Express Global Assist, call ☏ **800/554-2639.**

Area Codes The area code for San Francisco is **415;** for Oakland, Berkeley, and much of the East Bay, **510;** for the peninsula, generally **650.** Napa and Sonoma are **707.** Most phone numbers in this book are in San Francisco's 415 area code, but there's no need to dial it if you're within city limits.

Business Hours Most banks are open Monday through Friday from 9am to 5pm as well as Saturday mornings. Many banks also have ATMs for 24-hour banking. (See the "Money" section beginning on p. 1.) Most stores are open Monday through Saturday from 10 or 11am to at least 6pm, with shorter hours on Sunday. But there are exceptions: Stores in Chinatown, Ghirardelli Square, and Pier 39 stay open much later during the tourist season, and large department stores, including Macy's and Nordstrom, keep late hours. Most restaurants serve lunch from about 11:30am to 2:30pm and dinner from about 5:30 to 10pm. They sometimes serve later on weekends. Nightclubs and bars are usually open daily until 2am, when they are legally bound to stop serving alcohol.

Earthquakes There will always be earthquakes in California, most of which you'll never notice. However, in case of a significant shaker, there are a few basic precautionary measures you should know. When you are inside a building, seek cover; do not run outside. Stand under a doorway or against a wall, and stay away from windows. If you exit a building after a substantial quake, use stairwells, not elevators. If you are in your car, pull over to the side of the road and stop—but not until you are away from bridges, overpasses, telephone poles, and power lines. Stay in your car. If you're out walking, stay outside and away from trees, power lines, and the sides of buildings. If you're in an area with tall buildings, find a doorway in which to stand.

Emergencies   Call ⓒ **911** to report a fire, call the police, or get an ambulance anywhere in the United States. This is a toll-free call (no coins are required at public telephones).

Hospitals   Saint Francis Memorial Hospital, 900 Hyde St., between Bush and Pine streets on Nob Hill (ⓒ **415/353-6000**), provides emergency service 24 hours a day; no appointment is necessary. The hospital also operates a **physician-referral service** (ⓒ **800/ 333-1355** or 415/353-6566).

Internet Access   San Francisco is totally wired. You'll find that many cafes have wireless access, as do many hotels. Check www. wifi411.com for a huge list of Wi-Fi hotspots, or stop by one of the following locations around town: **Brainwash,** 1122 Folsom St., between Seventh and Eighth streets (ⓒ **415/861-3663;** www. brainwash.com); **Quetzal,** 1234 Polk St., at Bush Street (ⓒ **415/ 673-4181**); **Copy Central,** 110 Sutter St., at Montgomery Street (ⓒ **415/392-6470;** www.copycentral.com).

Laundry   Most hotels offer laundry service. But if you want to save money you can easily tote your gear to a local laundromat or dry cleaner. Ask your hotel for the nearest location—they're all over town. Or for a scene with your suds, go to SoMa's **Brainwash,** 1122 Folsom St., between Seventh and Eighth streets (ⓒ **415/861-3663**).

Newspapers & Magazines   The city's main daily is the *San Francisco Chronicle,* which is distributed throughout the city. Check out the *Chronicle*'s massive Sunday edition that includes a pink "Datebook" section—an excellent preview of the week's upcoming events. The free weekly *San Francisco Bay Guardian* (www.sfbg.com) and *San Francisco Weekly* (www.sfweekly.com), tabloids of news and listings, are indispensable for nightlife information; they're widely distributed through street-corner kiosks and at city cafes and restaurants.

Of the many free tourist-oriented publications, the most widely read are *San Francisco Guide* (www.sfguide.com), a handbook-size weekly containing maps and information on current events, and *Where San Francisco* (www.wheremagazine.com), a glossy regular format monthly magazine. You can find them in most hotels, shops, and restaurants in the major tourist areas.

Police   For emergencies, dial ⓒ **911** from any phone; no coins are needed. For other matters, call ⓒ **415/553-0123.**

Smoking If San Francisco is California's most European city in looks and style, the comparison stops when it comes to smoking in public. Each year, smoking laws in the city become stricter. Since 1998, smoking has been prohibited in restaurants and bars. Hotels are also offering more nonsmoking rooms, which often leaves those who like to puff out in the cold—sometimes literally.

Taxes In the United States, there is no value-added tax (VAT) or other indirect tax at the national level. Every state, county, and city has the right to levy its own local tax on all purchases, including hotel and restaurant checks, airline tickets, and so on, and is not included in the price tags you'll see on merchandise. This tax is not refundable. Sales tax in San Francisco is 8.5%. Hotel tax is charged on the room tariff only (which is not subject to sales tax) and is set by the city, ranging from 12% to 17% around Northern California.

Telephones Many convenience groceries and packaging services sell **prepaid calling cards** in denominations up to $50; for international visitors these can be the least expensive way to call home. Many public pay phones at airports now accept American Express, Master-Card, and Visa credit cards. **Local calls** made from pay phones in most locales cost either 25¢ or 35¢ (no pennies, please). Most long-distance and international calls can be dialed directly from any phone. **For calls within the United States and to Canada,** dial 1 followed by the area code and the seven-digit number. **For other international calls,** dial 011 followed by the country code, city code, and the number you are calling.

Calls to area codes **800, 888, 877,** and **866** are toll-free. However, calls to area codes **700** and **900** (chat lines, bulletin boards, "dating" services, and so on) can be very expensive—usually a charge of 95¢ to $3 or more per minute, and they sometimes have minimum charges that can run as high as $15 or more.

For **reversed-charge or collect calls,** and for person-to-person calls, dial the number 0 then the area code and number; an operator will come on the line, and you should specify whether you are calling collect, person-to-person, or both. If your operator-assisted call is international, ask for the overseas operator.

For **local directory assistance** ("information"), dial 411; for long-distance information, dial 1, then the appropriate area code and 555-1212.

Time San Francisco is in the Pacific Standard Time zone, which is 8 hours behind Greenwich Mean Time and 3 hours behind Eastern

Standard Time. The continental United States is divided into **four time zones:** Eastern Standard Time (EST), Central Standard Time (CST), Mountain Standard Time (MST), and Pacific Standard Time (PST). Alaska and Hawaii have their own zones. For example, when it's 9am in Los Angeles (PST), it's 7am in Honolulu (HST), 10am in Denver (MST), 11am in Chicago (CST), noon in New York City (EST), 5pm in London (GMT), and 2am the next day in Sydney.

Daylight saving time is in effect from 1am on the second Sunday in March to 1am on the first Sunday in November, except in Arizona, Hawaii, the U.S. Virgin Islands, and Puerto Rico. Daylight saving time moves the clock 1 hour ahead of standard time.

Tipping Tips are a very important part of certain workers' income, and gratuities are the standard way of showing appreciation for services provided. (Tipping is certainly not compulsory if the service is poor!) In hotels, tip **bellhops** at least $1 per bag ($2–$3 if you have a lot of luggage) and tip the **chamber staff** $1 to $2 per day (more if you've left a disaster area for him or her to clean up). Tip the **doorman** or **concierge** only if he or she has provided you with some specific service (for example, calling a cab for you or obtaining difficult-to-get theater tickets). Tip the **valet-parking attendant** $1 every time you get your car.

In restaurants, bars, and nightclubs, tip **service staff** 15% to 20% of the check, tip **bartenders** 10% to 15%, tip **checkroom attendants** $1 per garment, and tip **valet-parking attendants** $1 per vehicle.

As for other service personnel, tip **cab drivers** 15% of the fare; tip **skycaps** at airports at least $1 per bag ($2–$3 if you have a lot of luggage); and tip **hairdressers** and **barbers** 15% to 20%.

Toilets Those weird, oval-shaped, olive-green kiosks on the sidewalks throughout San Francisco are high-tech self-cleaning public toilets. They've been placed on high-volume streets to provide relief for pedestrians. French potty-maker JCDecaux gave them to the city for free—advertising covers the cost. It costs 25¢ to enter, with no time limit, but I don't recommend using the ones in the sketchier neighborhoods such as the Mission because they're mostly used by crackheads and prostitutes. Toilets can also be found in hotel lobbies, bars, restaurants, museums, department stores, railway and bus stations, and service stations. Large hotels and fast-food restaurants are often the best bet for clean facilities. Restaurants and bars in heavily visited areas may reserve their restrooms for patrons.

Index

See also Accommodations and Restaurant indexes below.

FROMMER'S® COMPLETE TRAVEL GUIDES

FROMMER'S® DAY BY DAY GUIDES

PAULINE FROMMER'S GUIDES: SEE MORE. SPEND LESS.

FROMMER'S® PORTABLE GUIDES

Acapulco, Ixtapa & Zihuatanejo
Amsterdam
Aruba, Bonaire & Curacao
Australia's Great Barrier Reef
Bahamas
Big Island of Hawaii
Boston
California Wine Country
Cancún
Cayman Islands
Charleston
Chicago
Dominican Republic

Florence
Las Vegas
Las Vegas for Non-Gamblers
London
Maui
Nantucket & Martha's Vineyard
New Orleans
New York City
Paris
Portland
Puerto Rico
Puerto Vallarta, Manzanillo &
    Guadalajara

Rio de Janeiro
San Diego
San Francisco
Savannah
St. Martin, Sint Maarten, Anguila &
    St. Bart's
Turks & Caicos
Vancouver
Venice
Virgin Islands
Washington, D.C.
Whistler

FROMMER'S® CRUISE GUIDES

Alaska Cruises & Ports of Call

Cruises & Ports of Call

European Cruises & Ports of Call

FROMMER'S® NATIONAL PARK GUIDES

Algonquin Provincial Park
Banff & Jasper
Grand Canyon

National Parks of the American West
Rocky Mountain
Yellowstone & Grand Teton

Yosemite and Sequoia & Kings
    Canyon
Zion & Bryce Canyon

FROMMER'S® WITH KIDS GUIDES

Chicago
Hawaii
Las Vegas
London

National Parks
New York City
San Francisco

Toronto
Walt Disney World® & Orlando
Washington, D.C.

FROMMER'S® PHRASEFINDER DICTIONARY GUIDES

Chinese
French

German
Italian

Japanese
Spanish

SUZY GERSHMAN'S BORN TO SHOP GUIDES

France
Hong Kong, Shanghai & Beijing
Italy

London
New York
Paris

San Francisco
Where to Buy the Best of Everything.

FROMMER'S® BEST-LOVED DRIVING TOURS

Britain
California
France
Germany

Ireland
Italy
New England
Northern Italy

Scotland
Spain
Tuscany & Umbria

THE UNOFFICIAL GUIDES®

Adventure Travel in Alaska
Beyond Disney
California with Kids
Central Italy
Chicago
Cruises
Disneyland®
England
Hawaii

Ireland
Las Vegas
London
Maui
Mexico's Best Beach Resorts
Mini Mickey
New Orleans
New York City
Paris

San Francisco
South Florida including Miami &
    the Keys
Walt Disney World®
Walt Disney World® for
    Grown-ups
Walt Disney World® with Kids
Washington, D.C.

SPECIAL-INTEREST TITLES

Athens Past & Present
Best Places to Raise Your Family
Cities Ranked & Rated
500 Places to Take Your Kids Before They Grow Up
Frommer's Best Day Trips from London
Frommer's Best RV & Tent Campgrounds in the U.S.A.

Frommer's Exploring America by RV
Frommer's NYC Free & Dirt Cheap
Frommer's Road Atlas Europe
Frommer's Road Atlas Ireland
Retirement Places Rated